ADHD
Achieving Success
in School and in Life

EDITED BY

Barbara P. Guyer, Ed.D.
Marshall University

FOREWORD BY

Edward M. Hallowell, M.D.

Allyn and Bacon
Boston • London • Toronto • Sydney • Tokyo • Singapore

Executive Editor: Virginia Lanigan
Series Editorial Assistant: Karin Huang
Manufacturing Buyer: Suzanne Lareau
Editorial Coordination: John Patrick Grace, Grace Associates, Huntington, WV
Packaging Services Coordinator: Solar Script, Inc.

Copyright © 2000 by Allyn & Bacon
A Pearson Education Company
Needham Heights, MA 02494

Internet: www.abacon.com

Library of Congress Cataloging-in-Publication Data

Guyer, Barbara P. (Barbara Priddy)
    ADHD : achieving success in school and in life / Barbara P. Guyer.
      p.   cm.
    Includes bibliographical references and index;
    Translation of: Attention-deficit hyperactivity disorder.
    ISBN 0-205-29229-1
    1. Attention-deficit disorder in adults.   2. Attention-deficit
disorder in adolescence.   I. Title.
    RC394.A85G95   1999
    616.85'89—dc21   99-37915
                                   CIP

Printed in the United States of America

10 9 8 7 6 5 4 3 2   03 02 01 00

This book is dedicated to my mother, who taught me that the most valuable things in life often cannot be seen by the eye alone.

Contents

v

Foreword

When Barbara Guyer asked me to write a foreword for this book, I happily agreed. But the book she has produced exceeded my already high expectations.

What distinguishes this book especially are two qualities rare in books like this one: it is written by practitioners who actually practice and see patients; and it is utterly practical.

The whole field of learning and attention deficit disorder is rife with theory. Indeed, debating theory is one of the most exciting aspects of working in this field. However, it lacks much practical value. As one of my old teachers said to me when I proposed to him a new theory of mine, "Well, Ned, that might be true, that might not be true, but in any case it's useless."

What you will find in this book is use-full. This book teems with useful information that will be of most benefit to others who are actively wrestling with real, live problems. You will not find rarefied pieties here. Instead, you will find tough, tried nuggets of actual practice.

In an entirely different context, the poet John Milton once wrote, "I cannot praise a fugitive and cloistered virtue that never sallies forth into the arena." The authors of the essays in this volume have indeed sallied forth into the clinical arena, the arena of human suffering and human perplexity, and they sally forth still. In this book they give the reader the tremendous benefit and comfort of what they have learned.

Edward M. Hallowell, M.D.

Acknowledgments

Sincere appreciation is expressed to the many children, adolescents, and adults who have taught us so much about ADHD. We are also grateful to their parents, who have willingly helped us to increase the depth of our knowledge in this new and changing field.

Our appreciation also goes to the following reviewers for their helpful comments on the manuscript: Rhoda Cummings, University of Nevada, Reno; Ralph Zalma, Hofstra University; Jean C. Faieta, Edinboro University of Pennsylvania; Charmaine Lepley, University of Rio Grande; and Janice Seabrooks, University of North Florida.

We are grateful to Deborah Painter, Marshall University, who compiled the section in the Appendix on Rating Scales for ADHD.

We are grateful to Dr. Edward N. Hallowell for his willingness to read this book and write the foreword.

Sincere appreciation is expressed to Diane Williams, Marshall University, for her careful and thorough proofreading of the material in this book.

About the Editor
and Contributors

About the Editor

Barbara Priddy Guyer, E.d. D., has extensive experience in the public schools, where she taught grades 2–6, remedial reading, and learning disabilities classes. She also taught remedial reading in a women's prison. She has been a consultant in special education as well as a principal in a city school system. Since 1975, she has been coordinator of the learning disabilities graduate program at Marshall University, Huntington, WV. In 1981 she began the H.E.L.P. Program (Higher Education for Learning Problems) as a support for undergraduate students with LD and ADHD. In 1985 she began Medical H.E.L.P., a unique remedial program for medical students and physicians who have LD and/or ADHD. She is co-author of *Studies of Multi-Sensory Structured Language Education and College: How Students with Dyslexia Can Maximize the Experience*. She is the author of *The Pretenders: Gifted People Who Have Difficulty Learning*. She is the mother of two daughters who have Learning Disabilities and ADHD.

About the Contributors

Lisa R. Deson, Ph.D., graduated from Fordham University with her doctorate in school psychology. Currently, she is the learning disabilities specialist at Andrus Children's Center, where she works with emotionally disturbed children and their teachers.

Kenneth E. Guyer, Ph.D., taught at the Medical College of Virginia prior to his current position as associate professor of biochemistry and molecular biology at the Marshall University School of Medicine. Among other areas, he has conducted research and published in the areas of learning disabilities, ADHD, and autism. He has served on admissions committees of the medical schools where he has taught. He is co-author of *How to Prepare for the Medical College Admissions Test*, published since 1976 and now in its eighth edition. He has been actively involved in the Virginia and West Virginia Learning Disabilities Associations.

Rosa A. Hagin, Ph.D., is a research professor of psychology in the Department of Psychiatry of the New York University School of Medicine. She holds the diplomate of the American Board of Professional Psychologists. With co-author Archie A. Silver, she has written *Disorders of Learning in Childhood* and *The Search and Teach Program*. She is an active member of the Learning Disabilities Association of America as well as former chair of the Professional Advisory Board. As a psychologist, Dr. Hagin's major work has been devoted to research, training, and clinical services for children and adults with learning disabilities and attention problems.

Patricia H. Latham, J.D., a graduate of the University of Chicago Law School, serves on the CHADD National Adult Issues Committee. **Peter S. Latham, J.D.,** is a graduate of the University of Pennsylvania Law School. The Lathams have co-authored four books: *Attention Deficit Disorder and the Law* (1992), *Learning Disabilities and the Law* (1993), *Succeeding in the Workplace* (1994), and *Higher Education Services for Students with Learning Disabilities and Attention Deficit Disorder: A Legal Guide* (1994). They are contributing authors to several books. The Lathams have broad experiences in law, including practicing in the areas of disability rights, employment, and education, to name a few. They co-founded an educational institution to serve the needs of students with learning disabilities, and they serve on many boards and committees, including Attention Deficit Disorder Association of America.

John P. MacCallum, M.D., is a child and adult psychiatrist who has had a special interest in ADHD for more than 20 years. While he has spent most of his medical career in the private practice of psychiatry, he was for two years a faculty member at the West Virginia University School of Medicine in the Department of Psychiatry. He, his wife, Susan, and their four children reside in Charleston, West Virginia. Dr. MacCallum is a popular speaker on the topic of ADHD as well as alternative medicine. He is the chief psychiatrist in a new alternative health center at a hospital in Charleston.

Peggy E. Ramundo, B.S., a former classroom teacher and adult with ADHD, has been specializing in the area of ADHD for 11 years. Nationally known for her work with children, adolescents, and adults who have ADHD, she currently works as an ADHD coach in private practice. She is the co-author of two books for adults who have ADHD, *You Mean I'm Not Lazy, Stupid, or Crazy?!* and *The ADDed Dimension*. She writes a regular column called "ADD-Libs" in *ADDvance, the Magazine for Women with ADD*. She is co-founder of the Attention Deficit Disorder Council of Greater Cincinnati, she serves on the advisory board of ADDvance for Women, and she is a staff member of The Optimal Functioning Institute (for ADD coach training). Ms Ramundo lives in Cincinnati, Ohio, with her husband and two children.

Mary McDonald Richard, M.A., is the Coordinator of Services for Students with LD/ADHD in the Office of Student Disability Services (SDS) at the University of Iowa. Annually, from 500 to 600 undergraduate, graduate, and professional school students with LD/ADHD are registered for accommodations and services with SDS. During 1995–1996, she was the National President of CHADD, an organization that provides support and research-based information about ADHD. Ms. Richard has authored a number of research and informational articles and textbook chapters. She is a frequent presenter at professional and organizational conferences on topics related to adolescents and adults with LD/ADHD.

Larry B. Silver, M.D., is an active member and supporter of the Learning Disabilities Association of America, serving both on its Board of Directors and its Professional Advisory Board. Dr. Silver is Clinical Professor of Psychiatry at the Georgetown University School of Medicine. Previously, he was Acting Director and Deputy Director of the National Institutes of Health. He is the author of *The Misunderstood Child: A Guide for Parents of Children with Learning Disabilities, Attention-Deficit Hyperactivity Disorder: A Clinical Guide to Diagnosis and Treatment,* and *Dr. Larry Silver's Advice to Parents on Attention-Deficit Hyperactivity Disorder.*

Suzanne Stevens, B.S., is a dynamic speaker at conferences and workshops. She has many years of experience as a teacher of children, adolescents, and adults who have LD and/or ADHD. She received her training in working with dyslexic students from the late June Orton, widow of Dr. Samuel T. Orton. She is the author of *The LD Child and the ADHD Child: Ways That Parents Can Help, Classroom Success for the LD and the ADHD Child,* and *Getting the Horse to Drink: How to Motivate Unmotivated Students,* books that are known and respected for being easy to read and full of practical information.

James Ward, Jr., M.D., has practiced pediatrics in Charleston, South Carolina, for many years. In addition to his medical degree, he has a master's degree in special education. He has worked diligently to improve the quality of education for children and adolescents who have LD and/or ADHD. While engaged in the active practice of medicine as a pediatrician, for 14 years he taught advanced biology and chemistry on his lunch hour. He has coordinated a research project involving adolescent males who were suspected of having ADHD. Dr. Ward is a popular national speaker on the topic of ADHD and is an active member of the International Dyslexia Association.

Chapter 1

Highlights

KENNETH E. GUYER

We speak of Attention Deficit Hyperactivity Disorder (ADHD), and one wonders if most people think of this as a new disorder. Has it always existed although it has only been recognized and labeled in the last 100 years? Does this actually exist as a disability, or does it represent the extremes in a continuum in each of the categories of motor activity, attention (inattention), and impulsivity? As of this writing, controversies abound, and there is little about ADHD that isn't controversial with parents, teachers, or other professionals.

Although problems result from impulsivity, hyperactivity, and inattention in other life functions, the greatest notice is taken in education. Classes in public schools often contain 25 students or more, and it is often necessary for all of the students to pay attention to the teacher if learning is to occur. Rarely is each student allowed to work independently for a significant part of the day. Rarely is a student afforded the luxury of individual instruction. Therefore, it is imperative that students attend rather closely to what the teacher is saying and that other students not be prevented from learning because of a student's problems with inattention, impulsivity, or hyperactivity. In earlier years, students were often given more individual instruction and then expected to complete related exercises on their own. They may have been given greater freedom of movement. If the symptoms of difference that we now call ADHD were sufficiently severe, the student was simply excluded from school.

Although impulsivity, hyperactivity, and inattentiveness often hinder the success of the individual with ADHD in the workplace, this is usually not as severe a problem as in the classroom. The individual in the workplace is more often doing rather than learning. But there is a decreasing demand for personnel involved only in physical activity. We recognize the rise in the demand for information-related personnel. Those personnel with ADHD may find it difficult to perform satisfactorily in tasks requiring concentration, the ability to solve problems, and the

1

preparation of reports. Combine this with the fact that many persons with ADHD are creative, and failure to meet their needs in the educational area and in the workplace may cause them to give up. This could result in a loss to society of the benefits of their creativity.

Since Learning Disabilities (LD) and ADHD are often mentioned in the same breath, many tend to use the terms somewhat interchangeably. This is unfortunate because it obscures just which disorder is being discussed.

LD refers to a disorder that is diagnosed and defined as failure to learn (as measured by educational achievement tests) up to the level predicted by the individual's ability (as measured by psychological tests of intelligence). Of course, allowance is also made for other problems such as blindness, deafness, psychiatric disorders, and cultural deprivation. Thus, individuals who are diagnosed as being LD are those who fail to learn up to their respective ability levels in the absence of other disabilities that could explain the achievement deficit.

In comparison to the LD term, which largely originated in the field of education, ADHD originated largely in the field of medicine. These individuals are characterized as being abnormally hyperactive, inattentive, or impulsive. (They may also exhibit two or three of these characteristics in combination.) The diagnosis is made by psychologists or physicians (usually psychiatrists).

Since we have differentiated between the terms LD and ADHD, one might wonder whether there is any "overlap" or comorbidity of the two disorders. Comorbidity is recognized by experts in the field, but it is difficult to pin down the numbers. Larry Silver (1998) reports that about 20% of children and adolescents with LD also exhibit ADHD. He also states that from 30% to 50% of children and adolescents with ADHD also exhibit LD. (The exact criteria for diagnosis of LD are subject to interpretation, thus affecting the percentages.)

In the United States the decision was made to provide for education of special needs students who were previously encouraged (or even required) to forego public education, including the physically disabled, the mentally impaired, the emotionally disturbed, the sensorially impaired, the learning disabled, and those with ADHD. This made it necessary to develop better methods to diagnose these disorders as well as methods to meet the educational needs of the various students.

Diagnosing ADHD

Diagnosis of ADHD involves multidisciplinary assessment by physicians, psychologists, and educational diagnosticians. Since such diagnosis involves substantial exercise of professional judgment by those making the diagnosis, criticism has been inevitable. It has been alleged that ADHD is not a disorder. If accepted as a disorder, it has been alleged to be overdiagnosed in this country, particularly among the privileged.

What would be the gain resulting from overdiagnosis? It might be argued that those involved in diagnosis and treatment of a disorder would receive greater income and/or job security. School systems receiving augmented funding from the state or federal government based on the count of students with ADHD might experience an easing of budgetary pressures. The individual who was inaccurately diagnosed might receive educational benefits to which he or she was not otherwise entitled.

Actually, although it is likely that ADHD may be overdiagnosed in some areas, it is probably underdiagnosed in other areas. Although it has been estimated that 3% to 6% of the school population may have ADHD, no more than 3% have been so diagnosed.

With diagnosis, there is the opportunity for additional assistance. The student may be assigned to smaller classes and/or one-on-one instruction for at least a part of the instructional day. Modifications (accommodations) in testing may also be allowed.

One of the problems in diagnosis of ADHD is that it requires so much subjectivity on the part of the examiner. The 1994 *Diagnostic and Statistical Manual (DSM-IV)* defines the disorder but does not unambiguously state how the diagnosis is to be made. It is described in terms of hyperactivity/impulsivity, inattention, or a combination of the two. These symptoms must have been noted before age seven years. The latter requirement that the symptoms must precede the seventh birthday has produced some problems. How may this be approached if the diagnosis is attempted decades later, when records may no longer be available regarding behavior that precedes age seven? At a more recent time teachers and parents may no longer survive or their memories may not be clear in this regard.

During the evaluation it is important that the diagnostician consider: (1) whether a pervasive developmental disorder such as autism exists, (2) whether attentional problems result from school learning problems, (3) whether attentional problems result from task demands that are out of keeping with intelligence, and (4) whether the characteristics of ADHD exceed a developmentally appropriate level, interfering with educational functioning.

Behavioral ratings (checklists) by parents and teachers are considered to be useful in alerting professionals to the need for further evaluation. In addition, these checklists can be incorporated into further evaluations and reports. It is often considered that when parent and teacher checklists are at variance, the teacher checklist may be more objective. Also, it may be that the parent evaluates the child in an arena devoid of significant pressure whereas the teacher evaluates in the more constrained, pressurized arena of the classroom.

Assessment instruments have been devised to avoid much of the subjectivity that may be present in other types of ADHD evaluations. On continuous performance tests (CPTs) the child is asked to watch a computer screen while various stimuli are projected. The child is instructed to push a button when a specified stimulus or combination of stimuli appears. The score reflects the number of correct responses, the number of omissions of responses to specified stimuli, and the number of responses when response was not called for. Although CPTs have the advantages noted above, they do suffer from a lack of standardization and lack of normative data. In addition, there is the subjectivity introduced by the need of the clinician to determine whether this performance reflects the child's performance in the classroom or at home. For a more detailed discussion of the diagnosis of ADHD, refer to Chapter 3.

Medical Treatment

The principal medications sometimes used today in the treatment of ADHD are methylphenidate (trademark Ritalin), dextroamphetamine (trademark Dexedrine), and pemoline (trademark Cylert). These have been used successfully to treat students in the public schools for several decades. Negative criticism has centered on (1) using medications to "drug" children into passive behavior, (2) the possibility that children exposed to these drugs might develop dependence on these and, later, other drugs, and (3) the possibility that these drugs may be abused by the patients or others. Research indicates that there has not been good evidence of significant chemical dependence or abuse in those for whom the medications are prescribed. There has also been little or no diversion of these materials by family members of the patients. It is difficult to argue that these persons should be deprived of useful medication because of the possibility of theft and abuse of the medication by others outside the family.

It was once argued strenuously that the problems of ADHD ended with adolescence. Perhaps that belief was influenced by the fact that the focus on ADHD at that time related mostly to motor hyperactivity or restlessness. Today significant numbers of post-adolescent patients with ADHD use psychostimulant medications during study and examination time. Some other individuals with ADHD use these medications only during times when they require their highest levels of concentration and performance. Refer to James Ward's discussion of the medical treatment of ADHD (in Chapter 4) for more information on this interesting topic.

Alternative Treatments for ADHD

Behavioral techniques and medication will ordinarily be tried with most individuals who have ADHD. Behavioral techniques may not achieve the desired results. Medication may not give acceptable results, or medication may be rejected because of the public conflict over its use.

Alternative treatments may be employed. In many cases these have little or no accepted scientific basis. Their success is also debatable. Often they are expensive and time-consuming.

These alternative treatments may be largely divided into physiological and chemical areas. The physiological category includes patterning, biofeedback, and treatment of "vestibular dysfunction." Patterning has been proposed for a variety of conditions, including mental retardation and learning disabilities. It requires a great deal of time taking the individual through successive developmental levels and its usefulness is not well accepted among professionals.

Biofeedback uses an electroencephalogram (EEG) to monitor brain waves. An attempt is made to train the individual to change the brain waves to a pattern that is believed to be inconsistent with ADHD.

The chemical category of therapies includes megavitamins, trace elements, avoidance of refined sugars and food additives, and use of herbs. Megavitamins are comparatively large doses of water soluble vitamins (vitamin C and various B vitamins).

Trace element therapy is based on a belief that the low-concentration chemical elements found in the body may not be at the optimal concentrations. Their concentrations are measured in hair or nails, and an attempt is made to correct the balance by element intake or by chelation therapy. The elements may be determined with high levels of accuracy, but it is not clear what treatment of hair or nails should be used to remove contamination. In addition, it is unclear what area of the head should be used as the source of the hairs and what segment of each hair should be used.

Food additive avoidance therapy arises from the observation that large numbers of additives (mostly flavor and color) are introduced into our foods. Adherents to this theory alter the diet to try to alleviate symptoms. For ADHD in particular they try to avoid foods containing certain additives or salicylates. Some medications (prescription and over the counter) are prepared to meet this market. An objective panel, having reviewed the literature, agrees that a small percentage (probably 1% or less) of individuals affected by ADHD may show improvement with this approach.

Refined sugar avoidance therapy relies on an observation by some parents that their children become hyperactive when eating refined sugar. This observation has not held up well in controlled studies. If refined sugar did pose a problem, it is unclear whether this theory blames an impurity introduced or important nutrients removed during the refining process.

Herbal therapy relies on the idea that certain herbs contain materials that alleviate ADHD. The medications offered contain such materials as pycnogenol, ginko biloba, colloidal minerals, multivitamins, amino acids, enzymes, dried plant extracts, or a combination of more than one of these. Some of these are not subjected to a high level of analysis, and the components may be present at variable concentrations.

Allergy therapy has also been suggested by some for treatment of ADHD. Although this initially sounds like what we have discussed with food additives, allergy therapy can also focus on nondietary allergens. The major nondietary allergens involved here are respiratory. Therapy can include removal of respiratory allergens as well as symptomatic treatment—e.g., with antihistamines. Refer to Larry Silver's chapter on "Controversial Therapies" (Chapter 5) for a stimulating discussion of this topic.

The Remediation of ADHD

After an individual has been diagnosed with ADHD, what happens next? If the individual is in elementary or secondary school, remediation may be attempted. This may involve behavior management, enhancement of self-image, or development of organizational skills. If impulsivity is a problem, this may be approached by counseling about negative behavior and by role playing to try to help the student to understand the problem. This approach can sometimes result in improvement.

Impulsivity may also be combated by close supervision and quick intervention. The intervention should consist of firm but minimally judgmental action. The student should be helped to see that impulsivity can be dangerous, and, at the very least, it can cause problems that could otherwise be avoided. Sometimes impulsivity may be decreased by counting to a certain number or even by reciting the alphabet. The student may sometimes have awareness heightened by role playing, placing himself or herself in the place of the person who is affected by the impulsivity. This allows the student to see that an attempt must be made to alleviate this alienating behavior.

Sometimes impulsivity and fidgety activity may be ameliorated by giving the student some freedom of movement beyond the norm. It may be possible for the student and teacher to work out silent signals that indicate the need for mutually approved activity during class time.

Children with ADHD also require assistance in developing better organization and time management skills. Early on, the teacher may find it necessary to monitor and correct the student in this area. Later it is probably advisable to try to provide for a transition to a level of less intensive supervision. The student must be assisted to develop skills in this area, effectively monitoring his or her own tasks and progress. A calendar with future tasks is often a good idea. The student can then see what is in the future and plan for it. For more detailed information, refer to the chapters by Suzanne Stevens and Barbara Guyer (Chapters 6–8).

Legal Protection of Those with ADHD

After secondary school some individuals with ADHD apply for admission to post-secondary education. It is usually necessary that they take either the SAT or the ACT in order to complete application to colleges and universities. With appropriate diagnosis of ADHD and recommendation from a qualified professional, accommodation is often allowed on such standardized examinations. Although accommodation varies with different disabilities, accommodation may include increased time, a separate room, or an assigned reader/scribe.

Colleges are also forbidden by federal legislation against discriminating on the basis of disability on the admission of the individual with ADHD (or other identified disability). Does the federal legislation mandate that an applicant be accepted? No, the legislation stipulates that an *otherwise qualified* applicant cannot be rejected solely on the basis of the disability. There is sometimes argument on the question of what constitutes an *otherwise qualified* applicant.

Having applied and been accepted into a private school for grades K through 12 or a college, the student who is diagnosed as having ADHD may be eligible for accommodation if recommended by a qualified professional. This may include increased time and/or separate room for tests, video recording of lectures, or audio recording of lectures as the most common accommodation.

As a part of the application for education beyond the bachelor's degree, there are frequently other tests, such as the Medical College Admission Test, Dental Aptitude Test, Graduate Record Exam, Law School Admission Test, and so on. These exams are also subject to request for accommodation.

Upon completion of professional school (e.g., medical school, dental school, or law school), there is often an examination required for admission into licensed practice of the profession (e.g., medicine, dentistry, or law). These exams are also regulated by federal law. The individual diagnosed as having a covered disability such as ADHD may request accommodation on an exam required to enter the practice of the profession. At this time it appears unclear as to whether federal judges will rule that the disability must be compared to the general population or to individuals having similar abilities and training. There is also confusion regarding whether the disability in certain functions in these individuals will be noted with or without respect to the benefits derived from compensatory techniques and/or medication. The chapter by Patrichia and Peter Latham (Chapter 11) provides insight into this topic.

The chapter by Mary Richard (Chapter 12) presents a look at myths and misconceptions about ADHD. She deals with myths about the very existence of ADHD as a disorder, its cause, its diagnosis, its features, and its treatment. Ms. Richard gives a perceptive view of these topics that strike at the very heart of the field of ADHD.

The authors of this text have varied backgrounds, but they share one common ground. They all have extensive experience in working with children, adolescents, and/or adults who have ADHD. They have come together to pool their knowledge so that you, the reader, may benefit from their many experiences in this controversial and rapidly changing field. It is the hope of everyone associated with this publication that the information contained herein will enable the parent, teacher, or other professional to deal more effectively with those who have ADHD.

Reference

Silver, L. B. (1998). *The misunderstood child* (3rd ed.). New York: Times Books.

Chapter 2

The History of ADHD

BARBARA PRIDDY GUYER

Until recent years, whenever we thought of someone with problems of attention and activity level, we thought of 10-year-old Billy, swinging from the light fixtures, a human tornado and a general nuisance to everyone who stood in his path. Today we know that much more variety is exhibited in different individuals with ADHD. In addition to problems with hyperactivity and attention, there may be difficulty with impulsivity or focusing, poor interpersonal relationships, poor impulse control. These and a lack of organizational skills are qualities that can easily lead to failure in the classroom and later in life.

Sometimes the ones most handicapped are those who are not noticeably affected. Even today it is not uncommon to blame students and accuse them of lacking motivation when they fail to thrive academically, when in actuality the cause may be directly related to ADHD. Girls are now diagnosed as having ADHD much more often than they were in earlier years. The presenting picture of what we today call ADHD has significantly changed over the years, and it is likely to continue to change as we learn more through experience and research.

Development and Changes in Education

The Early Years—Through the Eighteenth and Nineteenth Centuries

Problems with attention and hyperactivity are not new, but in earlier days they were seldom afforded the importance they are granted today (see Figure 2.1). Prior to the eighteenth and nineteenth centuries, children died more often than they lived. Life was so tenuous that until children had survived to approximately age

ADHD Time Line

Prior to 20th Century	• Plagues, cholera, poverty more important than behavior • Education of masses usually nonexistent
1900	
1917	• World War I — head traumas, etc., recognized to affect behavior and learning • Epidemics are recognized as affecting behavior
1930–1940	• Dominant hemisphere in brain for language discovered • Additional knowledge of brain from World War II • Additional research on effects of brain trauma on learning and behavior • Increased interest in effect of brain on language, movement, and behavior • Amphetamines used as treatment for symptoms of what we currently refer to as ADHD
1960s	• Research with "brain-injured" children who are not retarded • Strategies for education of "brain-injured" children • Recognition that some children have characteristics of "brain-injured" children without evidence of injury • Minimal Brain Dysfunction (MBD) substituted for "Brain-injured" when no evidence of injury • ADD and ADHD terms proposed • Treatment of children with amphetamines does not have a paradoxical effect
1970s	• PL94-142 guaranteed free appropriate public education to the handicapped • Feingold Diet and megavitamins to treat ADHD • Treatment of ADHD with vitamins B complex and C • Hundreds of studies on ADD conducted
1980s – 2000	• 20 – 25% of LD population has ADHD • 10 – 20% of general population has ADHD • Genetic cause of ADHD claimed • Central nervous system relationships claimed • Differences found between brains of those with and without ADHD • Medical treatment became more sophisticated • 1991 — Given protection provided by IDEA, Section 504 of Rehabilitation Act and ADA

FIGURE 2.1   ADHD Time Line

seven, they were often not regarded as a part of society. It seemed a waste of energy to be overly concerned about children who would probably not live long anyway. During those difficult years of our history, the problems of early childhood, which were frequently illustrated in literature and poetry, were seldom noticed unless they were very serious (Stills, 1902). The problems of being overly active or easily distracted paled in comparison with threats from pneumonia, the plague, cholera, etc. As life conditions improved and society became more sophisticated, things other than mere survival gained in importance. The education of children was one area that society began to see as important.

Education for the Masses

The derivation of the Greek word for *school* comes from "leisure time," specifically leisure to pursue philosophy, discussion, and learning in the tradition of the men of classical Greece. Influential scholars significantly affected the education of children, thus beginning a revolution in cultural attitudes towards learning. Many of the basic assumptions that we have today about education began during the eighteenth and nineteenth centuries. Jesuit educators in the seventeenth century felt that childhood should be a time of innocence and that children should be protected from the corruption of adults, reared apart, and taught the word of the Lord. Private tutors and governesses were used by the aristocracy to teach children during this time. Gradually, the middle class began to push to have their children educated as well. Following the Industrial Revolution, the village schoolhouse increased in enrollment until it reached the proportions of what we might call a middle-sized school (Renshaw, 1974).

Practices such as teaching the foundations of reading first and then branching out to more complex academic subjects began primarily with the Jesuit priests. The practice of remaining seated for long periods of time while learning was also instituted during this time. When children were tutored individually, more exceptions could be made for the individual who had a different learning style. When children were placed in groups, however, the individualization seemed to decrease, if not disappear almost entirely (Goldstein, 1990).

Changes in Expectations of Children

In today's society, children's toys display the trend toward action and movement in entertainment. Walking and talking toys, computerized miniature cars and planes, mini-bikes and hot rods, and so on, all add to the action that today's child has learned to expect and even demand. Many children are skilled at using the computer before they begin school, and they often know more than their parents about skillfully mastering video games such as Nintendo. When children begin kindergarten, they are accustomed to a never-ending barrage of color, noise, and frequent change. School can be quite a disappointment in comparison.

Unfortunately, especially for the student with ADHD, many classrooms today continue to require students to remain seated at their desks for long periods of time, participating passively in the act of learning. This is a particularly unfortunate practice for the student who has a high energy level and/or who has problems with attention. Each of us has different skill levels when we focus on a topic. If our attending skills are not highly developed, we find it extremely difficult to attend to one thought for a long period of time (Mercer, 1998). Some people are able to attend for 30 minutes or more without being distracted, whereas others may be distracted after a few seconds. When we reach the limit of our attending ability, it is not uncommon for the mind to begin to wander or for the person to become sleepy. Look around when you are in church or at a lecture, and see if your eyes don't confirm this statement. Better yet, observe your own behavior and evaluate how long you seem to be able to attend to a lecture before your thoughts wander. Don't use the ability to concentrate on video games or a television program to measure attention span. There seems to be a degree of self-hypnosis or hyperfocus involved here. Also, watching television requires no participation on your part whatsoever. Many people who have ADHD stare at TV for hours in a trance-like state. When someone speaks to them, they often are not aware of being spoken to and continue to stare at the TV. On the other hand, engaging in a game of Nintendo certainly requires involvement by the participant, and active learning is an integral part of the experience, requiring the person to be alert every second or else lose the game. (It also helps that winning brings immediate verbal and visual reward.) These immediate rewards may include a great deal of color and a variety of sounds as well as a score. The scenes change quickly and seem to be able to attract and hold even the most distractible person. Perhaps those of us involved in teaching need to profit from what we have learned from computer games and alter teaching techniques as much as possible. Becoming actively involved in the learning process makes it much more likely that the student with ADHD will succeed academically.

Some teachers try to alter their teaching style by asking questions that ask for answers as feedback. Unfortunately, it is not seen as "cool" to respond to teachers' questions. If the answer is wrong, the student is seen as dumb. If the answer is right, the student is seen as a braggart who makes the other students appear dumb or ill-prepared. This makes it even more socially acceptable for the student with ADHD to gaze out the window and refrain from participating in class.

Existence of ADHD in the United States and Other Countries

Hallowell and Ratey (1994) have theorized that the numbers of people with ADHD may be much higher in the United States because of the characteristics of the people who originally settled in the New World. People who were eager for adventure, had high levels of energy, or were not successful in established society were often those who became pioneers in the colonies. On the surface, this theory seems credible. Currently, however, most researchers agree that ADHD is a universal condition and has been found to exist wherever studies regarding diagnosis of this disorder have occurred (Barkley, 1997, 1998). Although estimates of the existence of ADHD seem to vary only slightly in different countries, ADHD is more widely recognized, treated, and accepted in the United States than elsewhere. However, we do not know if ADHD occurs more in the United States or if it is diagnosed more often because it is more acceptable as a condition amenable to diagnosis.

When using behavioral characteristics similar to those used in the United States (which had 3–8% of its population diagnosed as ADHD), several countries significantly exceed the United States in the percentages of the population diagnosed as having ADHD. New Zealand reported 13%, West Germany reported 8%, Spain reported 16%, Italy reported 12%, Great Britain reported 10%, and China reported 11% (Shaywitz & Shaywitz, 1988).

A favorite poem by Rudyard Kipling found in D. C. Renshaw's (1974) publication is included here because it seems to describe the ADHD population ideally:

> "I know a person small—
> He keeps ten million serving men
> Who get no rest at all!
> He sends 'em abroad on his own affairs
> From the second he opens his eyes—
> One million Hows, two million Wheres,
> And seven million Whys!"

The Twentieth Century

Head injuries that occurred in the two world wars showed physicians that brain trauma affects behavior as well as cognition and motor activity. Soldiers who had no reading problems or behavioral problems prior to wartime exhibited serious problems following a head injury (Stewart, 1970).

A number of outstanding researchers left Europe before or during World War II and fled to the United States. During the 1930s, Kurt Werner and Alfred Strauss were able to leave Nazi Germany and find employment in Detroit at the Wayne County Vocational School (Hallahan & Kauffman, 1999). While still in Germany, both Werner and Strauss had the privilege of working with Kurt Goldstein, who had studied the behavioral effects of head injuries in German soldiers who had fought in World War I. Goldstein concluded that brain damage in adults caused a variety of cognitive and behavioral problems that included poor impulse control, inattention, poor perceptual motor abilities, and difficulties with reading and memory.

The encephalitis epidemics of 1916 and 1917 seemed to produce similar effects in the children who survived. The brain damage documented in these cases included symptoms quite similar to those that Goldstein had seen in the German soldiers. These two sources of large amounts of data prompted researchers and clinicians to look more carefully at the possible neurobiological causes for the cognitive and behavioral problems exhibited by children and adults (Renshaw, 1974).

It is important to mention, although it does not bear directly on ADHD, that during this period Samuel Orton became interested in the non-brain-injured person who had serious reading problems. He labeled this problem *strephosymbolia* ("scrambled symbols") and stated that the cause was delayed cerebral lateralization. He believed that such persons lacked the neurobiological substrates for language and that there was not a dominant hemisphere in the language center of the brain (Orton, 1937). Orton was convinced that the result of this neurological difference was that children were unable to learn the complex linguistic tasks of turning printed abstract symbols into meaningful units (words). Although Orton was primarily interested in strephosymbolia (dyslexia), he did a great deal to convince professionals that there need not be a documented brain injury and that a structural or functional difference in the brain might be the cause of failure for the child to perform adequately. This led to an interest in brain-injured retarded children by several researchers, including Werner and Strauss in earlier years and, later, Strauss and Lehtinen (1947). They theorized that these brain injuries resulted from non-genetic causes (shortage of oxygen during the birth process, injury to the head, or a very high fever during infancy) rather than from genetic causes (inherited brain structures that caused impairments in learning). They reported that these injuries produced a cluster of symptoms, including disorders in language, perception, hyperactivity, distractibility, and inattention. Of equal importance, Strauss and his colleagues provided training for many educators and researchers. They began with the theory that "minimal brain injuries" caused deficits in language, movement, and behavior. They were very influential in the development of some of the leaders in the field of special education, such as Cruickshank, Kephart, Myklebust, Kirk, and Frostig. The introduction of racemic (dl-) emphetamine in pill form paved the way for the first scientific study of what we currently define as ADHD (Bradley, 1937).

Before 1940, whenever children experienced problems with learning, the general consensus of professionals was that these children had to be mentally retarded, emotionally disturbed, or socially or culturally disadvantaged (Silver, 1999). As a child, I can remember hearing older adults talk about children who were "different," and the comment of "bad blood" is one that I never forgot. My grandmother knowingly advised that "having bad blood was something a person simply couldn't overcome." My immediate thought was that I hoped I didn't have any of the "bad blood." Some of the terminology that has evolved has sounded as hopeless as "bad blood." What could offer less promise or potential than a "brain-injured child?"

Chess (1960) was one of several researchers who separated the symptoms of hyperactivity from those of brain damage. She wrote about the "hyperactive child syndrome," whose causes were of biological rather than environmental origin.

Later, professionals and other concerned individuals developed an awareness of children who were not mentally retarded but who also had problems that seemed to be caused by brain injury. Cruickshank (1967) and his colleagues developed remedial strategies for brain-injured children in the classroom. They stressed the importance of providing structure and reducing distracting stimuli. The typical classroom created specifically for the brain injured was bland, to say the least. Walls were painted white or gray. Cubicles were usually installed in a classroom so that children wouldn't distract one another. Teachers wore bland colors with little or no jewelry to act as distractors. What Cruickshank and his colleagues did not consider, and what we can easily see through hindsight, is that the children continued to distract themselves. Their ever-racing minds were never still, and during a typical arithmetic lesson, they thought about anything that might occur to them. Their thoughts might range from an argument at home to a fight on the school bus to a much anticipated birthday party. Their minds controlled them, rather than the other way around. During the sixties and early seventies Cruickshank's educational techniques could be seen in many classrooms designed for the "brain injured."

However, many professionals and parents were dissatisfied with the term *brain injured*. They felt that the term denoted a hopeless and permanent condition. In 1957, Stevens and Birch suggested that the term *Strauss syndrome* be used in lieu of *brain injured*. Some of the characteristics that apply to Strauss syndrome also apply to characteristics that are now associated with ADHD: (1) exaggerated behavior that is abnormal for an age group, (2) increased motor activity that is inappropriate for the stimulus (such as running around the classroom when excited while other students remain seated), (3) poor organization of behavior, (4) consistent hyperactivity, and (5) excessive distractibility.

The term *minimal brain dysfunction* (MBD) was introduced, and its popularity increased rapidly. MBD seemed to be a classification that appealed to many. It soon came to be used as a proverbial "dumping ground" for professionals trying to group together disruptive behaviors they observed in the classroom. To this educator, it seemed that whenever one didn't know exactly how to categorize a student, MBD became the label of choice. During the 1960s it was not unusual for teachers to have at least one child per class categorized as having MBD. After diagnosis, it was common to place those students in "brain-injured classrooms," where they could be taught "properly" and not be distracted by their peers (or, more honestly, where they would not distract others). It was also not unusual for the parent of an unruly child with MBD to be told by authorities that there was no place in the school for that child. The parent was requested to keep the child at home, and often homebound instruction was not provided. Behavior by professional educators such as this spurred the lobbying that finally brought about the passage of Public Law 94-142 in 1973. This law guaranteed to all handicapped children a free, appropriate public education equal in quality to that provided for normal children.

In 1966, Clements attempted to clarify MBD by providing ten of the most commonly recognized characteristics in rank-order listing. The most popular characteristics were (1) hyperactivity, (2) emotional lability (wide swings in moods), (3) disorders of attention (short attention span and distractibility, (4) impulsivity, and (5) disorders of memory and thinking. Another possible characteristic, learning disabilities (LD), was mentioned. As the label of MBD became less popular, the term *hyperkinetic reaction* or *hyperactive child* began to be used. *Hyperkinetic Reaction of Childhood or Adolescence* was the formal term used for the purposes of diagnosis as delineated in the *Diagnostic and Statistical Manual of Mental Disorders (DSM-II)* (American Psychiatric Association, 1968). This indicated a change from using a label that implied an underlying etiological process that seemed to be impossible to diagnose definitively to the use of a label that more correctly defined the disorder.

Shaywitz and Shaywitz (1988) reported that 25% of the LD population also had ADHD, with Silver (1998) reporting a similar percentage of 20% to 25%. It seems appropriate to note that ADHD in the general population is 10% to 20% (Silver, 1999). Silver also reported that between 30% and 70% of children with ADHD will continue to have these behaviors when they are adults. He also noted that LD affects the brain's ability to learn, whereas ADHD interferes with an individual's availability for learning. Silver's comment seems to be an especially helpful statement when one attempts to discern the difference between LD and ADHD.

Let us look at a typical situation that was all too common before federal legislation made a situation such as this illegal:

Marianne Royal opened her front door to see the principal of her son's school standing on the porch. Before she could ask him in, Mr. Johnson tipped his hat respectfully and blurted out, "Mrs. Royal, we have had a meeting at school about your son, Joe. He has been a big problem in his classroom this year, disturbing all the other children and making life very difficult for his teacher. We talked about it at length, Mrs. Royal, and we have decided that Joe should not return to school after today. So if you'll just keep him at home, everything will be just fine."

"But how will he learn?" the worried mother asked.

"I'm sure you can help him at home yourself. I'll be glad to lend you a few books, if you like." Mr. Johnson tipped his hat again and walked rapidly to his car, relieved to have this behind him. Mrs. Royal was crestfallen. It struck her that Joe had no chance now for "the good life."

By 1968, there were many concerns about the misuse of the MBD terminology. After the American Psychiatric Association introduced the term *hyperkinetic reaction to childhood* in 1968, in the third edition of the *DSM* (1980), the term *attention deficit disorder* (ADD) appeared. It was then stated that ADD interfered with learning processes. Two types of ADD were described (with and without hyperactivity). ADD with hyperactivity included inattention (failure to finish assignments and difficulty concentrating), impulsivity (acting before thinking), and hyperactivity. It was stated that in order to be identified as ADD, the condition had to occur before age seven, be present for a minimum of six months, and not be caused by other mental disorders. In ADD without hyperactivity, the hyperactivity component was deleted and the other characteristics were not as severe. In 1987, with the publication of the *DSM-III-R*, the name was changed to attention-deficit/hyperactivity disorder (ADHD). One list of characteristics that included all three classifications of ADHD (inattention, impulsivity, and hyperactivity) had only one threshold, and the number needed for a positive diagnosis was specified. There was a separate category for ADD without hyperactivity, and it was referred to as "undifferentiated attention-deficit disorder." The 1994 DSM-IV makes no adjustments for age or gender. Symptoms must appear in two of three settings of home, school or work. Those who have only ADD without hyperactivity are categorized as another type of ADHD. (American Psychiatric Association, 1994). Many experts feel that the differences are important enough to warrant classifying the two as separate disorders. A statement was made that there were no diagnostic criteria because of a lack of research. With each publication of the *DSM*, characteristics of ADHD have changed somewhat, and this trend may well continue for some time in the future.

The Causes of ADHD

Zametkin and Rapaport (1987) reviewed the neurobiological mechanisms affecting ADHD, stating that existing data suggested that a variety of neurotransmitters and neuroanatomical areas were an integral part of ADHD. Hynd, Hern, Voeller, and Marshall (1991) listed 18 neuroanatomical hypotheses implicating several regions including the reticular activating system, the septal region, and the frontal lobes.

One of the problems in understanding ADHD has been a disagreement about its origin. Is it totally a problem of psychopathology, brought on by some traumatic event or events, or does it also have a measurable anatomical and/or physiological basis (Goldman, Genel, Bezman, and Slanetz, 1998)?

The elegant studies in the Colorado twin project have offered evidence for a genetic basis (Gilger, Pennington, & DeFries, 1992). They report concordance as high as 92% in monozygotic twins and only about 33% in dizygotic twins. (Dizygotic twins would share the same fetal environment, of course, but their genetic similarity would be only that of siblings.)

It has also been reported that there are anatomical differences between the brains of ADHD individuals and those not so diagnosed (Castellanos, Giedd, Marsh, et al., 1996). These studies have been made possible in living subjects by the advent of the non-invasive procedure called magnetic resonance imaging (MRI).

At one point it was widely believed that a distinction could be made between ADHD individuals and others by the use of stimulants. A favorable response to psychostimulants was considered to be an indication of ADHD, whereas an unfavorable response (e.g., possibly heightened activity) was evidence that the subject was not ADHD (a "paradoxical effect"). It was difficult to justify testing "normal" children with a drug such as an amphetamine, especially since parents could not readily give informed consent. The problem was solved by using "normal" children whose parents were medical professionals at the National Institute for Mental Health. The study was completed, and it was found that ADHD children and "normal" children responded in the same direction when given the psychostimulant medication. Thus, successful administration of the drug was not an indication of ADHD (Rapaport, Buchsbaum, Zahn, et al., 1978).

Cerebral glucose metabolism has been studied by positron emission tomography (PET scan) using F18-fluorodeoxyglucose. In adults with ADHD there was decreased global and regional glucose metabolism in the cerebrum when compared with normal volunteers (Matochik et al., 1993). This difference was not found between adolescents with or without ADHD (Zametkin, Liebenauer, Fitzgerald, et al., 1993). The explanation of this is difficult to ascertain. Perhaps non-significant differences in cerebral metabolism in adolescence bring about changes in structure and function that result in significant differences in cerebral metabolism in adulthood.

Treatment of ADHD

Bradley (1937) was the first to study the effects of amphetamine pills as a treatment of what is now recognized as ADHD. With amphetamines, he found that the subjects, ages 5 to 13, became more goal directed than they had ever been previously.

During the early years of medical treatment for ADHD, treatment was strictly limited to children who exhibited symptoms of this disorder. The possible effects of medication on the adult were not considered in the early years, and it was not until the children who were treated successfully became adults that we began to discover that medication could be effective in treating the adult with ADHD.

Although not a treatment by medication in the classical sense, the Feingold diet should be mentioned here. Feingold, an allergist with an early health maintenance organization (HMO), noted that he was being asked to treat many hyperactive children. He developed the concept that these children were unusually sensitive to certain foods, particularly foods containing artificial colorings and flavors. He noted that many of these were related to salicylates and he developed diets avoiding such compounds. The approach was quite popular at one time, but it is not accorded significant acceptance by professionals or the public at this time. The scientific/medical community does not support the belief that any significant number of individuals with ADHD respond positively to dietary approaches such as the Feingold diet (Office of Medical Applications of Research, 1982). Another approach of "dietary" origin was advanced by Cott. This approach, consisting mainly of dietary supplementation with large amounts of vitamins B complex and C, receives little notice today. (Presumably the individual with ADHD, for whatever reason, required much larger than usual intake of these vitamins [Cott, 1985].)

Actual treatment of hyperactivity with drugs probably occurred first in children. It had long been realized that some drugs given to children would have the converse effect of what was noted in adults. Thus, mild sedatives given to some children bring about hyperactivity, the converse of what is seen in adults. Amphetamines, taken by some adults as a means of stimulation to maintain alertness (or to treat narcolepsy), were found to decrease the hyperactivity in some children (Silver, 1999).

Dextroamphetamine (e.g., Dexedrine) was one of the first stimulants given to children with ADHD. Today it has largely been supplanted by methylphenidate. It is reported that the latter drug accounts for over 90% of the stimulant medication used for individuals with ADHD in the United States. This is believed to be caused by overuse of dextroamphetamine in order to produce weight loss and the belief that methylphenidate offered less opportunity for abuse. Although the production and use of methylphenidate in the United States has increased from less than 200 kg in 1986 to 9000 kg in 1995, there was little evidence of abuse of the drug by patients with ADHD or by their families (Goldman et al., 1998).

Non-stimulant drugs have achieved some success as well. Tricyclic antide-pressants and the newer antidepressant Bupropion are used, especially in those for whom the stimulant drugs are ineffective or have unacceptable side-effects (Gold-man, et al., 1998; Fowler, 1995). Bupropion is known to function by blocking the reuptake of norepinephrine and dopamine (Conners, Casat, Gualtieri et al., 1996). Centrally acting alpha-blockers such as Clonidine have sometimes been used suc-cessfully, especially with those who are inclined to be aggressive (Silver, 1999; Elin, 1996).

The Adult with ADHD

In the early years, physicians often advised parents that symptoms of hyperactiv-ity and other accompanying problems would disappear by adolescence (Gallico, Burns, & Grob, 1991). Parents waited and waited, and by the time the hyperactive child reached voting age, they began to fear that the symptoms were a permanent fixture. For others, the excessive hyperactivity did disappear, but more socially acceptable behaviors often appeared. Foot tapping, fingernail biting, pencil twist-ing, and seat squirming were common occurrences with the adult who no longer exhibited the typical characteristics of hyperactivity.

However, the adult has seemed to become more defeated by other character-istics of ADHD (Banks, Guyer, & Guyer, 1995). The lack of organizational skills becomes much more serious with the adult, who no longer has a parent or teacher to structure the day and direct the sequence of activities. When left to one's own devices, it is easy to become distracted by anything and everything and to waste time without realizing it.

> Mark explains it this way: "I am studying in a quiet conference room at my uni-versity. Someone walks down the hall whistling. I stop to wonder who is in the hall. Several names flash through my memory, and I stop to think about each per-son—what they might be doing, where they are now, etc. Then the whistling reminds me of the time I was in charge of a whistling contest when I was in high school. I think of the problems I had with publicity, etc. By this time, I've wasted 45 minutes, and I am not even aware of it! When I take medication for ADHD, I hear the person walking down the hall just as I did before, but that's as far as it goes. I immediately get back to my studying and save 45 minutes." (Guyer, 1996).

Problems with interpersonal skills have a deleterious effect on establishing relationships, maintaining marriages, and so on (Hallowell & Ratey, 1994). Con-tributing to and possibly causing many problems are poor self-esteem, frequent feelings of failure, failure to interpret body language, and feelings of depression. Behavioral characteristics may be a part of the total picture as well and are typified by problems with impulsivity, distractibility, emotional lability, and immaturity, making it extremely difficult for the average adult with ADHD to establish and maintain intimacy.

Adults with ADHD sometimes have "racing minds," and this compounds their problems with interpersonal communication. For example, a man may want to discuss a personal problem with his girlfriend or spouse who has ADHD. He feels that the discussion has only begun when she skips to another, unrelated topic. She accuses him of "talking it to death" and of "dragging his feet." He becomes angry and shouts that it is impossible to discuss anything with her. After a few of these unproductive episodes, the relationship will be in serious trouble. Similar experiences can occur in the workplace as well, but here an employer often lacks the patience that a spouse may have. Meanwhile, the adult with ADHD is often completely unaware that he or she is a large part of the problem (Fowler, 1995).

Many changes have occurred in our recognition, diagnosis, and treatment of ADHD. In earlier years, we simply observed variant behavior such as hyperactivity and smiled. Sometimes we remarked that the parents didn't understand how to manage the behavior of their child, and we were grateful that the child wasn't ours. Today, however, when we observe children, adolescents, or adults who are impulsive, hyperactive, inattentive, etc., we are more likely to mention the possibility of the existence of ADHD. Most of us are aware, if only through the media, that treatment is possible. This is significant progress for the general public to make. With greater understanding, each year will witness an improvement in the treatment of ADHD so that this "difference" will cease to have such a deleterious effect on people of all ages who have ADHD.

There are several famous people who have been labeled as ADHD, often following death, by a variety of professionals. Included in this group are Wolfgang Amadeus Mozart, who is probably remembered as the most brilliant composer of classical music the world has ever known. He was able to hyperfocus for an unbelievable period of time, sometimes writing an entire opera in just a few weeks. At the same time, he left other pieces unfinished, although he had promised clients delivery dates. He seemed to be unable to deal with practical details such as finances, and it is noteworthy to mention that Mozart died penniless when he was in his mid-thirties.

Sir Winston Churchill had serious problems throughout his school career. He was described by his teachers as "hyperactive and naughty." He was frequently allowed to leave his classroom and run around the playground so that he could release his excess energy. In his biography, *My Early Life,* Churchill described his impulsivity, his frequency of accidents, and his many unpleasant experiences in school. Churchill's high energy level and creativity in problem solving served him well during World War II.

Thomas A. Edison experienced many difficulties during his brief stay in school. In retrospect, we can see that the characteristics of ADHD were actually an asset instead of a liability when he was unable to continue with just one investigation and was constantly going in directions that were ever changing. As a former teacher of Edison's wrote, "He alternated between letting his mind travel to distant places and putting his body in perpetual motion in his seat" (quoted in Sears & Thompson, 1998).

References

American Psychiatric Association. (1968). *Diagnostic and statistical manual of mental disorders* (2nd ed.). Washington, DC: Author.

American Psychiatric Association. (1987). *Diagnostic and statistical manual of mental disorders* (3rd ed., rev.). Washington, DC: Author.

American Psychiatric Association. (1994). *Diagnostic and statistical manual of mental disorders* (4th ed.). Washington, DC: Author.

Banks, S., Guyer, B., & Guyer, K. (1995). A study of medical students and physicians referred for learning disabilities. *Annals of Dyslexia, 45,* 233–244.

Barkley, R. (1995). *Taking charge of ADHD.* New York: Guilford.

Barkley, R. (1997). *ADHD and the nature of self-control.* New York: Guilford.

Barkley, R. (1998). The prevalence of ADHD: Is it just a U.S. disorder? *ADHD Reports, 6*(2), 1–6.

Bradley, C. (1937). The behavior of children receiving Benzedrine. *American Journal of Psychiatry, 94,* 577–585.

Castellanos, F., Giedd, J., Marsh, W., et al. (1996). Quantitative brain magnetic resonance imaging in attention-deficit hyperactivity disorder. *Archives of General Psychiatry, 53,* 607–616.

Chess, S. (1960). Diagnosis and treatment of the hyperactive child. *New York State Journal of Medicine, 60,* 2379–2385.

Clements, S. (1966). Minimal brain dysfunction in children. *NINDS Monograph 3,* U.S. Public Health Service Publication 1415. Washington, DC: U.S. Government Printing Office.

Conners, C. K., Casat, C. D., Gualtieri, C. T., et al. (1996). Bupropion hydrochloride in attention deficit disorder with hyperactivity. *Journal of the American Academy of Child and Adolescent Psychiatry, 35,* 1314–1321.

Cott, A. (1985). *Dr. Cott's help for your LD child: The orthomolecular treatment.* New York: Times Books.

Cruickshank, W. (1967). *The brain-injured child in home, school and community.* Syracuse, NY: Syracuse University Press.

Elin, J. (1996). Drug treatment for hyperactive children: Therapeutic guidelines. *Drugs, 46,* 863–871.

Fowler, R., & Fowler, J. (1995). *Honey, are you listening? How ADD could be affecting your marriage.* Nashville: Thomas Nelson.

Gallico, R., Burns, T., & Grob, C. (1991). *Emotional and behavioral problems in children with learning disabilities.* San Diego: Singular.

Gilger, J., Pennington, B., & DeFries, J. (1992). A twin study of the etiology of comorbidity: Attention-deficit hyperactivity disorder and dyslexia. *Journal of the American Academy of Child and Adolescent Psychiatry, 31,* 343–348.

Goldman, L. S., Genel, M., Bezman, R., & Slanetz, P. (1998). Diagnosis and treatment of attention-deficit/hyperactivity disorder in children and adolescents. *Journal of the American Medical Association, 279,* 1100–1107.

Goldstein, S., & Goldstein, M. (1990). *Managing attention deficit disorder in children: A guide for practitioners.* New York: Wiley.

Guyer, B. (March 3, 1996), Private conversation.

Hallahan, D., & Kauffman, J. (1999). *Introduction to learning disabilities.* Columbus, OH: Merrill.

Hallowell, E., & Ratey, J. (1994). *Driven to distraction.* New York: Pantheon.

Hynd, G., Hern, K., Voeller, K., & Marshall, R. (1991). Neurobiological basis of attention-deficit hyperactivity disorder (ADHD). *School Psychology Review, 20,* 186–194.

Matochik, J., Nordahl, T., Gross, M., Semple, W., King, A., Cohen, R., & Zametkin, A. (1993). Effects of acute stimulant medication on cerebral metabolism in adults with hyperactivity. *Neuropsychopharmacology, 8,* 377–386.

Mercer, C., & Mercer, A. (1998). *Teaching students with learning problems* (5th ed.). Columbus, OH: Merrill.

Office for Medical Applications of Research. (1982). *N.I.H. Consensus Development Conference summary.* Bethesda, MD: National Institutes of Health.

Orton, S. (1937). *Reading, writing and speech problems in children.* New York: W. W. Norton.

Rapaport, J., Buchsbaum, M., Zahn, T., et al. (1978). Dextroamphetamine: Behavioral and cognitive effects in normal prepubertal boys. *Science, 199,* 560–563.

Renshaw, D. (1974). *The hyperactive child.* Chicago: Nelson-Hall.

Sears, W. & Thompson, L. (1998). *The A.D.D. book: New understandings, new approaches to parenting your child.* New York: Little, Brown.

Shaywitz, S., & Shaywitz, B. (1988). Developmental disabilities: Current perspectives. In J. F. Kavanaugh & T. J. Truss, T. J. (Eds.), *Learning disabilities: Proceedings of the national conference.* Parkton, MD: York.

Shaywitz, S., & Shaywitz, B. (1998). Attention deficit disorder with hyperactivity. *Advances in Pediatrics, 44,* 331–367.

Silver, L. B. (1998). *The misunderstood child* (3rd ed.). New York: Times Books.

Silver, L. B. (1999). *Attention-deficit hyperactivity disorder: A clinical guide to diagnosis and treatment for health and mental health.* Washington, DC: American Psychiatric Press.

Stewart, M. A. (1970). Hyperactive children. *Scientific American, 222,* 94–98.

Stills, G. (1902). Some abnormal psychological conditions in children. *Lancet, 1,* 1008–1012, 1077–1082, 1163–1168.

Strauss, A., & Lehtinen, L. (1947). *Psychopathology and education of the brain-injured child.* New York: Grune & Stratton.

Zametkin, A., Liebenauer, L., Fitzgerald, G., King, A., Minkunas, D., Herscovitch, P., et al. (1993). Brain metabolism in teenagers with attention-deficit hyperactivity disorder. *Archives of General Psychiatry, 50,* 333–340.

Zametkin, A., & Rapaport, J. (1987). Neurobiology of attention deficit disorder with hyperactivity: Where have we come in 50 years? *Journal of American Academy of Child and Adolescent Psychiatry, 26,* 676–686.

Chapter 3

ADHD: Diagnosis

ROSA A. HAGIN   LISA R. DESON

Attention Deficit Hyperactivity Disorder (ADHD) is the third most common learning problem among children. It follows only reading and other language disorders (Gaddes & Edgell, 1994). A wide range of behaviors may lead to referral for diagnostic services. A child might be referred because of hyperactive behavior or difficulty sustaining attention in school. However, children may be brought to the attention of a clinician for other behaviors as well: disorganized schoolwork, sloppy handwriting, "bad" conduct such as blurting out answers or failing to take turns in games, truancy, academic failure, refusal to complete schoolwork, forgetting books and other study materials, and a lack of motivation. The clinician's job is to tease out the causes of these behaviors and to provide guidelines for intervention to teachers, parents, and others interested in the child's welfare—in short, to provide comprehensive diagnosis.

This is not an easy task. There is indeed great variation in behaviors, in causation, in contextual effects, and even in the definition of the disorder. Barkley (1990) has stated that the prevalence of ADHD is difficult to measure and that the incidence cannot be accurately determined because investigators have not agreed on definitions.

Approaches to Consensus

The Diagnostic and Statistical Manual of Mental Disorders (DSM-IV) of the American Psychiatric Association (1994) estimates that approximately 3% to 5% of all children have ADHD symptoms serious enough for professional attention. However, incidence depends upon how one chooses to define the disorder, the demographic characteristics of the population under study, the geographic locale of the survey, and the degree of agreement among parents, teachers, and other professionals who report the data. Over a decade ago, Douglas (1983) stated that some children were misclassified as ADHD on the basis of teacher and parent identification. Presently, there is little indication that the misclassification problem has been corrected.

Although *DSM-IV* does not provide specific procedures for assessing ADHD, it defines the disorder and describes characteristic behaviors. ADHD is seen as a persistent pattern of inattention, hyperactivity/impulsivity, or both, with this pattern more frequently observed in those with ADHD than in individuals at a comparable level of development. Some of the inattentive or hyperactive/impulsive symptoms that impair behavior must have been present before age seven, although the diagnosis may occur years after initial symptoms appeared. The behavior reported must be present in at least two settings—for example, at home, at school, or in play settings.

The *DSM-IV* structure is designed to enhance the reliability of the diagnosis across practitioners. Unlike the previous edition of the *Diagnostic and Statistical Manual,* the *DSM-IV* criteria highlight the importance of distinguishing inattentiveness from hyperactivity/impulsiveness, differences that are critical in identifying subtypes of the disorder. Specific symptoms provide a list of target behaviors that examiners should assess. Developmental histories of children are essential to determine the age of onset of the disorder and to obtain relevant medical and family history data. Finally, *DSM-IV* states that it must be established that the ADHD-related behaviors are chronic (occurring for at least 6 months). The requirement of pervasive symptoms occurring across environments implies the need for multiple sources of assessment data.

Causation

Although the cardinal symptoms associated with ADHD—inattention, distractibility, impulsivity, inability to delay gratification, motor restlessness, and hyperactivity—have been recognized for many years, they have been interpreted from different viewpoints. Such interpretations have often depended upon the prevailing views of child-rearing at the time. Early descriptions appear as bad examples in moralistic children's storybooks. For example, the 1845 story of *Das Struwwelpter* (unkempt Peter), written by a German physician, Henrich Hoffman, was reported by Gaddes and Edgell (1994), as was "Fidgety Phil" in an English storybook. These characters were portrayed as active, always in trouble, and never seeming to learn from their mistakes. In 1902, G. F. Still in the British journal *Lancet* described children who were inattentive, impulsive, unresponsive to discipline, wantonly mischievous, and destructive. He attributed these behaviors to a problem in moral development.

After the influenza epidemic during World War I, physicians began to recognize some of these behavior symptoms in children who suffered from influenza-related encephalitis. Laretta Bender wrote extensively about children who suffered insults to the central nervous system because of encephalitis (infections that were sequellae of influenza or of the infectious diseases of childhood, such as measles), because of exposure to lead or other toxic substances, or because of perinatal complications. The disordered behavior of these children came to be understood not as immoral and wicked, but as the result of organic factors, insults to the brain and central nervous system because of infections, toxic substances, or subtle injuries to the infant during the birth process.

Two important developments soon followed. In 1937, Bradley reported dramatic improvement in the behavior of these children when they were given amphetamine sulfate, a stimulant drug. Unlike the stimulant effect this drug induced with average people, the drug had a calming effect with hyperactive children. This contradictory response is still not completely understood, and, for a time, it was used as a sort of retrospective method of diagnosing attention deficit hyperactivity disorders—that is, if the child's behavior improved on the drug, it was regarded as confirmation of the diagnosis of hyperactivity.

A second important development occurred in 1947 with the publication of a book on the education of what some called "brain-injured children" by A. A. Strauss and Laura Lehtinen. This was one of the earliest approaches not only to more precise diagnostic techniques, but also to effective educational methods for teaching these children. This early work inspired others to develop educational approaches for these children, some modeling the work of Strauss and Lehtinen, some embodying other points of view. The following two decades saw an explosion of innovation and experimentation with educational methods and materials that enriched the special education movement in the schools.

Meanwhile, the question of nomenclature was a puzzling one. Not only did labeling children as "brain damaged" offend the sensitivities of their parents; in most cases, the label was false. Neurological examinations were at a loss to confirm what had been inferred from history and behavior. Terms such as minimal brain dysfunction, organic drivenness, Strauss syndrome, restless syndrome, and hyperkinesis were proposed and then discarded.

With the failure to find gross evidence of brain damage, people looked for other explanations of these children's disordered behavior. Impaired parent–child relationships became a convenient target; the problems in children were often attributed to poor child-rearing practices. Therapists found the parents less stressful to deal with than their offspring. Parent support groups and parent training activities proliferated.

Although ADHD was originally conceptualized as a childhood disorder, follow-up research and retrospective studies have shown it to persist into adulthood in many cases. Gaddes and Edgell (1994) estimate that 60% of the children diagnosed with ADHD continue to experience the disorder as adults, with all the implication of the effects on academic performance, interpersonal skills, self-esteem, and productivity.

Long-term studies of the disorder have contributed to the understanding of causative factors. Other scientific developments that have enhanced the knowledge of etiology have been technical advances in brain imaging and more specific methods in neuropsychology. Research continues in four major areas:

Neurological Causes

Although structural defects of the central nervous system have not been documented, a number of studies have focused on subcortical areas of the brain. Investigations of these deeper structures have focused on *gating*, the ability of the organism to select and control its response to environmental stimulation. Studies of blood flow have also shown decreased flow to the frontal lobes of the brain in subjects with ADHD. On the other hand, research on minor physical anomalies in development has found only weak associations with ADHD. Animal studies, in which it has been possible to induce alteration in neurotransmitter systems, have produced hyperactive behavior in some laboratories.

Heredity

Positive family histories in some cases and twin studies have been shown to bear some relationship to the disorder, but the mechanisms of transmission of the disorder are not clear.

Underarousal

Some investigators have explained the hyperactive behavior characteristic of these children as resulting from their need for stimulation because of underarousal. This stimulus-seeking behavior has been said to explain the paradoxical effect of stimulant medications on people with ADHD.

Allergies and Food Sensitivities

Although more than a decade of studies with foods and food additives failed to establish overall relationships to ADHD, it may be that allergies and food sensitivities may be significant in the cases of individuals. It has also been suggested that the physical stress created by allergens may increase the symptoms of ADHD or that the allergies and sensitivities may represent two symptoms of a common unknown cause.

To summarize current knowledge of the causes of ADHD, it can be said that causation varies with individual cases. Some symptoms are generated within the child's brain and central nervous system; others are secondary symptoms, responses to the environmental setting in which children live. These secondary symptoms may result from a mismatch between the demands of the classroom and the child's unique educational needs, or from the child's reaction to a chaotic home environment. Finally, some of the same symptoms associated with ADHD may be found in other disorders, such as the restless agitation manifested in some depressed children or the early precursors of tics in Tourette syndrome. Thus, the need for comprehensive diagnostic study is essential to understanding the meaning the symptoms have for the individual one is asked to help.

Need for Comprehensive Diagnosis

The need for a greater degree of concordance in diagnostic procedures is great. For example, in a review of 210 studies of hyperactive children, Barkley (1990) found that 64% of these studies used no specified criteria other than the opinion of the observer (parent or teacher) when classifying a child as hyperactive. In a survey of 131 school psychologists in New York State, McClure and Gordon (1984) found that only one of them used a direct measure of either attention or impulsivity when evaluating children referred for attentional problems.

A youngster may *appear* inattentive; however, appearance does not mean that the child actually suffers from ADHD. Some children are physically active and inattentive in school because of conduct problems, anxiety, learning disorders, depression, or academic demands that are not sufficiently challenging. Upon evaluation, they may be found to perform successfully on measures of attention and academic achievement (Fischer, Newby, & Gordon, 1993). Conversely, compliant, seemingly attentive children can exhibit clear deficits on tasks that require sustained attention. Diagnosis based on outward appearance may be misleading.

Distinguishing ADHD from other disorders may be a difficult task for clinicians and teachers. In view of the contradictory results from existing studies, Silver and Hagin (1990) suggested several methods in evaluating children who display attentional problems. They suggested that diagnostic identification be made over time and across settings to help distinguish "situational" from "pervasive" hyperactivity. Further, they suggested that the following questions be considered:

1. Are the children's attentional difficulties part of a more pervasive developmental disorder (e.g., autism)?
2. Are the attentional difficulties secondary to school learning difficulties?
3. Are the attentional problems secondary to a mismatch between task demands and the child's level of functioning (based on measures of intelligence and achievement)?
4. Are the behavior characteristics of ADHD present to a developmentally inappropriate degree so as to interfere with the child's functioning?

The term ADHD can be thought of as a descriptive label denoting a cluster of behaviors that commonly occur together. The task of the diagnostician is to determine whether the child is displaying behaviors at a developmentally inappropriate level and to a problematic degree in more than one setting. The very nature of questionnaires to assess behavior makes them a contextualized measure based on reports from parents who see the child in the home setting and teachers who see the child only at school.

This point is made in a study conducted by Deson (1998) in which she investigated agreement in rates of reporting hyperactive and distractible behavior by three different sources: parents, teachers, and the child's response to a continuous performance task. The measures used were the ADHD Rating Scale (completed by the parents and the teachers) and the Gordon Diagnostic System (GDS), a computerized continuous performance test administered to each child by the examiner. Agreement of the three data sources was found to be poor, with the parents' responses to the questionnaire identifying 15%, with teacher's responses identifying 4%, and with the GDS identifying 2% of the subjects as hyperactive and distractible. Although each source identified some children within the sample, overlap among the measures was almost nonexistent, with only one child identified by all three sources. These results suggest that children may exhibit different behaviors in different settings. Consequently, assessing a child in more than one environment is a necessity. Additionally, different raters may also have different standards of what is appropriate conduct; therefore, employing more than one rater to observe and report behavior will ensure more accurate diagnosis.

Deson (1998) concluded that the acceptance of universal definitions, guidelines for what is developmentally appropriate and what constitutes abnormal levels of hyperactive behavior, will help parents, teachers, and clinicians. Educating teachers to recognize off-task behavior that is not necessarily intrusive in a classroom might facilitate earlier identification and intervention with children who are not openly hyperactive. Classes for teaching parents how to establish rules with appropriate consequences for good and bad behavior may reduce the "hyperactive" conduct that mothers and fathers have reported so frequently.

Elements of Comprehensive Diagnosis

Sound diagnosis is data-based, using both clinical observations and formal measures. Although many well-engineered measures are available, test scores, by themselves, do not constitute effective diagnosis. Real diagnosis requires the judgment of a clinician who is able to evaluate and integrate results of observations and measures in a comprehensive formulation that leads logically to intervention strategies.

Good diagnosis is parsimonious. Although a wide variety of observation schedules, questionnaires, projective techniques, and behavior measures are available, quantity does not ensure quality. The measures to be used should be based on a well-articulated statement of the referring problem itself and on an understanding of previous attempts to diagnose and intervene.

For children suspected of having ADHD, diagnosis includes five major components:

- definition of the problem
- description of previous and current educational opportunities
- assessment of educational achievement
- assessment of cognitive and neuropsychological functioning
- description of behavioral and emotional resources

The range of information implies that the skills of more than one discipline are necessary, but it should be emphasized that no fixed group of professionals and no fixed battery of diagnostic procedure is necessary in every case. The disciplines and instruments involved should be determined by the needs of the individual, the availability of current information, the special aspects of the referral problem, and the history of previous services. Each element of diagnosis is discussed here in terms of basic clinical questions.

What is the problem? Answers to this question provide a focus for the information to be collected. Information is needed not only on the current problem, but also on the timing and severity of the problem's development. In addition, the developmental history of the child and descriptions of the child's strengths must also be recorded. Problem definition is important not only to guide the examiner, but also to achieve understanding by the child and his or her parents in order to secure their cooperation during the diagnostic process and in implementing recommendations that result from the study.

What kinds of educational opportunities has this child enjoyed? In addition to the conventional developmental history, the answers to this question should include a detailed history of educational development both at home and at school. Examiners should explore qualitative factors such as the nature of early care; the quality of adjustment to nursery school, day care, and kindergarten; and the consistency of school staffing and curriculum organization. Finally, a chronological description of previous interventions that have been recommended and results of their implementation should also be secured.

It is also useful to ask the youngster to describe the activities of a typical school day. This account may involve some degree of bias, but it is important for the examiner to understand the child's perceptions of the school program. On the one hand, an examination may elicit an account of well-organized, challenging activities; on the other, it may elicit a daily regimen of workbooks and ditto sheets with little opportunity for individualization as outlined in the individual educational plan. Classroom observation is also invaluable as a reality check on the child's perceptions of the educational program. Other rich sources of information include documentation provided by parents and teachers, report cards, school attendance records, copies of group test results, reports of previous psychological studies, individual educational plans, letters from camp, and baby books kept by parents. The quality and quantity of previous educational experiences must likewise be considered in any diagnostic study.

What is the current educational status? Objective measures of the skills areas through individual tests are important in assessing a child's current educational strengths and weaknesses. It is also useful to request samples of younger children's current schoolwork and to review the notebooks and textbooks of older students. This will provide information not only about current achievement levels, but also about the extent to which the school's expectations are being met and the kind of support the school is providing in day-to-day work. The clinician also needs to consider whether current levels of achievement are in keeping with the educational opportunities described in the earlier question. Are there intra-individual differences (e.g., language versus quantitative skills, written work versus oral participation)? Are gaps in achievement explainable as a mismatch between the school setting and the child's educational needs? Particularly with children reported to have attention problems, does the child possess generally adequate skills but fail to apply them in accomplishing the goals of an effective educational program? When answers to these questions are unclear, further diagnosis is necessary.

How does this child function on general cognitive measures and specific neuropsychological measures related to the referral problem? Clinicians assess cognitive functioning in nearly every aspect of a youngster's behavior: use of language, ability to attend to and to process information, logical thinking, and common sense as demonstrated in interviews and in dealing with educational measures. Psychological science has also provided a number of formal measures of cognitive abilities. Individual intelligence tests in the hands of a skilled examiner provide a good deal more information than do test scores. Such tests can be used to assess complex intellectual and motivational factors in a standardized way. Some relevant information can be obtained through observations of the child's response style to a series of structured tasks; other relevant information is available through analysis of known statistical properties of the various scales that have been subjected to intensive research. One method is scatter analysis, which is dependent upon the presence of statistically significant differences among various scale or subtest scores. Thus, an uneven profile, often characteristic of records of children with attention problems, can show the effects of atypical cognitive development. The examiner's task is not only to document these effects but also to determine how these effects influence the child's ability to learn.

Quantitative results of individual intelligence tests may underestimate the abilities of children with attention disorders because their difficulties in sustaining attention and limited frustration tolerance may interfere with their response to even the most patient examiner. Their inattention also represents a threat to the validity of their scores on cognitive measures in the area of social judgment and interpersonal relationships. These children may fail to pick up the social cues (such as raised eyebrows) that other children absorb casually in the course of life experiences. The cumulative effect of this loss may be reflected in their social and cognitive development in later years.

Recent interest in brain/behavior relationships has produced some application of neuropsychological methods on diagnostic work with children. Unlike adult neuropsychology, which emphasizes the detection and localization of brain pathology, work with children is directed toward the dynamics of brain function and how they relate to the unfolding demands of a child's immediate and long-range environment. For children with attention problems, the assessment of the subskills that underlie social learning guide the selection of the best ways of improving a child's capacity to focus.

What are this child's behavioral and emotional resources? The number of techniques for assessing emotional factors is large and varied. They range from those (such as interviews) that are clearly under the conscious control of the youngster to those in which the child may have little idea of the purpose of the task, much less any idea of what the nature of a "good" response might be (as with such projectives as the Thematic Apperception Test and the Rorschach). Choices among techniques may depend upon the ability of a child to take part in direct discussion of his or her problems, and also upon the orientation and training of the examiner. Whatever the choice, the purpose of this part of the evaluation is to provide data with which the clinician can describe the personality structure of the child and his or her resources, to be used in intervention planning.

In addition to an understanding of basic personality structure, adequate diagnosis of children referred for attention problems must include a balanced description of characteristic behavior. These descriptions must be normative across settings and reporters, because basic treatment decisions depend to a large extent upon accurate descriptions of children's behavior.

Behavior Rating Scales

Typically, although symptoms of ADHD may be observed prior to the age of 6, not until formal schooling begins is the seriousness of the symptoms formally noted. Teachers, who see many students of the same age, can readily make age and gender comparisons through which ADHD symptoms become apparent.

There is evidence that teachers are able to distinguish between children with and without ADHD symptoms. However, teacher rating scales can be subjective. For example, defiance toward a teacher can increase the likelihood that a child will be rated as hyperactive or inattentive (Schachar, Sandberg, & Rutter, 1986). Therefore, it is suggested that teacher reports be used as *part* of a comprehensive assessment battery, not depended upon as a complete diagnosis.

Behavior rating scales describe a behavior, and the rater determines if it is observable in the subject. Rating scales are easy to administer and efficient in the use of time, energy, and finances. However, there are drawbacks to this source of data:

1. Rater bias occurs when the rater overestimates or underestimates the frequency of particular behaviors.
2. Halo effects are possible.
3. Item overlap may occur.
4. A reporter may not recall or note the frequency of a particular behavior.
5. Vague or misunderstood rating criteria may inaccurately represent a subject's behavior.

Lack of agreement among raters can also occur because of situational or environmental differences (e.g., the contrast of a quiet home versus a noisy classroom) or different tolerance levels among raters (a teacher who wants students to sit up straight and look at the chalkboard versus a teacher who allows children to read sitting on the floor, or the teacher who sees the child alone versus the teacher who sees the child in a classroom group). Because of these issues of basic reliability and the indirect nature of reported data, rating scales are not always corroborated by other measures of ADHD. These problems tend to decrease confidence in the exclusive use of behavior rating scales for diagnosis.

Although behavior rating scales alone are not sufficient to generate specific diagnosis, in reality they are often used as the sole diagnostic tool (Young, O'Brien, Gutterman, & Cohen, 1987). The reasons lie in their cost efficiency and their provision of apparently objective assessment of severity of symptoms. Some of the commonly used behavior rating scales include the following:

- Comprehensive Behavior Rating Scale for Children (Lahey, Neeper, & Frick, 1990)
- Conners Teacher Rating Scale—Revised (Conners, 1985; Goyette, Conners, & Ulrich, 1978)
- Iowa Conners Parent Rating Scale (Loney & Milich, 1982)
- Child Behavior Checklist Parent Form (Achenbach & Edelbrock, 1983)
- Child Behavior Checklist Teacher Form (Achenbach & Edelbrock, 1983)
- Child Attention Problems (Edelbrock, 1984)
- ADHD Rating Scale (Du Paul, 1990)
- ADHD Rating Scale IV (Du Paul, Anastopoulous, Power, Murphy, & Barkley, 1994, 1996)

Some writers have reported that conduct problems may artificially inflate ratings on a scale purported to assess attention problems and hyperactivity. The item composition of the scale itself may also artificially inflate scores. Schaughency, Frick, Christ, Neeper, and Lahey (1990) examined profiles of children in different diagnostic groups when their teachers completed the Comprehensive Behavior Rating Scale for Children (CBRSC). Their finding that the profile of these clinic-referred children generally differed from other national normative samples on the CBRSC supported the use of teacher ratings as an efficient screening method for suspected adjustment difficulties. However, they did not find that ratings for the different diagnostic groups differed from one another. Children with clinical diagnoses of ADHD, conduct disorder, and ADHD plus conduct disorder did not have unique profiles of the CBRSC. Schaughency and colleagues concluded that the presence of conduct problems increased the likelihood that a child would be inaccurately rated as hyperactive or inattentive.

The Conners Scales have been shown to be sensitive to stimulant drug effects (Barkley, Fischer, Newby, & Breen, 1988), to effects of parent training in child management (Pollard, Ward, & Barkley, 1983), and to self-control training of hyperactive children (Horn, Ialongo, Popovich, & Peradotto, 1984). However, because the Hyperkinetic Index of the Conners Rating Scales contains a mixture of items related to non-compliance and aggression, it is difficult to separate problems due to overactivity and conduct disorder. Furthermore, the Conners' scales have been found to identify children with overactivity, but not attention deficit (Ullman, Sleator, & Sprague, 1984). Therefore, clinicians need to be wary of depending upon the Conners Rating Scales in initial assessments of children with attention problems.

In response to the item overlap on the Conners scales, Loney and Milich (1982) developed the Iowa Conners Rating Scale. This scale provides individual scores for inattention/overactivity and aggression. Empirical evaluations have demonstrated considerable evidence for the validity of the Iowa Conners as a measure of ADHD with derived normative data by age and gender. Unfortunately, observational and peer measures of aggression showed low correspondence with actual aggressive behavior in school (Atkins, Pelham, & Licht, 1985).

The Child Attention Problems Scale (CAP), developed by Edelbrock (1984), has been shown to be sensitive to stimulant drug effects. It also appears to be useful in classifying children with ADHD into two subtypes: (1) those with predominantly hyperactive symptoms and (2) those with predominantly attentional symptoms. Unlike other scales, the CAP's Inattention subscale is relatively "pure" and not confounded by items relating to conduct, affective disturbance, or overactivity.

Behavioral checklists that have demonstrated agreement with psychiatry's *Diagnostic and Statistical Manual IV* are regarded as among the most valid (Meents, 1989). The ADHD Rating Scale (Du Paul et al., 1994, 1996) incorporates *DSM-IV* criteria into questionnaire form. It can be used by both parents and teachers and has substantial normative data for each gender gathered from a general sample of 2,000 children ages 5 to 18 years. The scale has been shown to differentiate children who exhibit distractible and hyperactive behavior from those who display distractible behavior without hyperactivity (Barkley, Fischer, Edelbrock, & Smallish, 1990). Confirmatory factor analysis supports a two-factor model for both the home and school versions that conforms with the breakdown of symptoms in *DSM-IV*. Test–retest reliability after a 4-week interval was found to be .75, and scores on both scales were significantly correlated with ratings on the Conners Parent and Teacher Rating Scales, as well as with direct observations of classroom attention and productivity.

In conclusion, the item composition of the scales used is important. A qualitative assessment is needed to ensure that the scale does not have items that could produce false positives or items that pertain to disorders other than ADHD. As has been shown, certain questions about conduct may inflate the hyperactivity scores on some scales. It is important to characterize which behaviors, if any, are unique to ADHD. Techniques used in diagnosis document impairment at the same time; therefore, information collected may be used at a later date to evaluate treatment outcomes.

Using the Checklists

When parents and teachers disagree on the ratings of a child's behavior, it is important for clinicians to consider whether one rater is wrong, or whether the disagreement represents differences in the child's behavior in different settings. When sources disagree, clinically relevant information may surface through further investigation. Children who appear inattentive but test as attentive may show higher levels of anxiety, depression, and other internalizing disorders (Gordon, Di Niro, Mettelman, & Tallmadge, 1989). *If children have ADHD, they will exhibit hyperactivity, impulsivity, and distractible behavior in multiple settings.* Accurate diagnosis (and consequent treatment) requires that clinicians reconcile differences that may appear among informants for interviews, rating scales, and observations.

Many studies have examined the efficacy of rating scales, but conclusions are contradictory. Although some studies report a high degree of concordance of data from different sources, others show low correlations between reports from different sources. It is important that the clinician consider discrepant reports in terms of the varying causes of hyperactivity (e.g., situational, one-to-one attention, inappropriate academic challenge) in the light of a given child's functioning.

Some studies report that teacher ratings have been found to be more reliable than parent ratings in identifying children with ADHD (Loeber, Green, & Lahey, 1990). High interrater reliability between teachers and parents ($r = .83$) has been found; however, this correlation does not establish factually that the range of symptoms observed by both groups was similar. Instead, it may suggest that parents and teachers communicated and agreed on what was important in the classroom (Loeber, Green, & Lahey, 1990). Over the past several years, consensus has been reached that multiple measures are needed both to ensure accurate diagnosis and to pin down cross-situational as well as situation-specific ADHD symptoms (Douglas, 1990).

Continuous Performance Tests

Most instruments used for the diagnosis of ADHD fall into three basic categories: those intended for the measurement of other aspects of behavior that have been adapted to assess impulsivity, those that are largely limited to laboratory investigations, and questionnaires for reporting behavior. Continuous performance tests (CPTs), along with direct systematic behavioral observations of ADHD symptoms, are attempts to bring laboratory observations into real-life settings.

Although several types of CPTs are available, the most common require a child to watch a computer screen while letters, numbers, or other stimuli are projected on it at a rapid rate. The child is instructed to press a button when a certain stimulus or pair of stimuli in sequence appear on the screen. On a CPT, the scores derived include the number of correct responses, the number of target stimuli missed (omission errors), and the number of responses to nontarget or incorrect stimuli (commission errors). The last score is presumed to tap the child's ability to sustain attention and to control impulses; the first two measures are thought to assess sustained attention only. CPTs have been shown to be one of the most reliable methods for discriminating between ADHD and normal children (Douglas, 1983). They also appear to be sensitive to stimulant drug effects (Coons, Klorman, & Borgstedt, 1987). However, in this technique, lack of standardization and normative data—and cumbersome apparatus—are limiting factors. Finally, the clinician must decide whether the behavior sample obtained by the CPT validly represents the child's typical behavior at home and at school.

Although there are software programs for use on personal computers and several CPT microcomputers dedicated to CPT, research on the validity of the CPT technique is limited. The Test of Variables of Attention (TOVA) is a software program designed for use in diagnosis and treatment of ADHD. The TOVA measures inattention (through errors of omission), impulsivity (through errors of commission), response time, and variability (Greenberg & Waldman, 1993). One problem is that the TOVA was normed in one Midwestern suburban area with upper-middle-class children, 99% of them Caucasian. Little information is provided about them except that they were "normal." Additionally, research on the TOVA is lacking; papers supplied by the developer are unpublished in refereed journals. A detailed critique of the TOVA appears in the *Thirteenth Mental Measurements Yearbook* (Hagin & Della Bella, 1998).

There is more research reported on the Gordon Diagnostic System (GDS), a separate microcomputer providing continuous performance and vigilance tasks (Gordon, 1987). The GDS provides data on a child's ability to inhibit behavioral responses by reporting errors of omission, commission, and efficiency ratios. Through observation of the child's performance and from responses to post-test inquiries, the GDS also yields qualitative data, as well as behavioral information useful in the diagnostic process (McClure & Gordon, 1984).

CPTs have an advantage in that they are direct measures of a child's behavior, unlike rating scales that rely on an observer's ability to be objective. The apparatus provides data based on the child's responses in actual situations that require delay of action and sustained attention. A disadvantage of CPT is that it is administered to the child individually, it is of short duration, and it is a novel task (and therefore may attract the attention of the ADHD child). These essential conditions in its administration may keep it from providing an accurate picture of the child's typical behavior. Children with ADHD tend to respond better in a one-to-one setting than in a group. They also attend better with tasks that are novel and brief in duration. Readministration of the CPT over a period of a week or two may help with some of these limitations.

Tests of continuous performance may be useful, but are not sufficient for assessing children suspected of having difficulties with impulsivity or sustained attention. Like the rating scales and questionnaires, continuous performance tests provide one source of information to be integrated with other sources in reaching a comprehensive diagnosis.

Current Diagnostic Issues

ADHD is an imprecise and inconclusive set of behavior symptoms that can have serious impact upon the cognitive, educational, emotional, and social adjustment of children and adults. Because the diagnosis depends to a large extent upon observations of typical behavior, refinement of the descriptors is needed. Behavior checklists that demonstrate agreement with the *DSM-IV* criteria are regarded as the most valid. Currently, the behaviors most likely to characterize children with ADHD (hyperactivity, poor impulse control, and off-task behavior) are reflected in the *DSM-IV criteria* (Meents, 1989).

It has become clear that good clinical diagnoses call for the use of multidimensional criteria. These should include

- a thorough developmental history to assess how long the symptoms have been present and to determine familial patterns
- multiple behavioral assessments using questionnaires to determine whether the behaviors occur across settings and if they are seen by different observers in order to ascertain whether the problems are observed by all reporters or if they are task-specific, person-specific, or time-specific
- evaluation of cognitive functioning to assess current and potential abilities and to sample the child's problem-solving abilities
- assessment of current educational achievement through observations of classroom behavior, work samples, and formal tests of educational skills
- interview with the child and, if resources permit, administration of a continuous performance test

Finally, all data need to be collated and integrated in summary. This summary might use the structure of the five diagnostic components discussed earlier in this chapter to organize the findings. It should present, in addition, a clearly stated diagnosis and show how the problems that originally brought the child to the attention of clinicians relate to this diagnosis. Moreover, the summary should provide realistic plans for intervention, growing logically from the diagnostic data. Interventions should be prioritized so that the child and his or her family are not overwhelmed with advice; rather, the interventions that are most promising in terms of immediate payoff should be introduced first, with alternative strategies reserved as back-up procedures. Responsibility for each intervention should be incorporated in the plan. Finally, methods for evaluating results of intervention and modifying the original plan where needed should be stated clearly.

References

Achenbach, T. M., & Edelbrock, C. (1983). *Manual for the Child Behavior Checklist and Child Behavior Profile.* Burlington: University of Vermont, Department of Psychiatry.

American Psychiatric Association. (1994). *Diagnostic and statistical manual of mental disorders* (4th ed.). Washington, DC: Author.

Atkins, M. S., Pelham, W. E., & Licht, M. H. (1985). A comparison of objective classroom measures and teacher ratings of attention deficit disorder. *Journal of Abnormal Child Psychology, 13,* 155–167.

Barkley, R. A. (1990). *Attention deficit hyperactivity disorder: A handbook for diagnosis and treatment.* New York: Guilford.

Barkley, R. A., Fischer, M., Edelbrock, C. S., & Smallish, L. (1990). The adolescent outcome of hyperactive children diagnosed by research criteria: I. An 8-year prospective follow-up study. *Journal of the American Academy of Child and Adolescent Psychiatry, 29,* 546–557.

Barkley, R. A., Fischer, M., Newby, R., & Breen, M. (1988). Development of a multi-method clinical protocol for assessing stimulant drug responses in ADHD children. *Journal of Clinical Child Psychology, 17,* 14–24.

Bradley, W. (1937). The behavior of children receiving Benzedrine. *American Journal of Psychiatry, 94,* 577–585.

Conners, C. K. (1985). *The Conners Rating Scales: Instruments for the assessment of childhood psychopathology.* Unpublished manuscript, Children's Hospital National Medical Center, Washington, DC.

Coons, H. W., Klorman, R., & Borgstedt, A. D. (1987). Effects of methylphenidate on adolescents with a history of ADD: II. Information processing. *Journal of American Academy of Child and Adolescent Psychiatry, 26,* 368–374.

Deson, L. R. (1998). *Comparison of parents' and teachers' perceptions of children's behavior: A study of attentional problems in a natural setting.* Unpublished doctoral dissertation, Fordham University, New York.

Douglas, V. I. (1983). Attention and cognitive problems. In M. Rutter (Ed.), *Developmental Neuropsychiatry* (pp. 280–329). New York: Guilford.

Douglas, V. I. (1990, August). *Diagnosis and treatment of attention deficit hyperactivity disorder: Has research helped?* Paper presented at the 98th annual meeting of the American Psychological Association, Boston.

Du Paul, G. J. (1990). *The ADHD Rating Scale–IV: Normative data, reliability, and validity.* Unpublished manuscript, University of Massachusetts Medical Center, Worcester.

Du Paul, G. J., Anastopoulous, A. D., Power, T. J., Murphy, K., & Barkley, R. A. (1994). *The ADHD Rating Scale–IV.* Unpublished manuscript, Lehigh University, Bethlehem, PA.

Du Paul, G. J., Anastopoulous, A. D., Power, T. J., Murphy, K., & Barkley, R. A. (1996). *The ADHD Rating Scale–IV: Normative Data.* Unpublished manuscript, Lehigh University, Bethlehem, PA.

Edelbrock, C. S. (1984). Developmental considerations. In T. H. Ollendick & M. Herson (Eds.), *Child behavioral assessment: Principles and procedures* (pp. 20–37). New York: Pergamon.

Fischer, M., Newby, R., & Gordon, M. (1993). *The ADHD/Hyperactivity Newsletter, 19.*

Gaddes, W. H., & Edgell, D. (1994). *Learning disabilities and brain function: A neuropsychological approach.* New York: Springer-Verlag.

Gordon, M. (1987). How is a computerized attention test used in the diagnosis of attention deficit disorder? In J. Loney (Ed.), *The young hyperactive child: Answer's to questions about diagnosis, prognosis, and treatment* (pp. 53–64). New York: Haworth.

Gordon, M., Di Niro, D., Mettelman, B. B., & Tallmadge, J. (1989). Observations of test behavior, quantitative scores, and teacher ratings. *Journal of Psychoeducational Assessment, 7,* 141–147.

Goyette, C. H., Conners, C. K., & Ulrich, R. F. (1978). Normative data for the revised Conners Parent and Teacher Rating Scales. *Journal of Abnormal Child Psychology, 6,* 221–236.

Greenberg, L. M., & Waldman, I. D. (1993). Developmental normative data on the Test of Variables of Attention (T.O.V.A.). *Journal of Child Psychology and Psychiatry, 34,* 1019–1030.

Hagin, R., & Della Bella, P. (1998). Review of Test of Variables Attention. In J. C. Impara & B. S. Plake (Eds.), *The thirteenth mental measurements yearbook.* Lincoln, NE: Buros Institute of Mental Measurements.

Horn, W. F., Ialongo, N., Popovich, S., & Peradotto, D. (1984, August). *An evaluation of a multi-method treatment approach with hyperactive children.* Paper presented at the 92nd annual convention of the American Psychological Association, Toronto.

Lahey, B. B., Neeper, R., & Frick, P. J. (1990). *Comprehensive Behavior Rating Scale for Children*

(CBRSC): *Manual.* San Antonio, TX: Psychological Corporation.

Loeber, R., Green, S. M., & Lahey, B. (1990). Mental health professionals' perception of the utility of children, mothers, and teachers as informants on childhood psychopathology. *Journal of Clinical Child Psychology, 19,* 136–143.

Loney, J., & Milich, R. (1982). Hyperactivity, inattention, and aggression in clinical practice. In M. Wolraich & D. K. Routh (Eds.), *Advances in behavioral pediatrics* (Vol. 2, pp. 113–147). Greenwich, CT: JAI.

McClure, F. D., & Gordon, M. (1984). The performance of hyperactive and non-hyperactive children in an objective measure of hyperactivity. *Journal of Abnormal Child Psychology, 12,* 561–572.

Meents, C. K. (1989). Attention deficit disorders: A review of the literature. *Psychology in the Schools, 26,* 168–178.

Pollard, S., Ward, E. M., & Barkley, R. A. (1983). The effects of parent training and Ritalin on the parent–child interactions of hyperactive boys. *Child and Family Therapy, 5,* 51–69.

Schachar, R., Sandberg, S., & Rutter, M. (1986). Agreement between teachers' ratings and observations of hyperactivity, inattentiveness, and defiance. *Journal of Abnormal Child Psychology, 14,* 331–345.

Schaughency, E. A., Frick, P., Christ, M. A., Neeper, R., & Lahey, B. (1990, April). *Correspondence of profiles on teacher ratings of psychiatric diagnosis.* Paper presented at the convention of the National Association of School Psychologists, San Francisco.

Silver, A. A., & Hagin, R. A. (1990). *Disorders of learning in childhood.* New York: Wiley.

Strauss, A. A., & Leehtinen, L. E. (1947). *Psychopathology and Education of the Brain-injured Child.* New York: Grune & Stratton.

Ullman, R. K., Sleator, E. K., & Sprague, R. L. (1985). A change of mind: The Conners Abbreviated Rating Scale reconsidered. *Journal of Abnormal Child Psychology, 13,* 553–566.

Young, J. G., O'Brien, J. D., Gutterman, E. M., & Cohen, P. (1987). Research on the clinical interview. *Journal of the American Academy of Child and Adolescent Psychiatry, 26,* 613–620.

Chapter 4

Medical Management of ADHD

JAMES WARD   KENNETH E. GUYER

Before we discuss the controversial topic of medication for the person who has been diagnosed as having Attention Deficit Hyperactivity Disorder (ADHD), it is important to first address the neurophysiology of the brain. Probably the most complex object in our universe is the human brain, and to say that we do not understand completely how it functions is an understatement.

The Brain and Its Functions

The typical human brain weighs only three pounds, and it has an estimated ten billion nerve cells. Some have said that the least complex brain cell is as complicated as a modern computer. Every cell is unique in the manner in which it functions, but each cell is interwoven with hundreds of other cells to form a network of more than one quadrillion connections. Is there no wonder that we find the brain "a puzzlement" as Yul Brynner sang so unforgettably in *The King and I*?

Within the brain lies the human ability to think and reason, to understand, to feel emotion, and to have desires. It is the brain that makes it possible for people to create and to attempt to reach selected goals. When the brain doesn't react normally because it has been damaged or is dysfunctional, the life of that person can become a living nightmare. One may experience the uncontrolled firing of neurons in a seizure disorder or lead the life of a schizophrenic—filled with terrors we can only imagine. Parkinsonian spasms may cause unwanted and uncontrollable muscle movements, and whatever it is that causes ADHD may fill a person's life with disorganization, inattention, impulsivity, and/or hyperactivity. The brain may be our greatest ally, but it can also create problems that make life almost unbearable (Copeland, 1996).

Basic Neurochemistry

The nervous system is often compared to a system of wires for communication. We tend to think of a system of wires as being continuous. By comparison, there are gaps along the length of the nervous system. Between the units of the nervous system, which we call neurons, there are gaps called synaptic clefts. The impulses from the brain are transmitted across the synaptic clefts by neurotransmitters. In many cases, the neurotransmitters are catecholamines, particularly norepinephrine and dopamine.

Movement of the neurotransmitters across the synaptic clefts brings about the transmission of excitatory or inhibitory impulses. The transmission of neurons is a very complicated process; both excitatory and inhibitory neurons are involved. It is interesting to note that inhibition is as important as excitation, if not more so. The more sophisticated the nervous system is, the more inhibitory neurons are present. Every physiological response represents a complex interweaving of all of the inhibitory and excitatory neurons being stimulated and then transmitting the appropriate responses.

Norepinephrine, one of the catecholamines, is released into the synaptic cleft in some nerve pathways. The neurostimulants such as methylphenidate or dextroamphetamine increase the availability of catecholamines. Antidepressants decrease the re-uptake of catecholamines, whereas some other drugs prevent the metabolism of catecholamines.

Studies using neuroimaging techniques have begun to give validity to the theory about involvement of the frontal lobes in ADHD. Information obtained when treating patients who have sustained brain injuries from conflicts during wartime or from accidents, as well as from strokes, have helped to provide needed data. These data have indicated that the frontal lobes are responsible for response inhibition as well as attention. This area of the brain is also involved in executive function and problem solving (Hallahan, Kauffman, & Lloyd, 1998).

The basal ganglia, which may be found beneath the cortex and behind the frontal lobes, are felt to be responsible for controlling movement, and patients who have Parkinson's disease have been found to have damage to this area. Castellanos (1997) found that the connections between the frontal lobes and the basal ganglia do not function properly in persons who have been diagnosed as having ADHD.

How Does This Affect the Person with ADHD?

For many years ADHD has been considered a disorder of neurotransmitters. There are some medications that are used to treat ADHD that increase the availability of norepinephrine specifically on the presynaptic dendrites. Ritalin and Dexedrine are two medications that reportedly do this. Other medications, such as Norpramin and Tofranil, leave more norepinephrine at the synaptic cleft. Although there is a great deal more to be said, it is not our purpose to go into more detail at this time. If additional information is required, the reader is referred to Barkley (1998).

We conclude by stating that the mechanism of the brain is a complex process, one that we do not entirely understand at this time. A rudimentary understanding of the neurological development and function of the brain gives us a degree of knowledge that should enable us to understand the general effect of most medical interventions. Such knowledge is very important because neurological development often seems to be delayed in the person with ADHD (Copeland, 1996).

A Case History

Andy is 13 years old. If you were to see him today, you would think to yourself that he is an accident looking for a place to happen. It would be an understatement to say that he is poorly coordinated. He trips over his own feet, the stairs, other people's feet, the door sill, and so forth. His activity level may equal that of five people combined. He never seems to be able to sit still, and when he isn't actively moving, it is apparent to those who know him that his mind is racing. Andy repeated grades one and five because he hadn't turned in most of his assignments, seldom listened to his teacher, and had some learning problems in addition to his difficulties with ADHD. Andy's teacher began complaining during the second week of school. Because of Andy, she couldn't seem to teach anyone else either.

At the teacher's insistence, Andy was seen again by the school psychologist and evaluated for ADHD (which should have been done in his earlier diagnosis). The psychologist concluded that Andy had a severe problem with ADHD and should be seen by his physician as soon as possible.

Dr. Brown felt that medication was imperative if Andy was to learn in school and also not keep everyone else from learning. He prescribed 5 mg doses of Ritalin to be administered with breakfast and lunch. Later the dosage would be increased if it seemed warranted. When Andy was given 10 mg Ritalin twice a day, everyone noticed that Andy was a different person. He was able to sit still for longer periods of time, and he seemed to be able to pay attention for more than an hour at a time. The learning disabilities teacher began working with Andy to help him learn new study strategies and to take various kinds of tests more successfully. Andy's parents helped him organize his room and his study space so that he could begin to lead a more organized life.

With everyone working together, Andy's grades soared. He made the Honor Roll last semester for the first time in his life! He is beginning to make friends with some of his classmates, and he is no longer shunned by most of his peers. Andy's life has changed significantly for the better. Not just because of Ritalin—but because everyone is working together to help Andy learn to deal with ADHD in a positive manner.

I think I know why he's here to see the doctor!

FIGURE 4.1   Hyperactivity cries for attention.

Medical Management of ADHD

Medical management of ADHD often places the physician in a difficult position. Too often parents and educators turn to the physician for a quick fix when structure at home and the institution of certain teaching strategies at school might suffice to make the child with ADHD successful. Crowded classrooms don't allow the teacher time to adequately cope with the child with ADHD, and the ADHD "latchkey" child is a loose cannon in the neighborhood. Parents and educators often frantically turn to the physician for a behavioral straitjacket, and the result is inappropriate and overprescribing of psychostimulant medication. *The child who has mild or mild moderate ADHD should not usually require medication.* (These categories represent degrees of severity. They vary somewhat from one diagnostic instrument to another. These categories represent the mildest ones.)

Many classroom teachers often fall into two large groups. One group of classroom teachers is absolutely convinced that no child should be placed on psychostimulant medication. These teachers believe that the courses they took in college in classroom management techniques will ensure that every child participate in the educational process in an appropriate and successful manner. Such teachers may assure parents and principals that children do not need medication while they are attending classes. Even a master in classroom management techniques will fail at controlling the child who has severe or profound ADHD. Less severely affected children may appear to attend adequately and may have acceptable academic records; however, if this child has the intellect to make straight As and is making straight Cs, something may be amiss with the classroom management techniques.

The other group of teachers has seen children with moderate ADHD but without any learning problems or differences placed on psychostimulant medication, and because these children have superior intellects, they become the high school valedictorians and have highly distinguished academic records in college. These teachers begin to believe that almost any child with an exuberant lifestyle needs to be placed on psychostimulant medication.

Of course, both positions fall short of the truth, and if I (Dr. Ward) have offended all of my friends in the teaching profession, I beg that you recall that for 14 years I taught advanced biology and chemistry on my lunch hour. I have been in that same arena with you, and I have suffered when that impulsive teenager with ADHD almost made the chemistry laboratory a spectacular event. I am also in sympathy with the parents. The economy of today often requires that both parents work. A disastrous work day is one when the school calls and shares with the parent exactly what happened in the classroom because Johnny's medication was inadvertently omitted. The guilt is enormous, and the school suspension, the parents feel, is not their fault.

Another unfortunate fact associated with taking psychostimulant medication is that God and everyone else are aware which children take medication for ADHD. I have no problem with God knowing, but there is no need for everyone else to know. A real problem exists at the school due to the incidence of substance abuse, especially among secondary students. Rightfully, the schools require that all students taking medication must receive that medication at the nurse's or principal's office; as a consequence, all of those with ADHD line up at the appropriate time and place to receive their "hyper" medication. God forbid that the student with ADHD should forget to appear, because he will probably be reminded over the public address system for the school.

Ideally, of course, a responsible student could carry the day's supply of medicine and take it at appropriate times, possibly reminded by the teacher. Possible carelessness or perhaps abuse by the student makes this unlikely to be allowed. Popularity of some of these medications among other students presents even more of a danger that the drugs might be abused.

Alternatively, the teacher might store the medication in a locked area, allocating it to each student at the proper time and without attracting the attention of the other students. Unfortunately, it would probably be necessary for each teacher to store and dispense medication for several students. This would be an awesome responsibility considering the teacher's educational duties with a number of students. We must also remember that the teacher has little or no background in dealing with medications. And we must also remember the potential legal ramifications. The teacher and the school system would likely bear responsibility and possible liability if the medications were not stored and dispensed properly.

Storage and dispensing of medications by a nurse is often a better choice. The nurse has some background in pharmacology and dispensing of medication. The nurse may more adequately be covered by malpractice insurance and will probably not expose the school to as great a legal liability. This choice would require the individual students to go to the nurse's office to obtain medication, however, and would probably make it more difficult to shield the student from the curiosity of other students. And there are many schools, of course, that have no nurse assigned to them.

Administration of medication has become such a headache that some school systems have refused to participate. The courts have ruled that such refusal is not legal.

Having said all of this, it is easy to understand why the development of medication taken once a day (or morning and night) has become such a priority. Such medication need not involve the school personnel.

Now that we have blown off some steam over psychostimulant medication, we will try to discuss the major psychostimulant medication in a user-friendly manner for the non-physician. One must keep in mind that ADHD, like dyslexia, has a strong familial or genetic base. The familial factor in ADHD was noted some years ago. Immediate family members of individuals with ADHD are themselves more likely to have ADHD than are individuals who are not closely related to an individual with ADHD. Of course, this could be a matter of genetics, or it could be simply the behavioral activity of one family member affecting the behavior of other family members. Evidence favoring a genetic base has been reported in a study of children adopted at an early age. The incidence of ADHD among biological parents and siblings of those with ADHD was found to be higher than its incidence among adoptive parents and adoptive siblings (Anastopoulos & Barkley, 1988). Additional investigation will be required to prove which chromosome is involved. Indeed, between 20% and 40% of dyslexic individuals have an intertwining of ADHD and dyslexia. These individuals will need the team of the school psychologist, the teacher, and the physician to be successful. We also know that 70% of individuals who were diagnosed as having ADHD in childhood will carry the handicap into adult life. We now see many physicians dealing with ADHD in the adult.

ADHD is a medical diagnosis because it is a neurological entity. The definitive diagnosis should be made by a physician because medical intervention will be required. Dyslexia is an educational diagnosis and should be made by an educator or school psychologist. Treatment for dyslexia, however, consists of appropriate teaching strategies. The diagnostic criteria for ADHD are presented in Tables I, II, and III and are from the *Diagnostic and Statistical Manual of Mental Disorders* (fourth edition) (1994).

In 1995, L. L. Greenhill coined a wonderfully simple acronym for the cardinal features of attention deficit hyperactivity disorder (Table IV), and it is this acronym

Table I   DSM-IV Diagnostic Criteria for ADHD

Inattentive Type Symptoms

1. Six or more of the following symptoms of *inattention* have persisted for at least 6 months to a degree that is maladaptive and inconsistent with developmental level:

    a. Often fails to give close attention to details or makes careless mistakes in schoolwork, work, or other activities
    b. Often has difficulty sustaining attention in tasks or play activities
    c. Often does not seem to listen when spoken to directly
    d. Often does not follow through on instructions and fails to finish schoolwork, chores, or duties in the workplace (not due to appositional behavior or failure to understand instructions)
    e. Often has difficulty organizing tasks and activities
    f. Often avoids, dislikes, or is reluctant to engage in tasks that require sustained mental effort (such as schoolwork or homework)
    g. Often loses things necessary for tasks or activities (e.g., toys, school assignments, pencils, books, or tools)
    h. Is often distracted by extraneous stimuli
    i. Is often forgetful in daily activities

Adapted from *Diagnostic and Statistical Manual of Mental Disorders*, 4th Edition, American Psychiatric Association (1994).

Table II   DSM-IV Diagnostic Criteria for ADHD

Hyperactive-Impulsive Type Symptoms

2. Six or more of the following symptoms of *hyperactivity-impulsivity* have persisted for at least 6 months to a degree that is maladaptive and inconsistent with developmental level:

Hyperactivity
a. Often fidgets with hands or feet or squirms in seat
b. Often leaves seat in classroom or in other situations in which remaining seated is expected
c. Often runs about or climbs excessively in cases when it is inappropriate (in adolescents or adults, may be limited to subjective feelings of restlessness)
d. Often has difficulty playing or participating in leisure activities quietly
e. Is often "on the go" or often acts as if "driven by a motor"
f. Often talks excessively

Impulsivity
g. Often blurts out answers before questions have been completed
h. Often has difficulty standing in line or waiting for turn
i. Often interrupts or intrudes on others (e.g., butts into conversations or games)

Adapted from *Diagnostic and Statistical Manual of Mental Disorders*, 4th Edition, American Psychiatric Association (1994).

Table III   Three Diagnostic Subsets of ADHD

- Attention Deficit/Hyperactivity Disorder, Predominantly Inattentive Type (if Criterion a1* is met but Criterion a2** is not met for the past 6 months)
- Attention Deficit/Hyperactivity Disorder, Predominantly Hyperactive-Impulsive Type (if Criterion a2* is met but Criterion a1** is not met for past 6 months)
- Attention Deficit/Hyperactivity Disorder, Combined Type (if both Criteria a1* and a2** are met for the past 6 months)

*a1: Six or more of the symptoms described for inattention have persisted for at least 6 months to a degree that is maladaptive and inconsistent with developmental level.

**a2: Six or more of the symptoms described for hyperactivity-impulsivity have persisted for at least 6 months to a degree that is maladaptive and inconsistent with developmental level.

Adapted from *Diagnostic and Statistical Manual of Mental Disorders,* 4th Edition, American Psychiatric Association (1994).

Table IV   Cardinal Features of ADHD

Remember the Acronym "HIDE":

H = Hyperactivity (excessive gross motor activity)
I = Inattentiveness (inability to sustain attention)
D = Disorganization of Behavior
E = Easy Distractibility

Adapted from Greenhill (1995).

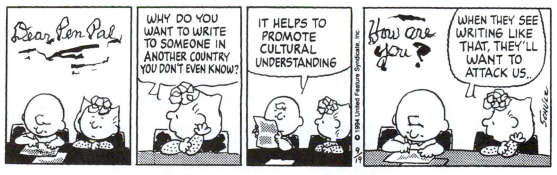

PEANUTS reprinted by permission of United Feature Syndicate, Inc.

FIGURE 4.2   Impulsivity and hyperactivity can have a significant effect on handwriting, among other things.

(H.I.D.E.) that the physician primarily addresses with the administration of psychostimulant medication in the treatment of ADHD.

The label of "hyperactive syndrome" was used in the early 1900s for overactive, impulsive, and uninhibited children. A close look at these children revealed many who had neurological damage from trauma, meningitis, encephalitis, etc. As early as 1937 a racemic form of amphetamine was given to children who were diagnosed with "hyperactive syndrome," resulting in rather dramatic improvement in academic performance and behavior (Bradley, 1937). Since 1960, controlled studies on psychostimulants have reported marked reduction in symptoms of ADHD, especially impulsivity and inattentiveness. Medline (Internet computer database) retrieval of such studies between 1982 and 1991 revealed some 990 controlled studies on psychostimulant treatment of ADHD individuals. Many of these studies report that the condition is more prevalent in boys. Reports of ratios from 4 to 1 of boys to girls to 9 to 1 of boys to girls have been published. The true sex incidence is probably closer to 4 to 1 or even less. There probably exists a selective bias since girls with ADHD exhibit inattentive, cognitive symptoms, whereas boys often exhibit more aggressively impulsive symptoms. (The hyperactive young people are the ones who forcefully call attention to themselves.) A search of the literature will also reveal that ADHD comorbidity occurs with conduct disorders and dyslexia. Some of the latest studies are finding the salient symptoms of ADHD in narcolepsy, some sleep disorders, and sleep apnea (Table V).

The pharmacology of the major psychostimulants is presented in Table VI. Cylert is presented for completeness; however, this medication has been shown to produce liver damage and possible hepatic failure and is not presently considered a first-line medication for ADHD. Note that all of the medications (possibly excluding Cylert) cross the blood brain barrier and are thus available to the neurotransmitter sites in the brain. Note also that all of the medications cross the placental barrier and are thus not appropriately taken during pregnancy.

Table VI contains additional pharmacology facts that are essentially self-explanatory. Some classification is given in regard to the mechanisms of action. All

Table V   Comorbidity of ADHD and Other Disorders

1. Comorbidity is seen in all age groups and may be as high as 65% in children with ADHD.
2. Comorbidity includes mood disorders, anxiety disorders, substance abuse disorders, eating disorders, oppositional defiance disorder, conduct disorders, and Tourette syndrome.
3. Symptoms of comorbidity make differential diagnoses more difficult.
4. It is important to diagnose and treat the comorbid disorder as well as the symptoms of ADHD.
5. About 10–20% of children with ADHD are reported to have mood disorders, 20% have conduct disorders, as many as 40% have oppositional disorder, about 7% have tics or Tourette syndrome, and at least 11% seem to have learning disabilities.

Adapted from Copeland (1996); Cantwell (1996); and Goldman, Genel, Bezman, & Slanetz (1998).

Table VI Pharmacology of Drugs for Treatment of ADHD

Generic Name	Ritalin* Methylphenidate	Ritalin SR* Methylphenidate ER	Dexedrine* Dextro Amphetamine	Dexedrine Spansule* Dextro Amphetamine SR	Adderall* Mixed Amphetamine Salts	Cylert* Pemoline
Tablet Size	5, 10, 20 mg	20 mg	5, 10 mg	5, 10, 15 mg	5, 10, 20, 30 mg	18.75, 37.5, 75.0 mg
Dose	2.5–60 mg	20–60 mg	2.5–40 mg	5–40 mg	2.5–40 mg	18.75–112.5 mg
Dose/Day	2–4	2–3	2–4	2–4	1–2	1–2
Crosses the Placenta	+	+	+	+	+	+
Half-Life	1–2 hrs.	2.5–3.4 hrs.	6–7 hrs.	6–7 hrs.	7.5–15.4 hrs	7–8 hrs
Peak Serum Levels	1.5–2.5 hrs.	1–4 hrs.	2–3 hrs.	2–3 hrs.	2–3 hrs.	2–4 hrs.
Mechanism by Availability	DA^>NE^	DA^>NE^	DA^ and NE^	DA^ and NE^	DA^ and NE^	
Organ of Metabolism	Liver	Liver	Liver	Liver	Liver	Liver and unchanged in urine
Excretion Route			Urine	Urine	Urine	Urine

*Registered trademark of the manufacturer.

DA—dopamine   NE—norepinephrine

Adapted from Shire Richwood, Inc. (1999). Spender, J., Biederman, J., Wilens, T., et al., 1996; Swanson, J., Wigal, S., Greenhill, L., Browne, R., Waslik, B., Lerner, M., et al., 1998; and Fisher, B., 1998.

of the psychostimulants increase the availability of dopamine and norepinephrine in the brain stem, thalamus, and cerebral cortex. The critical point of interest here is that Ritalin increases the availability of dopamine to a greater extent than it increases norepinephrine. Adderall and Dexedrine increase the availability of norepinephrine and dopamine in more equal ratios. Adderall is composed of four salts of amphetamine and contains 75% dextro-amphetamine and 25% levoamphetamine (optical isomers). The dextro isomer has more effect on dopamine availability, and the levo isomer has more effect on norepinephrine availability. This mixture accounts for the longer sustained release of Adderall. This balance is not found in any of the other medications. Methylphenidate (Ritalin) has been used for treatment for 25 to 30 years and has been highly effective in the treatment of many children with ADHD (Copeland, 1996).

(Editor's note: The next several paragraphs were written by James Ward, M.D., based on his practice of medicine with patients who have ADHD.)

In my experience, the sustained-release Ritalin has been very erratic in covering the entire school day, and I seldom prescribe it. When the proper dose of the short-acting Ritalin is prescribed, it is very effective for approximately a 4-hour period. This necessitates a midday dose at school, and many children and adolescents resent lining up at the nurse's office at lunchtime for their medication. Suppression of appetite is found in some children who take Ritalin; however, this tends to diminish as the medications are taken during the school year. The children usually make up this deficit with an afternoon snack and a good supper. Even though Ritalin has been a great adjunct in the educational life of many thousands of children, it has received a lot of "bad press" from the media and from persons of certain religious sects. One fact I have had to deal with in the past 5 years is that Ritalin has become a "recreational drug" among some high school and college students. This continues to be a growing concern for the physician as more adolescents and adults must be treated and monitored.

Dexedrine also has some history of abuse, and doses greater than the therapeutic level tend to produce a euphoric high. Dextrostat has the same potential. When I first heard some of the information on the pilot studies of Adderall 5 years ago, I had great reservation about the medication because it was composed of amphetamine salts.

I began cautious trials of Adderall 3 years ago with college students and felt that the results were quite rewarding. The students had all been previously on Ritalin, and "hands down" they preferred the Adderall. Focus and attending were excellent; however, the college students did not feel "medicated" on the Adderall. Rebound when Adderall was wearing off was infrequent, and if the dose was over the therapeutic level, these students did not feel euphoric. They felt "jumpy and jittery" instead. The medication does not have the "street value" of Ritalin and does not seem to be celebrated by the college community as a new recreational drug. Experiences with younger teens and children on Adderall have also been similar to those with the college student. One of the most rewarding facts about Adderall is that when the therapeutic dose is determined, its effectiveness is 7.5 to 8 hours.

This alleviates the midday medication crisis of the child or adolescent with ADHD. Adderall will suppress appetite, and the weight of growing children must be monitored closely. Weight loss is usually a minor problem in children taking psychostimulants as appetite returns to normal in the afternoon and evening when the medication wears off. If the medication is not required on weekends, appetites will rebound vigorously and weight will usually be maintained in very acceptable ranges.

Skeletal growth is another concern of parents and physicians, and is another reason for close monitoring of growing children on psychostimulant medication. There was initial reservation about psychostimulants due to the fact that administration might produce insomnia or bizarre sleep patterns, and it was a physiological fact that growth hormone was released during sleep. Methylphenidate, Dexedrine, and Adderall are prescribed only for daytime activities and are essentially out of the system by bedtime. Cylert (pemoline) was given daily to maintain a therapeutic blood level; however, this medication is used less frequently now due to its liver toxicity potential. Observations and studies indicate that any suppression of growth is minimal. If it does occur at all, it may be due to an interference with cartilage physiology during the mid and late teens (Copeland, 1996).

Another point to be made in comparing the usefulness of Cylert lies in its classification by the Drug Enforcement Agency (DEA) as a Schedule IV controlled drug. Thus, it must be obtained by prescription, but it may be written for more than a 30-day supply. The physician may indicate refills and may phone this prescription in to the pharmacy. Both dextroamphetamine and methylphenidate are Schedule II drugs. A prescription must be hand-carried to the pharmacy within a few days, may not be written for more than a 30-day supply, and may not include pre-authorized refills. Presumably, this difference reflects the DEA assessment of a lesser danger of abuse of Cylert. As noted before, however, the concern about possible liver damage limits its use.

Adderall, Ritalin, Dexedrine, and Dextrostat are the primary medications used in my practice for ADHD, with Adderall being my first choice and Ritalin a second reliable choice. All of these medications address inattentiveness, hyperactivity, and impulsivity. There are other medications that I will mention only briefly. However, some are widely used by many clinicians. Two medications that have been in existence for a long time are Imipramine and Desipramine. Both of these are tricyclic antidepressants. They work by suppressing the uptake of norepinephrine at the synapse, thus increasing the amount of norepinephrine at the synaptic cleft. These tricyclics address the problems of hyperactivity and inattentiveness, but they seem to be ineffective in controlling impulsivity. In my opinion, this is a significant pharmacological deficit as impulsivity is the characteristic that is going to produce "Armageddon" at the school and in the neighborhood. Another reservation some clinicians have with the tricyclics involves cardiac arrhythmias and cardiac arrest. At therapeutic doses this type of catastrophe is probably remote; however, such an event in any practice is unacceptable. I personally do not use these medications, but I do not wish to criticize their use. Clonidine is not a tricyclic. Pharmacologically, it works in a similar way as the tricyclics in increasing available norepinephrine at the synapse. Clonidine has been used rather effectively for many years to reduce some of the characteristics of Tourette's syndrome. Clonidine does reduce hyperactivity markedly and to some extent impulsivity; however, I am not convinced that it addresses the problem of inattentiveness in ADHD. Clonidine is a very difficult drug to regulate at a therapeutic level, as even minute doses really "zonk" the child in the initial weeks of administration. I have great reservations about starting this medication during the school year and find that I need the summer vacation to regulate the medication appropriately. Clonidine will effectively address the problem of hyperactivity and will induce rest if the child with ADHD suffers from insomnia.

Wellbutrin (Bupropion) also suppresses the uptake of norepinephrine in a manner similar to the tricyclics and has been used effectively in the treatment of ADHD, but the effect is not as dramatic as with the psychostimulants (Casat, Pleasants, & Fleet, 1987). One reservation with Wellbutrin is the fact that it lowers the seizure threshold. Wellbutrin is a very effective adjunct in breaking the addiction to nicotine and probably addiction to alcohol. I have found it extremely helpful in treating the teenage alcoholic as well as those who wish to break the nicotine habit. I seldom use Wellbutrin as the initial medication for ADHD unless there is a significant element of depression. Several other medications reported to be helpful in the medical management of ADHD are Mellaril, Tegretol, and lithium. While there is apparently a place for these medications in the treatment of ADHD, my experience with these drugs is minimal.

I have used Mellaril in the management of some autistic children, but not for children who have ADHD. Whereas I have seizure patients on Tegretol with excellent control, I have no ADHD patients on this medication. Lithium has been used effectively for bipolar (manic depressive) disorder, but I have never treated a patient for ADHD with this medication.

Even the most astute and experienced clinician will be able to bring help to only 80% of the individuals with ADHD. Why 20% will not respond to medical interventions is an enigma to the physician. When all of the factors indicate ADHD and yet there is no favorable response to medication, it may be that these symptoms indicate that another primary problem is operational and the ADHD symptoms are simply a spin-off. These individuals may very likely have central nervous systems that are "wired" differently. These refractory individuals need in-depth neurological, endocrinological, or psychiatric evaluations.

ADD without Hyperactivity

Children who are not hyperactive or impulsive but who are inattentive and possess many of the cognitive deficits associated with attention deficit are frequently undiagnosed during childhood. Retrospective diagnosis can be very difficult to obtain. For example, school records may lack the detail required. Former teachers may have left the area or may have no memory of former students whose behavior was unremarkable. Establishing a childhood history of abnormal behavior is even more difficult with gifted students. We know several physicians who were not diagnosed as having ADD until they were failing in medical school. In spite of their attention and organizational problems, they were able to function well academically, thereby preventing others from knowing of their deficits until they were able to compensate no longer.

Parents often accurately report current childhood experiences. However, parents of adults may fail to report ADD symptoms. They sometimes react defensively, afraid that a diagnosis later in life may indicate that they have been poor parents. Other parents may have blocked out unpleasant memories, or perhaps there is little awareness of the symptoms of ADD. There are others who are reluctant to describe their adult children in negative terms (Biggs, 1995).

This classification, which *DSM-IV* refers to as AD/HD, Predominantly Inattentive Type, seems to be more susceptible to anxiety disorders (Lahey, Schaughency, Hynd, Carlson, & Nieves, 1987). Many agree that this condition is more difficult to diagnose, especially in those women who are only distractible.

Women with ADD who do not have hyperactivity often report that adolescence was a period of isolation and unhappiness. Many experts are now convinced that ADD without hyperactivity is much more common in women than in men. Medication is often a major part of the solution to the distractibility, organizational problems, and so on, that these women may face (Ratey, Miller, & Nadeau, 1995).

The Teacher's Role in Monitoring Medication

The importance of the role of the teacher in communicating with the physician regarding medication for ADHD cannot be overemphasized. No one but the teacher sees the child or adolescent in situations that are crucial in the learning process. It is the teacher who

- sees the child in an academic setting
- sees how the child responds in a distracting environment
- observes the effect that medication has on the child
- observes the effect that changes in dosage have on the child
- observes the duration of positive effects of medication (which will affect frequency of dosage)
- observes possible side-effects of medication
- observes changes in behavior of the student
- notices changes in academic performance
- notices changes in impulsivity, attentiveness, activity level, frustration level, organizational skills, and interest in schoolwork

When the teacher reports to the physician regarding the student's reactions to medication, it is very important to be specific. Comments such as "doing better" or "I can't even tell when he's taking medication" can be difficult to interpret. More helpful comments from the teacher could be as follows:

- "Peter was able to complete a test today without leaving his seat."
- "Joe hasn't been in a fight this week, and that's the first time this semester."
- "Susan's handwriting is so much easier to read. She doesn't seem to rush through everything now as she did earlier."

Individuals need to be closely monitored when they are on any medical regimen for ADHD as the medication can be titrated and kept at therapeutic levels only when the patients are seen at regular, frequent intervals. Good data from teachers and parents are essential for the physician to keep the dosage of the medication at an optimal level. Parents need to be active in attending seminars presented by knowledgeable researchers and clinicians who have dealt with ADHD. Parents need to subscribe to journals that are devoted to the diagnosis and treatment of ADHD. Parents also need to accept the fact that, at present, there is no cure for ADHD. Ideally, ongoing research will allow us someday to prevent ADHD or to treat it without side-effects. Parent support groups can be found in most communities, and many behavioral scientists teach classes for parents to learn the non-medical approaches for treating ADHD. We must remember that success for the person with ADHD is dependent upon professionals, parents, and the affected individual all learning to work together. Finally, many parents of children who have ADHD find that prayer is very helpful to them in relieving frustration and in helping them deal more effectively with their children. With a great deal of cooperation, empathy, flexibility, and patience, it is indeed possible for the person with ADHD to find success in school and in life.

In conclusion, let us summarize points that must be remembered in the effective medical management of ADHD:

- Medication is often a necessity in treating someone with ADHD; however, it is not the only component.
- Medication does not work for everyone.
- Careful observation by parents and teachers is crucial if proper dosage of the best medication for that person is to be found.
- Communication with the physician must be no less than once a month when dosage levels are being determined.
- Most medications have some common side-effects. Learn what they are for the medication in question, and watch for them.
- Keep and date a log in which the behavior of the person with ADHD is described.
- Always remember that medication may alleviate only part of the symptoms. A total program is required where the parents, teachers, psychologist or counselor, patient, and physician work together.

• Don't expect miracles. ADHD may continue well into adulthood. And contrary to what was once accepted, continuation of relief of some symptoms of ADHD may require long-term use of medication. As with diabetes mellitus and some other chronic disorders, we are fortunate that relief of symptoms is usually possible with medication.

References

American Psychiatric Association. (1994). *Diagnostic and statistical manual of mental disorders* (4th ed.). Washington, DC: Author.

Anastopoulos, A. D., & Barkley, R. A. (1988). Biological factors in attention deficit hyperactivity disorder. *Behavior Therapist, 11,* 47–53.

Barkley, R. (1998). *Attention-deficit hyperactivity disorder: A handbook for diagnosis and treatment.* New York: Guilford.

Biederman, J., Newcorn, J., & Sprich, S. (1991). Comorbidity of attention deficit hyperactivity disorder with conduct, depressive, anxiety, and other disorders. *American Journal of Psychiatry, 148,* 564–577.

Biggs, S. (1995). Neuropsychological and psychoeducational testing in the evaluation of the A.D.D. adult. In K. Nadeau (Ed.), *A comprehensive guide to A.D.D. in adults.* New York: Brunner/Mazel.

Bradley, C. (1937). The behavior of children receiving Benzedrine. *American Journal of Psychiatry, 94,* 577–585.

Cantwell, D. (1996). Classification of child and adolescent psychopathology. *Journal of Child Psychiatry, 37,* 3–12.

Casat, C., Pleasants, D., & Fleet, J. (1987). A double blind trial of bupropion in children with attention deficit disorder. *Psychopharmacology Bulletin, 23,* 120–122.

Castellanos, F. (1997). Toward a pathophysiology of attention deficit/hyperactivity disorder. *Clinical Pediatrics, 36,* 381–393.

Copeland, E. (1996). *Medications for attention disorders and related medical problems.* Atlanta: Southeastern Psychological Institute.

Fisher, B. C. (1998). *Attention deficit disorder misdiagnosis.* New York: CRC.

Goldman, L. S., Genel, M., Bezman, R. J., & Slanetz, P. J. (1998). Diagnosis and treatment of attention-deficit/hyperactivity disorder in children and adolescents. *Council on Scientific Affairs, American Medical Association. Journal of the American Medical Association, 279,* 1100–1107.

Greenhill, L. (1995). Attention-deficit hyperactivity disorder: The stimulants. *Child and Adolescent Psychiatric Clinics of North America,* 4(1), 123–168.

Hallahan, D., Kauffman, J., & Lloyd, J. (1998). *Introduction to learning disabilities.* Boston: Allyn & Bacon.

Lahey, B., Schaughency, E., Hynd, G., Carlson, C., & Nieves, N. (1987). Attention deficit disorder with and without hyperactivity: Comparison of behavioral characteristics of clinic-referred children. *Journal of the American Academy of Child and Adolescent Psychiatry,* 26(5), 718–723.

Lavenstein, B. (1995). Neurological comorbidity patterns in adult attention deficit disorder. In K. Nadeau (Ed.), *A comprehensive guide to attention deficit disorder in adults.* New York: Brunner/Mazel.

Ratey, J., Miller, A., & Nadeau, K. (1995). Special diagnostic and treatment considerations in women with A.D.D. disorder. In K. Nadeau (Ed.), *A comprehensive guide to A.D.D. in adults.* New York: Brunner/Mazel.

Shaywitz, B. E., Fletcher, J. M., & Shaywitz, S. E. (1997). Attention-deficit/hyperactivity disorder. *Advances in Pediatrics, 44,* 331–367.

Shire Richwood, Inc. (1999). Adderall package insert.

Spencer, T., Biederman, J., Wilens, et al. (1996). Pharmacotherapy of attention deficit hyperactivity disorder across the life cycle. *Journal of American Academy of Child & Adolescent Psychiatry, 35,* 409–432.

Swanson, J. M., Wigal, S., Greenhill, L. L., Browne, R., Waslik, B., Lerner, M., Williams, L., Flynn, D., et al. (1998). Analog classroom assessment of Adderall in children with ADHD. *Journal of The American Academy of Child and Adolescent Psychiatry, 37*(5), 519–526.

Chapter 5

Alternative Treatments for ADHD

LARRY B. SILVER

Attention Deficit Hyperactivity Disorder (ADHD) is a neurologically based disorder caused by a deficiency of a specific neurotransmitter in specific areas of the brain. The initial treatment of choice is to use one of the medications that increase the relative level of this neurotransmitter in these areas of the brain. Once the level of this neurotransmitter is close to or at the appropriate level, the behaviors associated with ADHD significantly lessen or disappear. After the appropriate medication is used and adjusted to reach maximum benefit with no or minimal side-effects, the non-medication treatments are initiated. The individual and family members are educated on ADHD. The residual psychological, social, and family problems are evaluated and addressed. Within the school system appropriate services and accommodations must be developed and implemented. When developing these plans, two critical issues must be addressed: (1) Does the individual also have a learning disability (50% will). If not, might this student have deficiencies in skills and knowledge because she or he was not fully available for learning during the school years prior to diagnosing and treating the ADHD? (2) Is the student successfully on medication or not? (Silver, 1998). The use of appropriate medication and each of these non-medication concerns are discussed in other chapters of this book.

Our knowledge of ADHD is not complete. We do have approaches to treatment that are based on research and are considered to be accepted practices. The less acceptable or more controversial, alternative approaches to treatment will be discussed in this chapter. The controversy related to these alternative therapies might be based on the theory behind the treatment, on the way the treatment is done, or on the lack of research data to support the findings reported by the people using the treatment approach.

Controversial therapies have been with us throughout history. There have been claims for curing cancer or other diseases that are challenged by the "established" medical profession. Professionals who study controversial therapies comment on specific themes that exist for most, whether for cancer or ADHD:

1. The individual who publicizes and pushes for the treatment claims to have research to prove what is being stated, yet no research is provided from respected journals.
2. The individual stresses that "traditional medicine" is too conservative and refuses to accept anything that does not fit what he or she already knows.
3. Claims for cure or improvement are made with literature provided by that individual to prove these claims. One is left to wonder why, if what is claimed is accurate, the treatment is not used by most professionals in the field.
4. The person seems to be saying "I'm a genius or I'm a quack," and it is up to the public and the establishment to prove which is true.

Often, parents and educators turn to their family physician for guidance only to learn that she or he does not know any more than they do. The difficulty is that there are many professionals and nonprofessionals proposing approaches for helping. If research has been done to support a particular approach, it will be published in professional journals that are carefully reviewed to ensure that the results reported are accurate. Usually, others try to replicate the findings found by the first researcher. If others support the treatment findings, the approach is accepted by the professional groups. When information is communicated in books that are often written and published by the person making the statements or in a popular book, in newspapers, in popular magazines, or discussed on a television show, it is difficult to evaluate the claims (Silver, 1999). Thus, professionals know only what they read or hear through these sources or from parents who tell them about the treatment.

The controversial approaches to treatment reviewed have been proposed and are still in use. Controversial research that focuses on cause but that has not resulted in proposed treatment approaches will not be discussed. Where there is research to show that the proposed treatment does not work, it will be presented. When all of the facts are not yet in or agreed upon, the information known will be reviewed from both perspectives.

Many parents are apprehensive about putting their son or daughter on medication over an extended period of time. In addition, the treatment for ADHD works only during the hours the child or adolescent is on medication. After the medication wears off, she or he is ADHD again. Back come the hyperactivity, inattention, and/or impulsivity. Thus, it is very understandable that parents would want to try almost any approach that might work better and faster for their son or daughter. It is especially understandable that a parent would want a cure rather than an intervention. When it comes to the controversial alternative treatments discussed in this chapter, parents are left with minimal information and only what the proposed therapist presents. Parents and teachers must be informed and intelligent consumers (Silver, 1998). Parents need to know that before committing their daughter or son to any new or different approach, they must ask questions. There is a general rule of thumb to consider. If the treatment approach that is about to be tried is so successful, why isn't everyone in the country using it? No professional, regardless of discipline, would avoid using a treatment that has been shown to work.

These controversial therapies for treating ADHD will be grouped by the proposed mechanism of action—physiologic changes or chemical changes. A few proposed treatments do not fit this model and will be listed separately. *Physiological changes* refers to the concept that by stimulating specific sensory inputs or exercising specific motor patterns, one can retrain, recircuit, or in some way improve the functioning of a part of the nervous system. *Chemical changes* refers to the concept of orthomolecular medicine. This is a term introduced by Linus Pauling, referring to the treatment of mental disorders and other disorders by the provision of the optimum concentrations of substances normally present in the human body (Pauling, 1968).

The Controversial Therapies for Treating ADHD

Physiological

Patterning
Vestibular Dysfunction
Biofeedback

Chemical

Megavitamins
Trace Elements
Food Additives
Refined Sugars
Herbs

Other Approaches

Allergies

Patterning

The theory and technique known as patterning was initially developed by Glenn Doman and Carl Delacato (Doman & Delacato, 1968). The underlying concept follows the principle that failures to pass properly through a certain sequence of developmental stages in mobility, language, and competence in the manual, visual, auditory, and tactile areas reflect poor "neurological organization" and may indicate "brain damage." The proposed treatments involve repetitive activities using specific muscle patterns in the order the child should have learned if development had been normal—for example, rolling over, then crawling, then standing, then walking, and so forth. The method is described in their literature as reaching ". . . all of the stimuli normally provided by this environment but with such intensity and frequence as to draw, ultimately, a response from the corresponding motor systems" (*Mental Retardation*, 1965, p. 27; Doman, Spitz, Zueman, et al., 1960).

Reports from the American Academy of Pediatrics (American Academy of Pediatrics, 1965) and other professional organizations (American Academy of Cerebral Palsy, 1965; United Cerebral Palsy Association of Texas, 1965), based on a review of all the literature, deny any evidence of success. In 1982 the American Academy of Pediatrics issued a policy statement concluding ". . . that the patterning treatment offers no special merit, that the claims of its advocates are unproven, and that the demands on families are so great that in some cases there may be harm in its use" (American Academy of Pediatrics, 1982).

This approach remains popular in the United States and around the world. Parents must know that patterning will not improve their son's or daughter's ADHD.

Vestibular Dysfunction

Several investigators have suggested that the vestibular system is important in learning. The vestibular system consists of a sensory organ in each inner ear that monitors head position and the impact of gravity and relays this information to the brain, primarily to the cerebellum. These investigators claim that there is a clear relationship between vestibular disorders and poor academic performance involving children with learning disabilities (DeQuiros, 1971; Frank & Levinson, 1972, 1977; Ayres, 1978).

The first to stress this view was Jean Ayres (1978). She proposed a theory of sensory integration needed to allow for the development of higher learning and intellectual functioning. Her theories propose the interrelationship among the visual, vestibular, tactile, and proprioceptive senses. Much of her research and that of others explore these interrelationships. There is controversy about aspects of her theory of sensory integration. These will not be discussed since the focus of this chapter is not on theory but on treatments. The treatment model that evolved from her theories is sensory integration therapy. There are individuals who question the usefulness of this therapy approach for children and adults with learning disabilities who have visual perception, motor planning, vestibular, and tactile difficulties. However, the majority view of the field is positive about sensory integration therapy.

Harold Levinson has written several books describing his views on the causative role of the vestibular system and the vestibular–cerebellar systems with dyslexia (Levinson, 1980, 1984, 1993). In the later books he proposes this treatment approach for ADHD as well. Levinson proposes treatment with anti-motion-sickness medication to correct the vestibular dysfunction. His books do not present research published in scientific journals. Most of the research presented is his and is published in his books. There is little evidence to support his theory or the effectiveness of his treatment. In one of his recent books he proposes multiple other interventions along with anti-motion-sickness medication, including many other medications (among them, Ritalin).

Much research has been done on the vestibular system. The consistent finding is that there is no significant differences either in the intensity of vestibular responsivity or in the prevalence of vestibular dysfunction between children who are normal learners and those with learning disabilities or ADHD (Polatajko, 1985). Furthermore, these researchers point out that the technique used by Levinson to diagnose vestibular dysfunction (i.e., a rotating cylinder with a picture on it with the child reporting when the picture is no longer clear) is a measure of "blurring speed" and, thus, a measure of visual stimulation and not of vestibular stimulation.

Levinson continues to write and publish his books. Much of the publicity for his approach is through these books and appearances on television talk shows. Other professionals have not started to practice what he proposes. Yet he remains busy, with a long waiting list.

Biofeedback

It is proposed that ADHD is a result of an altered pattern of brain waves and that this pattern can be identified on an electroencephalogram (EEG). This approach is presented as a diagnostic instrument. It is proposed that by using a biofeedback technique, it is possible to teach an individual to change his or her brain wave pattern. Once the pattern is corrected, the ADHD is improved or treated (Othmer, 1992, 1994; Othmer, Kaiser and Othmer, 1993.)

There is controversy about this theory relating to diagnosis and to treatment. There is greater controversy relating to EEG biofeedback as a treatment for ADHD. Yet the equipment is sold, and many professionals throughout the United States do this form of treatment.

Recently, the Professional Advisory Board of the organization known as Children and Adults with Attention Deficit Disorder (CHADD) published a position statement (CHADD, 1995). These professionals reviewed all of the literature on these concepts. In their statement, the use of EEG biofeedback for ADHD was challenged, and parents were advised not to use this treatment approach.

Megavitamins

Using massive doses of vitamins to treat emotional or cognitive disorders was first proposed in the 1940s for the treatment of schizophrenia (Hoffer, Osmond, & Smythies, 1954; Hoffer & Osmond, 1960). It was argued that this disorder was the result of a biochemical problem and that this problem could be avoided by the use of massive amounts of vitamins, especially the B vitamins. No research supported the theory or the treatment, and few professionals consider this approach today.

In the early 1970s, Allen Cott proposed that learning disabilities could be successfully treated with megavitamins (Cott, 1985). As with other professionals mentioned in this chapter, he presented this concept in his own book, citing no research to support his concepts. The American Academy of Pediatrics issued a report specifically focusing on megavitamin therapy to treat learning disabilities (American Academy of Pediatrics, 1973). The conclusion: "There is no validity to the concept or treatment."

Within the past several years the concept of megavitamins to treat learning disabilities as well as ADHD surfaced again. These approaches will be discussed later, in the section on herbs.

Trace Elements

Trace elements are chemicals found in the body in minute amounts that are essential to normal functioning. They include copper, zinc, magnesium, manganese, and chromium, along with the more common chemicals calcium, sodium, and iron. In recent years iodine, aluminum, and cadmium have been discussed.

Individuals are evaluated for the level of these trace elements in their body. Hair or nail clippings are used for this analysis. If deficiencies are found, replacement therapy is given. Alan Cott suggested the possible linkage of such deficiencies with learning problems and attentional problems (1985). No data have been published to support the theory that deficiencies in one or more of these elements are a cause of learning disabilities or ADHD. No formal studies by professionals other than those offering the diagnosis and treatment have validated the proposed successes.

This concept remains popular in this country. Centers are available to diagnose deficiencies and to treat learning disabilities and ADHD with trace elements.

Food Additives

In 1975, Benjamin Feingold published a book, *Why Your Child Is Hyperactive* (Feingold, 1975). He proposed that synthetic flavors and colors in the diet were related to hyperactivity. He reported that the elimination of all foods containing artificial colors and flavors as well as salicylates and certain other additives stopped the hyperactivity. Neither in this book nor in any of his other publications did Feingold present research data to support this theory. All findings in the book were based on his clinical experience. He and his book received wide publicity. Parent groups advocating the Feingold diet formed all over the country. It was left to others to document whether he was correct or incorrect.

Because of a hope that he might be correct and a need to either counter his claims or to prove he was correct, the federal government sponsored several major research projects to study this theory and the treatment. Two different types of clinical studies were done: dietary-crossover design and specific-challenge design. These studies were reviewed by the American Council on Science and Health (Sheridan, 1979).

In 1982, the National Institutes of Health held what is called a "consensus conference" on "Defined Diets and Childhood Hyperactivity" *(Defined Diets and Childhood Hyperactivity,* 1982). A panel of experts was brought together by the National Institute of Child Health and Human Development. This panel reviewed the results of these major research studies, read all available literature, held hearings to allow anyone who wished to present to do so, and questioned experts. The panel members then spent time synthesizing what was known and finally wrote a consensus on the topic.

They concluded that there does appear to be a subset of children with behavioral disturbances who respond to some aspects of Feingold's diet. However, this group is very small, possibly 1% of the children studied. They also commented that with notable exceptions, the specific elimination of synthetic food colors from the diet does not appear to be a major factor in the reported responses of a majority of these children. They concluded that the defined diets should not be used universally in the treatment of childhood hyperactivity.

Two studies done after this conference reached the same conclusions (Kavale & Forness, 1983; Mattles, 1983). The Feingold diet is not effective in treating hyperactivity in children. There may be a small group, perhaps 1%, who appear to respond positively to the diet for reasons that are not clear.

There is no way for physicians to identify in advance which patients might be part of this 1% group. Sometimes a parent will report that if their child eats foods with specific food colors (e.g., Kool Aid, Hawaiian Punch, certain cereals) or takes a medication with specific food colors (e.g., penicillin with red or yellow food dye), he or she will become more hyperactive. Perhaps this is the child with ADHD who might respond to a diet that eliminates that specific food color. However, the basic ADHD behaviors would still be present and need treatment.

Refined Sugars

Clinical observations and parent reports suggest that refined sugar promotes adverse behavioral reactions in children. Hyperactive behavior is most commonly reported (Prinz, Roberts, & Hartman, 1980). Two theories have been proposed for this possible reaction. There is the possibility that certain sugars (e.g., glucose) could influence brain neurotransmitter levels and thus the activity level in hyperactive children. This concept is based on the observation that platelet serotonin levels in hyperactive children have been found to be elevated above the norm. The other concept is that carbohydrate intake influences the level of essential fatty acids. These fatty acids are essential for the synthesis of prostaglandin in the brain. Insulin is required in the critical step to activate the prostaglandin precursors. Thus, a role for essential fatty acid levels in producing hyperactivity could be influenced by carbohydrate intake, which could influence insulin production.

Several formal studies have been done to clarify and/or verify these parent claims. Each used what is called a "challenge study." Children who were reported by parents to become more hyperactive when they ate refined sugar were challenged with refined sugar (glucose), natural sugar (fructose), or a placebo. The results failed to support the parent observations.

As an example, one research team (Conners & Blouin, 1982/1983) studied the relationship of sugar intake to conduct disorders, learning disorders, and attentional disorders in children. Behavioral and classroom measures were made after intake of sucrose, fructose, and placebo. The results did not distinguish the normal effects of increased energy intake from sugar effects per se. They could not conclude that deviant behavior was increased by sugar. Another sugar-challenge study in children reached the same conclusions (Rapoport, 1982/1983).

Another study explored whether the reported increase in activity level with children who ate a high sugar snack or meal might be related to the amount of refined sugar eaten and not to the exposure to the sugar (Conners, Caldwell, & Caldwell, 1985). In this study, each child was given a breakfast. This breakfast was high in fat, carbohydrates, or protein. The children were then given the challenge test with refined sugar, natural sugar, or a placebo. The study found that some children appeared to be more active after a high carbohydrate breakfast and exposure to refined sugars. Possibly, then, some children with ADHD will become more hyperactive if they eat high levels of refined sugar in foods and snacks throughout a period of time (sugared cereal for breakfast, cookies for snack, jelly sandwich and candy for lunch, cake for after-school snack . . .).

Herbs

The use of alternative medicines is popular around the world. Herbs, spices, and other ingredients have been known to be therapeutic in certain situations. These concepts as a treatment for ADHD and possibly for learning disabilities have become very widespread within the past several years. As with most of the controversial treatments discussed in this chapter, much of what is known is found in flyers and advertisements distributed by the individuals selling the product. No research is presented. Claims are made about the effectiveness of the treatment.

To date, there are no published studies, on the use of these products for children and adolescents who have ADHD. In preparation for this chapter, I wrote for more information on each product I saw advertised in magazines, found exhibited at a meeting, or received advertisements in the mail. I was struck by the absence of anything more than advertisements. I was also struck by the fact that three of the products I wrote "for more information" included an offer for me to be the exclusive salesperson for the product in my area. I was told how much good I would do for children by making them aware of this treatment.

I list those products I know of now. The uniform theme is that there is no research provided to defend the claims made. Testimonials were common. Large, technical words were used. There was a feeling that if I did not use the product, I was preventing my child from making progress. This list is meant to inform parents of the most common products available at the time this book was finalized. It is not a complete list. I'm sure there are others.

- *God's Recipe:* a mixture of colloidal minerals, antioxidant with ginkgo biloba, and multi-enzymes. (No scientific definitions were given for these ingredients.)
- *Pedi-Active ADD:* Phosphatidy/serine, stated to be the "most advanced neuronutrients available," including a diversified combination of other ingredients. (No scientific definitions were given for these ingredients.)
- *Kids Plex Jr:* multivitamins, amino acids, a mixture of "Ergogens and Krebs Cycle Intermediates and Lipotropics." (No clarification was given as to which multivitamins or aminoacids or a definition of what ergogens, krebs cycle intermediates, or lipotropics are.)
- *Calms Kids:* a mixture of vitamins, minerals, and amino acids. (No clarification was given as to which vitamins, minerals, or amino acids.)
- *Pycnogenol:* a "water processed extract from the bark of the French Maritine Pine Tree . . . (the most) potent nutritional antioxidant discovered by science." (No further explanation was provided.)
- *New Vision:* a mixture of 16 juices and 18 fruit blends made into a capsule. (No details were provided.)
- *Super Blue Green Algae:* this product comes in many forms and its benefits are stated to be based on the fact that algae is the "very basis of the entire food chain—it is largely responsible for creating and renewing all life on earth." (No references were given for such dramatic claims about algae.)

None of the producers of these products gives details. For example, what vitamins or amino acids are included? Many of the terms used were not defined and make little sense. No evidence to support the claims is provided. Parents and teachers need to think carefully before recommending or buying these products.

Allergies

Professionals who work with children have reported for many years that they see a higher percentage of children and adolescents in their practice with allergies who also have learning disabilities and/or ADHD. Most studies have been done on the possible relationships between allergies and learning disabilities. Feingold focused on ADHD (Feingold, 1975).

There does appear to be a relationship between allergies and brain functioning. No clear cause and effect has yet been clarified. Two clinicians have written about specific issues relating allergies to ADHD. Each has proposed a treatment plan. As with other approaches, the theory and treatment concepts are presented in books written by these clinicians, sometimes published by the clinician. Little, if any, research is presented. The established profession of pediatric allergy does not accept these treatments.

Doris Rapp believes that there is a relationship between food or other sensitivities and learning as well as with hyperactivity (Rapp, 1986). She proposes a diet that eliminates the identified foods or the avoidance of other suspected allergens as a treatment. She believes that the traditional allergy skin testing for foods does not always detect the foods that cause problems. Her critics say that her challenge test, with a solution placed under the tongue, is not a valid measure of allergies.

Rapp identifies certain foods or food groups that children might be allergic to: milk, chocolate, eggs, wheat, corn, peanuts, pork, and sugar. She suggests that parents try a specific elimination diet described in her books. This diet consists of eliminating all of the possible allergy-producing foods, then adding one back each week to see if there is a change in behaviors.

She studies other possible allergens in her tests by using a food extract solution placed under the tongue. If the child is found to be sensitive to certain foods or chemicals in the environment (e.g., paste, glue, paint, mold, chemicals found in new carpets), these items are eliminated or avoided. She reports an improvement in the behaviors of the child. Most specifically, she reports less aggressive or oppositional behavior and less hyperactivity. Other professionals have not been able to duplicate her findings or claimed successes.

William Crook has written extensively on the relationship between allergies and general health, learning disabilities, and ADHD (Crook & Stevens, 1987). He writes of the "allergic-tension-fatigue syndrome." He also reports that specific allergies can result in hyperactivity and distractibility.

Much of Crook's more recent publications and presentations focus on a possible allergic reaction to specific yeasts and the development of specific behaviors following a yeast infection. He reports that treatment of the yeast infection improves or corrects the problem. No clinical or research studies have confirmed his theories or proposed treatment program.

Summary

There is a relationship between brain function and nutrition as well as between brain function and allergic reactions. These relationships appear to be true for learning disabilities, ADHD, and other neurological disorders. However, at this time we do not understand these relationships, and there are no known treatments based on these relationships that are clinically successful.

When a parent or teacher learns of a new treatment or technique, it is understandable that he or she will show interest. We all want a better and faster way to help these children and adolescents. Each must take the time to become as informed as possible. Ask why this amazing approach is not used by everyone. If the person proposing the treatment tells you that "most professionals are biased and do not believe my findings because they are different from the usual treatments," ask to see the data supporting the concept and treatment. Don't accept as validated facts popular books published by the person proposing the theory or treatment. Discuss the approach with the family's physician, with school professionals, and with other parents.

Don't put a child or adolescent through something unproven and unlikely to help. It is critical to spend as much time researching these treatments as one does at a supermarket, when every label is read in detail before deciding which product to buy.

References

American Academy of Cerebral Palsy. (1965). Statement of the Executive Committee, February 15.

American Academy of Pediatrics. (1966). Statement of the Executive Board. *American Academy of Pediatrics Newsletter, 16,* 1.

American Academy of Pediatrics. (1982). The Doman–Delacato treatment of neurologically handicapped children. A policy statement by the American Academy of Pediatrics. *Pediatrics, 70,* 810–812.

American Academy of Pediatrics, Committee on Nutrition. (1973). Megavitamin therapy for childhood psychoses and learning disabilities. *Pediatrics, 58,* 910–911.

Ayres, A. J. (1978). Learning disabilities and the vestibular system. *Journal of Learning Disabilities, 11,* 18–29.

CHADD. (1995). Report from the Professional Advisory Board, February 1995. Plantation, Florida.

Conners, C. K., & Blouin, A. G. (1982/1983). Nutritional effects on behavior of children. *Journal of Psychiatric Research, 17,* 192–201.

Conners, C. K., Caldwell, J. A., & Caldwell, J. L. (1985). Effects of breakfast and sweetener on the cognitive performance of children. *Psychophysiology, 22,* 573.

Cott, A. (1985). *Help for your learning disabled child. The orthomolecular treatment.* New York: Times Books.

Crook, W. G., & Stevens, L. (1987). *Solving the puzzle of your hard-to-raise child.* Jackson, TN: Professional Books.

Defined Diets and Childhood Hyperactivity. (1982). Bethesda, MD: National Institutes of Health Consensus Development Conference Summary, Vol. 4, No. 3.

DeQuiros, J. B. (1971). Diagnostico deferencial de la dislexia especifica. *Fonoaudiologica Buenos Aires, 17,* 117–123.

Doman, G., & Delacato, C. (1968). Doman–Delacato philosophy. *Human Potential, 1,* 113-116.

Doman, R. J., Spitz, E. D., Zueman, E., et al., (1960). Children with severe brain injuries: Neurological organization in terms of mobility. *JAMA, 17,* 257–261.

Feingold, B. F. (1975). *Why your child is hyperactive.* New York: Random House.

Frank, J., & Levinson, H. N. (1973). Dysmetric dyslexia and dyspraxia. Hypothesis and study. *Journal of the American Academy of Child Psychiatry, 12,* 690–701.

Frank, J., & Levinson, H. N. (1977). Anti-motion sickness medication in dysmetric dyslexia and dyspraxia. *Academic Therapy, 12,* 411–424.

Hoffer, A., & Osmond, H. (1960). *The chemical basis of clinical psychiatry.* Springfield, IL: Charles C. Thomas.

Hoffer, A., Osmond, H., & Smythies, J. (1954). A new approach: II. Results of a year's research. *Journal of Mental Science, 100,* 29–54.

Kavale, K. A., & Forness, S. R. (1983). Hyperactivity and diet treatment. A meta-analysis of the Feingold hypothesis. *Journal of Learning Disabilities, 16,* 324–330.

Levinson, H. N. (1980). *A solution to the riddle of dyslexia.* New York: Springer-Verlag.

Levinson, H. N. (1984). *Smart but feeling dumb.* New York: Warner.

Levinson, H. N. (1994). *A scientific watergate. Dyslexia.* Lake Success, NY: Stonebridge.

Mattles, J. A. (1983). The Feingold diet: A current reappraisal. *Journal Learning Disabilities, 16,* 319–323.

Mental Retardation. (1965). Philadelphia Institutes for the Advancement of Human Potential, p. 27.

Othmer, S. (1994). Personal communication, May 22, 1994.

Othmer, S., Kaiser, D., & Othmer, S. F. (1993). EEG biofeedback training for attention deficit disorder: A review of recent controlled studies and clinical findings. From a newsletter issued by EEG Spectrum, Inc., Encino, CA, June 1995.

Othmer, S. F., & Othmer, S. (1992). Evaluation and remediation of attentional deficits. From a newsletter issued by EEG Spectrum, Inc., Encino, CA, December 1992.

Pauling, L. (1968). Orthomolecular psychiatry. *Science, 160,* 265–271.

Polatajko, H. J. (1985). A critical look at vestibular dysfunction in learning-disabled children. *Developmental Medicine and Child Neurology, 27,* 283–292.

Prinz, R. J., Roberts, W. A., & Hartman, E. (1980). Dietary correlates of hyperactive behavior in children. *Journal of Consultant Clinical Psychology, 48,* 760–769.

Rapoport, J. (1982/1983). Effects of dietary substances in children. *Journal of Psychiatric Research, 17,* 187–191.

Rapp, D. J. (1986). *The impossible child in school and at home.* Buffalo, NY: Life Sciences.

Sheridan, M. J. (1979). *Diet and hyperactivity: Is there a relationship?* New York: American Council on Science and Health.

Silver, L. B. (1998). *The misunderstood child.* New York: Times Books.

Silver, L. B. (Ed.). (1999). *Attention-deficit hyperactivity disorder: A clinical guide to diagnosis and treatment for health and mental health professionals.* Washington, DC: American Psychiatric Press.

United Cerebral Palsy Association of Texas. (1965). The Doman–Delacato treatment of neurologically handicapped children. *Information Bulletin,* United Cerebral Palsy Association of Texas.

Chapter **6**

A Teacher Looks at the Elementary Child with ADHD

SUZANNE STEVENS

Recognizing the ADHD student is not always easy, particularly with a tangle of state guidelines to complicate the issue. As often as not, it is the child with the most outrageous behavior, or the most persistent mother, who gets officially identified and provided with appropriate accommodations. Significant patterns of behavior that are easy to detect in research data and clinical observation are not so obvious when viewed from the blackboard side of the teacher's desk.

When classroom teachers see an ADHD student in action, they often fail to recognize what they're looking at. They see the blurting out of answers and the constant talking, and think "Can't take turns. Bad manners." They see fidgeting, wiggling, and bounding up out of the seat, and decide "immature." They see acting without thinking and conclude "undisciplined." It isn't that the behaviors of ADHD students go unnoticed. They are observed. But then they are misinterpreted. They are experienced, commented upon, and then explained away (Stevens, 1997).

It is highly probable that a large percentage of our genuinely ADHD students go through school totally unrecognized. Instead of compassion and modifications, they get criticism and punishment. Classmates reject them socially; teachers eject them from the classroom, so they populate detention centers and halls; schools expel them for their bad attitude, offensive behavior, lack of motivation, unexcused absences, and general lack of interest and success.

Yet in every school there are a few teachers who have a combination of personal temperament and instructional styles that make it easy for students with ADHD-type behavior to succeed without causing undue frustration to either classmates or teacher. What is the secret to designing a learning environment that is immune to the disruptive capacities of ADHD youngsters? It seems to rest on three major factors: (1) attitude: educators who view nontraditional learners as an exciting challenge that make teaching a worthwhile adventure find ADHD students a delight; (2) teaching techniques: educators who create a structured classroom environment and teach organizational skills within the regular curriculum rarely find ADHD pupils to be unmanageable; and (3) teamwork development tactics: educators who consider effective teamwork and cooperative social interaction to be teachable skills find ADHD students to be apt pupils who are extremely grateful for even the tiniest boost to their social status and self-esteem (Stevens, 1995).

Attitude

Within the walls of our schools, the behaviors and personality traits associated with ADHD are frequently thought of as entirely negative. Such a grossly unbalanced perspective prevents teachers from providing assistance to youngsters who are struggling to overcome limitations that could thwart their attempts to develop to their full creative and intellectual potential. And, even worse, such a one-sided mind-set prevents educators from seeing the unusual talents so typically found among individuals with attention deficit hyperactivity disorder. It is within the ranks of this wiggling, distractible, disorganized part of the student body that we are likely to find our outstanding athletes, artists, musicians, actors, poets, adventurers, architects, innovators, inventors, visionaries, mechanics, dancers, plumbers, entrepreneurs, pilots, astronauts, and other such creative types. When students come to us with the one-sided label ADHD, it is important that we learn to recognize the giftedness that so typically balances out the areas of deficiency (Stevens, 1996).

Those teachers who have very little difficulty with ADHD students usually see them as well-rounded individuals with about the same number of flat sides as all the rest of us. When asked about their uncanny ability to get along with these disruptive youngsters, these educators quickly reveal attitudes that allow them to be flexible while maintaining high standards, to hold strong positive expectations while accepting the students' limitations, and to sustain a clear and obvious belief that these students can succeed both in the classroom and in the world at large. When looking at ADHD children, these teachers see beyond wiggles, work habits, grade books, and labels. Part of the trick is that they admire these youngsters and recognize many of their differences as gifts. They applaud their inventiveness, love their quick sense of humor, appreciate their startling insights, savor their outrageously sprung logic. They may also wish they had the energy of their pupils with ADHD, and are constantly amazed by the persistence with which these students devote themselves to the things they find interesting. Such a balanced perspective allows educators to capitalize on the natural traits that others see as obstacles. In classrooms where the prevailing attitude trusts students to draw on their unique personal talents and inner resources to solve their own academic problems, the ADHD student's natural creativity becomes a powerful tool for success. Here the teacher moves from the role of adversary to that of trusted coach, partner, and friend (Stevens, 1997).

Darryl was in a fifth-grade academically gifted (AG) class. Ritalin enabled him to sit still and pay attention, but it was of no value in helping him to learn long division. The boy hated everything about math. When his classmates got out their arithmetic books, he would sneak a library book into his lap. While his teacher and his gifted peers discussed challenging concepts and worked problems, Darryl drifted off into a fictitious world where there were no numbers.

Everybody in the class had learned the multiplication tables back in the third grade. Despite a year and a half with tutors and nightly drills at home, Darryl had not managed to master even the threes, fours, and fives. His parents were frantic. Darryl was extremely discouraged and very sensitive about his problem. It was embarrassing to have an IQ of over 140 and not be able to memorize the multiplication tables! In math class, he shunned all special help, claiming, "It makes me look stupid."

Since the boy's attitude made overt intervention impossible, his teacher took a lateral approach that would allow this bright ADHD child to apply the combined forces of his high intellect and his unusual creativity. In a brief private exchange, she gave Darryl a biography of Albert Einstein and told him that the great mathematical wizard had had a similar difficulty with memorizing the multiplication tables—but had apparently found a way to work around it. She gave her frustrated student a pocket calculator and a small laminated chart of the troublesome facts. When he began protesting, "The other kids don't use calculators. They'll say I'm cheating," she avoided the trap of endless persuasion and restated the simple rule that would have to guide his behavior: "Reading a library book during math class is not an option." With a smile and a parting wink, Darryl's teacher left him with a final word of encouragement: "You're a clever boy. You'll think of something."

After a few days, this inventive AG/ADHD 10-year-old came up with a solution that not only solved the basic problem, but offered the bonus of letting him look cool in front of his classmates. Instead of discretely taping the wallet-size chart of the tables into some corner of his notebook, he laboriously hand-copied a full set of the facts onto a sheet of legal paper, which he then rigged up with a cardboard backing and some duct-tape hinges so he could swing it out of his desk and into his lap for easy reference. It was an elegant solution to the problem; Darryl's swiveling multiplication table not only helped him remember his math facts, but also acted to remind him of his own ability to find creative ways to overcome personal limitations.

Although medication can do much to help youngsters control tapping fingers and a wandering mind, it does not provide them with a comprehensive solution to problems that are likely to cause lifelong difficulties. And it does not address their unusual weaknesses in handwriting, spelling, written expression, organization, math computation, and/or social skills. Getting ADHD children to sit down and shut up helps teachers establish a tranquil learning environment that serves the best interests of everyone in the classroom, but dealing with the academic glitches that these youngsters face daily requires ingenuity, persistence, and a good-natured spirit of experimentation from both the student and the teacher.

Any educator who encourages ADHD students to use an exploratory approach to finding nontraditional solutions to their problems helps them build confidence in their own resourcefulness and develop lifelong attitudes of trust in their own competence. And any educator who leads students to this level of success earns their boundless gratitude, their respect, and their cooperation.

Teaching Techniques

Teachers who operate on the premise that it is their job to make every subject they teach interesting and accessible to every student often lead ADHD students to otherwise unattainable levels of academic success. Such instructors are keenly aware of the fact that youngsters who are not actively involved in learning will get into trouble. They prevent difficulties from arising by maintaining a quiet, productive classroom environment and by ensuring that all students fully participate in class activities. For most youngsters, active involvement in schoolwork will produce satisfying academic success.

To make it possible to achieve such lofty goals, an *organizational system* must be created to help every student keep track of books and materials, and live comfortably within a carefully structured time management system.

Organizational Skills

Without direct instruction and supervision, very few ADHD students learn to keep track of their school supplies so that they are always equipped for class. Teachers who choose to provide materials management training must make a commitment to take a very active part in leading the entire class through the process of setting up a system of carefully organizing notebooks, desks, lockers, and book bags. The teacher should also take time daily to monitor the students as they learn to implement the system.

Be prepared to closely monitor ADHD students for several months. Although most children can perfect the use of such a materials management program in six to eight weeks, many ADHD students, even when closely supervised, will have trouble organizing their belongings over the period of an entire semester (Stevens, 1997). There will always be one or two who will require continued monitoring—possibly forever.

Watch for the benefits that improve the atmosphere for everyone in the classroom. Getting an entire class organized all but eliminates the constant disruptions caused by ADHD students digging through cluttered desks for books that got left on the bus or wandering the halls while fuming classmates wait for them to return from their locker. It saves wear and tear on the teacher and helps avoid much of the resentment that classmates feel toward any student who robs them of their fair share of the teacher's attention and ruins her otherwise sunny disposition. Teaching ADHD children to keep track of their stuff brings awards for valor and unending praise from parents, future employers, and spouses.

Do not expect parents to take a very active role in supervising their child's efforts to develop organizational skills. Since the parents of ADHD children are usually just as disorganized as their offspring, it is unrealistic to expect parents to be very effective in monitoring their children's management of materials or time.

Be sure to provide a full array of scheduling materials when setting up students' notebooks and school supply storage systems. They will need calendars, schedules, assignment books, weekly and monthly planners, and detailed instructions on how to use them.

Systematically teach students to enter assignment information on calendars and memory joggers. Since the whole purpose of these time management tools is to teach students to develop the scheduling habits that will enable them to be reliable and self-sufficient, ongoing item-by-item supervision will be required for some time. It won't be enough to write the page numbers on the board, tell the class to take out their assignment books, and give students a minute to copy down the information. Teachers will have to check and correct every entry as a matter of routine. As youngsters demonstrate proficiency in getting essential details into their memory joggers, supervision can ease off gradually to spot checks once a day or even once a week.

Provide continued encouragement and support for those who have trouble learning to accurately record necessary information about homework, class preparation, and independent assignments.

Impose the same high standards on every member of the class. Students who are highly resistant to using these organizational control techniques are almost always the ones who need it most. To get the cooperation of these reluctant youngsters, teachers need to impose the system of organization on all their students, adhere to it themselves, monitor compliance, and provide rewards as reinforcement.

Continue to oversee the system for the whole school year for those few truly scatterbrained youngsters who are completely unable to acquire orderly habits. That's a lot of work—but well worth it when one considers the alternatives.

Teachers who take the time to implement an organizational program report startling improvement in classroom tranquillity and student participation. ADHD students who have gone through such organizational training say that they no longer feel so frantic and uptight. They boast of a whole new outlook on life now that they're "in control." Teaching students to be in control makes a profound difference in their attitude and their performance.

If very active supervision is not available for the first six to eight weeks of a materials control and time management system, it should not be attempted. Such a program can produce the desired results only if the student is provided with the necessary materials *and* is systematically taught *how* to use them (Stevens, 1997).

Provide temporary stopgap measures when necessary. If circumstances force a postponement of materials management training, a few precautions can prevent most disastrously disruptive patterns from developing. At all costs, the forgetful, disorganized work habits of ADHD students must not be allowed to contaminate the serenity of the classroom atmosphere.

Purchase a small supply of emergency materials. It's well worth a small investment at the beginning of the school year to procure essential materials for those times when a student's own equipment is not readily available. Some teachers make it a loan arrangement by holding a shoe or a driver's license as security. Others just keep an old coffee can full of pencils and a stack of notebook paper in a place where they are easily accessible, and consider it an investment in stress management.

Keep at least one extra textbook on hand for use during class to guard against ADHD students' tendency to lose books. **Make sure that participation in today's lesson is not contingent on successful completion of last night's homework.** Never let an ADHD youngster's unreliable habits about completing home assignments provide an excuse for begging off on classwork. Highly creative and energetic students can always find ways to keep themselves amused while others take part in the activities of the day's lessons, a situation guaranteed to lead to disruptive behavior and unpleasant confrontations.

Establish a firm policy: Class participation is not optional. Henry Ford used to say, "If you've got a difficult job to do, give it to the laziest man in the factory, and he'll find the easiest way to do it." Be a lazy teacher. Save yourself aggravation by planning ahead: keep ADHD students fully involved in all classroom activities.

Daily sign-off systems can be very helpful for students who cannot be trusted to record homework details accurately in their assignment book. This requires the teacher to check over a pupil's record of the day's homework at the end of each class. The instructor then initials the sheet to verify that the information is complete and accurate. This supervision method is particularly effective when there is a reliable homework monitor available to follow through with the sign-off process at home. Very few slip-ups get through when a well-organized teacher and a truly persistent parent team up on a sign-off system.

Weekly assignment sheets can be very efficient. Instead of a daily homework record, some teachers opt for a weekly assignment sheet that they hand out to an entire class every Monday. In addition to relieving students of the burden of copying down detailed information for themselves, it allows every class member to have advance notice of upcoming tasks and helps them keep abreast of due dates for reports, long-term projects, and tests. Teachers who use this technique report that it is a great time saver and much appreciated by parents, tutors, and other homework helpers.

Emphasize Time Limits

Set time limits. Getting ADHD students stopped usually causes as much difficulty as getting them started. When told, "Time's up," students with an attention deficit disorder almost always resist with loud protests: "I'm not finished yet." This unpleasant little routine can usually be avoided by making a habit of bringing scheduled activities to a smooth conclusion with a 5-minute warning, a three-minute reminder, and a final one-minute countdown. When this technique is used, it's easy to stand firm in a non-negotiating position on "Turn in your paper—now."

Enforce time limits. Most people with ADHD (adults even more so than children) have a very poor concept of time and no natural inclination toward punctuality. By enforcing time limits in the classroom, teachers prepare youngsters to live successfully in a world full of "cutoff dates" and "deadlines." There's no need to be brutal or hard-hearted. Lectures and tirades are pointless. Hints, helps, gimmicks, tricks, and a cheerful acceptance of the fact that the child has an unreliable inner clock will be necessary (Stevens, 1996). But teaching children to meet deadlines is a life skill that cannot be ignored, even in the youngest students.

Teach students to plan ahead

- To be considered "satisfactory," an assignment must be done according to the directions, get a passing grade, and be turned in on time. That's a life rule that applies to everybody.
- ADHD students will often need an assignment modified or a deadline extended, but such adjustments should be arranged well before the moment when the work is actually due.
- By closely monitoring long-term projects, teachers put themselves in a position to intervene or suggest scheduling options well before a student's time management difficulties blossom into disasters.

Transition Tactics

Without close monitoring and special schedule management training, students with an attention deficit disorder are likely to spend much of their lives in a time warp. The typical school day is a continuous procession of different activities separated by brief transitions. "Hand in your papers, put your math workbook away, and take out this week's vocabulary list." This simple series of instructions poses no problem for most students.

For ADHD youngsters, every shift of activities offers a new opportunity for their minds to drift. Long after the new assignment has been given and the rest of the class has settled down to work, students with attention problems will be digging in their desk, staring off into space, talking to a neighbor, playing with a toy. It's at the transition points that ADHD students typically get into trouble and sorely try the patience of their teacher and their classmates (Stevens, 1997).

Supervise transitions by carefully monitoring every step of the process so that assistance and encouragement can be provided throughout every phases of the undertaking. Concluding one activity, handing in completed work, getting out new materials, listening to directions, starting the new activity—all of these loosely structured operations are fraught with dangers for ADHD students.

When teachers employ instructional methods that require active physical involvement from their class, ADHD students find it easy to "get into" the lesson and sustain interest and concentration. After the activity gets rolling and the students become engrossed in the project, ADHD youngsters tend to slide into the total absorption of "over focus" and need no special monitoring until the next transition.

Instructional Methods

Teachers who systematically teach and monitor organizational and time management skills create a classroom environment where disorganized youngsters have a chance to succeed. Students who keep track of their materials and keep up with their assignments are in an ideal position to fully participate in class activities. By incorporating just a few alternative techniques into regular classroom instruction, teachers can guide these distractible youngsters to use simple study methods that can enhance their concentration, decrease their frustration, increase their patience, and improve their memories (Lazear, 1991b).

Get whole-body involvement. ADHD students have their best chance for success when instructional techniques actively engage the entire body, not just the mind, eyes, and pencil. By requiring all the sensory channels to operate at once, teachers can tremendously increase students' level of concentration. Teaching techniques that allow physically interactive learning—such as manipulative devices, demonstrations, and role playing—can help even the most distractible youngsters stay on task.

Keep hands busy. To keep their attention focused, whole-body learners need a strong hands-on component like drawing, building, writing, or manipulating something. Since many ADHD students have great difficulty with written language, note taking is rarely the ideal way to draw them into deep concentration. On the other hand, working at a computer provides a type of multisensory activity that usually helps them develop the strong focus of attention required for sustained effort and clear thinking.

Allow for postures other than sitting. Since posture has a profound effect on concentration, it's important to allow students to explore a larger range of body positions than those allowed by seating at standard tables and desks. Many ADHD students thrive when teachers deliberately create opportunities for them to work standing up at charts, bulletin boards, or the chalkboard. Projects that require kneeling on the floor to write on paper or poster board can also be helpful. Standing up, pacing around, chewing gum, fiddling with a rubber band, pointing at words as they're read, or handling some item related to the subject being studied can all act to engage attention and interest while increasing recall (Dunn & Dunn, 1992). As long as unorthodox activities or positions don't disturb classmates, they should be encouraged.

A very bright fourth-grader was having trouble keeping up with the other children in his math class for the gifted and talented. After 10 or 12 minutes of concentration, he'd go into a state he called "brain slide." And his wiggly, fun-loving nature would take over. When warnings and corrections didn't stop this energetic imp from moving into his class clown routine, the teacher tried some preventive measures. The one that was the most effective required moving him to the end of a row, where he could be close to a blackboard so he could do his math standing up at the first sign of the wiggles. He rarely worked more than three or four problems at the board before his concentration was reactivated and he could return to a more normal classroom posture.

Provide strong visual input. Whole-body learners need strong visual input. This can be achieved by choosing instructional methods that emphasize visual thinking:

- **Teach by showing rather than by telling,** and encourage students to demonstrate their proficiency through methods of communication that do not rely entirely on the written word.
- **Use charts, graphs, maps, manipulatives,** and other visual aids. Rely on demonstrations as much as explanations.
- **Write key words on the chalkboard or overhead**—preferably in color.

Add a touch of color. In almost any assignment, it helps to add a touch of color. Crayons, chalks, felt-tip markers, and drawing pencils come in a wide range of hues that can create visual interest to make information easier to digest and remember. Rather than underlining subjects and verbs, write action words in green and names of things in red. When working math problems on the board, lay them out in color-coded columns or make the symbols in some bright day-glow tone that stands out from the numbers. When introducing students to different note-taking methods, encourage them to use colors for writing as well as highlighting. Every time color is introduced, visual thinking becomes a more significant component in the cognitive processing (Lazear, 1991a).

Encourage students to think and read to themselves out loud. Many children need to talk their way through thought processing in order to hear themselves think. They shouldn't be discouraged from moving their lips while reading or discussing things with themselves quietly when thinking. When studying and reviewing are done out loud, a powerful auditory component adds verbal cues to the facts being stored in memory. Mnemonic devices almost always include a strong verbal element. Rhymes, jingles, songs, and chants help most learners fix sequences in chains that are easily remembered. Many youngsters never learn to do alphabetizing without using the ABC song.

Use visual language when speaking so that the verbal component of class instruction makes a stronger imprint on memory. By simultaneously providing verbal and visual input, mnemonic devices and illustrative stories help ADHD students compensate for their weakness in remembering sequences. Though it's been over forty years since my last biology class, I can still rattle off the sequence kingdom, phylum, class, order, family, genus, species, because a clever teacher permanently imprinted my mind with a quirky little story about a soldier on KP whose need to COF led to an invasion of gremlin Girl Scouts. She made KP COF GS into a mnemonic device for kingdom, phylum, class, order, family, genus, species. Memory tricks that rely on absurd visual images can be tremendously valuable to any student when a list of items must be remembered in order.

Create mental pictures. Graphic explanations that create mental pictures are almost always helpful to these whole-body thinkers. Even when the visual component is all in their imagination, it acts to enhance both concentration and recall. For example, telling a class that Germany is 95,000 square miles in area is a purely verbal method of introducing students to the size of this European nation and highly unlikely to make much of an impression on the mind of an ADHD student. On the other hand, telling students that the German Republic is about the size of North and South Carolina put together gets students to use more of their own thinking power by forcing them to refer to their visual memory's set of familiar maps in order to make the comparison. Every time a student does "more thinking," concentration is enhanced.

Encourage whole-body learners to apply their special talents to normal classroom activities. This helps improve their attitude as well as their concentration and level of achievement. By introducing color-coded files and notebooks to help them stay organized, by allowing them to use drawings and illustrations in place of verbal explanations, by valuing models and collages as highly as formal written reports, teachers can provide the kind of environment in which the natural talents of ADHD students can help them learn (Armstrong, 1993).

Teamwork Development Tactics

Some youngsters with an attention deficit disorder have wonderful social skills and a natural talent for leadership. They can read the set of an eyebrow or the slope of a shoulder, and know just what to say in every situation. They may have all the usual problems with organization, concentration, procrastination, restlessness, and impulsive behavior—but their people skills are so outstanding that they can slick-talk their way out of almost any difficulty. Some seem destined to be great salesmen, politicians, or, perhaps, con artists.

Many children with ADHD have extremely limited social skills. They can't read social signals, never seem to know when to shut up, say all the wrong things, and stand out in all the wrong ways. They are usually found at the bottom of the classroom pecking order. Many reside in the boisterous ranks of the troublemakers in the back. Some become solitary outcasts who stay on the peripheries, where they are quietly ignored. A few grow to be so actively disliked by their classmates that they become victims of teasing and bullying. When the situation degenerates to this level, the teacher is forced into the role of police officer to protect the despised "weirdo" from those who would steal clothing and lunch money, or pull a knife or throw a few punches when not under the watchful eye of an authority figure.

Help ADHD students develop appropriate behaviors. Getting ADHD youngsters to fit comfortably into the classroom community requires some serious preventive measures. Children who get away with ignoring rules, assignments, and schedules tend to be resented by the rest of the class. Those who destroy the peaceful atmosphere of the classroom with odd or disruptive behavior will find disapproval from their peers. Students who take more than their fair share of the teacher's time and keep the entire room in turmoil are likely to meet rejection by their classmates. Thus, every time a teacher helps an ADHD student avoid behaving in a way that carries a high social penalty, there has been an improvement in that child's social status.

Establish a structured classroom environment. By carefully maintaining a structured classroom where organizational skills are taught and closely monitored, the teacher helps students with an attention deficit disorder succeed with their schoolwork. If they complete their assignments within the time allowed, their classmates won't grow impatient and angry because they're always being forced to wait for this one slow worker. If they can do their math, they won't unleash the shrieking outbursts and fits of sulking that make the other children think they're weird. Everything that helps ADHD students succeed in the classroom gains them more acceptance from their classmates (Stevens, 1997).

Build a "team spirit" with the entire class. Special remedial programs designed to teach social skills to students with an attention deficit disorder are best run in small groups under the supervision of a psychologist or school counselor. For classroom use, teachers usually have to develop their own techniques through workshops or materials that outline procedures others have found effective. Regardless of the methods, the success of any social skills program seems to hinge on how well the teacher can get students to see one another without reference to linear ranking systems such as the social ladder or the classroom pecking order. As long as group members treat one another in accord with each individual's standing in the classroom social status, no cooperative attitude of mutual respect and interdependence can develop to pull the members together into a single working "team." And, of course, since ADHD youngsters are so low on the acceptance totem pole, their attempt to participate in any group activity usually leads to friction, complaints, and rejection.

Teach students to see one another from a positive perspective. Teachers who wish to break through this ostracism barrier need powerful instructional techniques to reform personal attitudes and improve the classroom atmosphere:

- **Lead the class through a learning styles analysis.** A systematic investigation of personal approaches to learning can be very enlightening to individual students, the teacher, and the class as a whole. The research findings of Rita and Kenneth Dunn are particularly appropriate for such a project (Dunn & Dunn, 1992).

- **Teach students about the seven types of intelligence.** Howard Gardner's theory of seven intelligences offers an especially useful and interesting format for exploring the strengths and weaknesses of an entire class. Once students develop an appreciation of the special talents of others, they find it much easier to work in a cooperative fashion (Armstrong, 1987, 1993).

At a large teacher training workshop in Texas, things were not going well. One hundred teachers and supervisors had volunteered to participate in the week-long hands-on seminar. But nobody wanted to get their hands dirty. Everybody paid close attention during lectures and demonstrations, but bureaucratic protocol prevented team members from interacting in ways that allowed them to apply serious thought or creativity to the teaching materials they were supposed to be designing. Superintendents leaned back in their chairs, drank coffee, and socialized with other white males of equally imposing stature. Supervisors with a no-nonsense attitude and sensible shoes made all the decisions, but never touched scissors or glue. The classroom teachers did most of the actual work while young aides scurried around gathering supplies, looking up information, copying facts onto charts, and measuring and holding things.

On the third day the presenter got so disgusted with this unproductive gathering of educators that she reorganized the groups. As a preface to the actual reshuffling of personnel, she introduced Gardner's theory of multiple intelligences. Participants were given charts and questionnaires to guide them in analyzing their personal strengths and weaknesses in each of the seven types of intelligence: verbal/linguistic, mathematical/logical, visual/spatial, kinesthetic, musical, interpersonal, and intrapersonal. When the new teams were assembled, each group had to have one member for each of the seven types of intelligence (Lazzear, 1991a, 1991b; Armstrong, 1987, 1993).

As work resumed, everybody assumed roles that fit their temperaments and talents, and the room buzzed with a new level of productivity and cooperation. Shy teacher's aides had no trouble asserting their authority in the area of their personal responsibility. Superintendents understood their specific function in the enterprise and participated with great enthusiasm. The lesson plans and materials they designed were extremely creative and beautifully executed. For the first time that week, these educators produced work that strongly demonstrated their qualifications as "modification managers."

Reorganizing the teams so that each member could contribute from an area of personal interest and strength transformed the dynamics and interactions of every person in the room. Children rarely have trouble working together cooperatively after they have been taught to see one another from a perspective that allows honest appreciation of talents and compassionate acceptance of weaknesses.

Teach ADHD youngsters to prevent problems before they develop. Any kind of realistic attempt to help ADHD youngsters improve their social skills must include direct instruction that teaches them to recognize difficult situations that come up repeatedly and then guides them in creating a specific plan for dealing with them effectively.

Kathleen was a cute, bubbly third-grader, but she was very sensitive about showing classmates her report card. When asked "What'd you get?" she would start to cry. Her anxiety level sometimes got so high that she went home sick before ever even seeing her grades. To avoid the unpleasant scenes that were undermining her social status, Kathleen's teacher helped her devise a one-line script. When classmates asked about her grades, she simply replied, "I promised my mother I wouldn't tell." Armed with the little speech that she had prepared in advance, report card day no longer forced this pert little girl to deal with snubs and snide remarks from her classmates. It changed her whole outlook on grades.

By scripting and rehearsing responses, students can make the small, day-to-day behavior changes that gradually build up to improve their level of social acceptance. Even the most modest gain in social skill helps students with ADHD build confidence, self-esteem, and social status.

Conclusion

Teachers who wish to take an active part in leading ADHD students to success will find that the tools to do so are available. Within the privacy of each classroom, educators have the power to create a structured environment and adjust their teaching techniques so that students with ADHD-type difficulties can stay actively engaged in learning. It's not a matter of changing the children; we are the ones who need to change.

Educators do not *cause* learning. However, they do have the power to enhance students' chances for development, growth, and acquisition of skills. By consciously taking control of the classroom environment, teachers can create an atmosphere where every class member feels totally confident that it is safe to try, it is possible to succeed, and it is worth the effort.

References

Armstrong, T. (1987). *In their own way.* Los Angeles: Tarcher.

Armstrong, T. (1993). *Seven kinds of smart.* New York: Penguin.

Dunn, R., & Dunn, K. (1992). *Teaching elementary students through their individual learning styles.* Jamaica, NY: Learning Styles Network.

Lazear, D. (1991a). *Seven ways of teaching.* Palatine, IL: Skylight.

Lazear, D. (1991b). *Seven ways of knowing.* Palatine, IL: Skylight.

Stevens, S. H. (1995). *Getting the horse to drink: How to motivate unmotivated students.* Columbia, MO: Hawthorne Educational Services

Stevens, S. H. (1996). *The LD child and the ADHD child: Ways that parents and professionals can help.* Winston-Salem, NC: Blair.

Stevens, S. H. (1997). *Classroom success for the LD child and the ADHD child.* Winston-Salem, NC: Blair.

Recommended References and Materials

Barkley, R. (1995). *Taking charge of ADHD.* New York, NY: Guilford.

King, D. (1990). *Writing skills.* Cambridge, MA: Educators Publishing Service

Levine, M. (1990). *Keeping ahead in school.* Cambridge, MA: Educators Publishing Service

Margulies, N. (1991). *Mapping inner space: Learning and teaching mind mapping.* Tucson, AZ: Zephyr.

McCarney, S., & Bauer, A. (1995). *The parent's guide to attention deficit disorders.* Columbia, MO: Hawthorne Educational Services.

Meirovitz, Marco, Dods, & Stuart. (1990). *Verbal thinking: Building the thinking–communication connection.* Monroe, NY: Trillium.

Richards, R. (1993). *L.E.A.R.N.: Playful techniques to accelerate learning.* Tucson, AZ: Zephyr.

Rose, C. (1987). *Accelerated learning.* New York: Dell.

Rudginsky, L., & Haskell, E. (1985). *How to teach spelling.* Cambridge, MA: Educators Publishing Service.

Stevens, S. H. (1996). *The LD child and the ADHD child: Ways that parents and professionals can help.* Winston-Salem, NC: Blair.

Chapter 7

Reaching and Teaching the Adolescent with ADHD

BARBARA PRIDDY GUYER

Andy is 15 years old and on the move. Finding it painful to remain seated for an entire class period he either drums his fingers on his desk or swings his foot recklessly. This is very distracting to those around him. His attention wanders constantly. He usually loses his homework before he reaches his classes; at times, he is unaware of his assignments. His grades? They are not good. Though Andy has been diagnosed as having ADHD, his parents refuse to consult a physician. It is up to his teachers to make the best of a difficult situation.

What can Andy's classroom teacher do? For one thing, she can allow Andy opportunities for "legal movement"—prearranged activities in which he may engage when he feels the need. The teacher could contract with Andy to let him do the following when he is restless or can't seem to pay attention: (1) sharpen his pencil without asking, (2) get a drink of water, or (3) use the permanent hall pass to go to the bathroom or perhaps walk up and down the stairway several times. (When the other students ask why Andy gets special privileges, the teacher can respond that this is an arrangement between her and Andy.) When Andy's mind seems to be wandering, the teacher can stand in front of him as she talks to the class. Sometimes she might gently put her hand on his shoulder (or just put her hand on his desk) to get his attention. Whenever possible, she should use nonverbal cues to get his attention and tell him privately in advance how she will do that. One reason for this is that Andy will tune out a lot of what he considers "verbal garbage." Another reason is that Andy needs to understand why the teacher is doing something.

Possibly, Andy's parents don't understand the severity of his ADHD problems at school. It may be helpful to speak to the principal about the possibility of video-taping a class session. When his parents come in for a conference, the video might reveal Andy as perpetually restless and not focusing well on his studies.

An educator should never say, "I believe your child should take Ritalin." This is practicing medicine without a license. Instead, if testing at school has found that ADHD is a distinct possibility, a teacher may suggest that the parents consult Andy's physician (or preferably a specialist in ADHD) to determine what might improve his life at school. Medication may not be what the physician will recommend, at least in the beginning.

Other Suggestions for Reaching and Teaching Adolescents

The teenager diagnosed with ADHD may have so many problems in the classroom that the untrained observer may miss the underlying cause. For example, Andy's social studies teacher may notice his constant fidgeting, talking in class, frequent yawning, tendency to be the class clown, and failure to respond to her meaningful glares (Mercer & Mercer, 1998). Not understanding that these are characteristics of an ADHD student, she may treat the presenting problems as if they are the willful result of poor behavior and total lack of interest in school.

As more teachers are educated regarding the symptoms of ADHD, their responses can be quite different. Consequently, Andy and his peers with similiar problems may respond differently when they are treated with techniques that have a good chance of succeeding in middle and high schools.

ADHD may be divided into three categories: inattention, impulsivity, and hyperactivity. Some youngsters have problems with all three areas, whereas others are plagued by one or two (Silver, 1999). Let us first look at inattention.

PEANUTS reprinted by permission of United Feature Syndicate, Inc.

FIGURE 7.1   Easy isn't always easy with ADHD.

Inattention

Teachers' comments: "He knows more about what's going on out the window than in class!"

"She never seems to keep up with a class discussion, but she doodles beautifully."

Parents' comments: "I don't believe my son ever listens to what I say."

"He can watch TV for hours on end, but he can't do homework for 20 minutes."

These are typical comments from parents and teachers who live or work with teenagers who have ADHD. The most frequently seen characteristic of inattention is a serious difficulty in focusing attention properly. One of the common behaviors that one sees in the classroom is a *short attention span*. These students seem to "flit" from one thing to another with little regard for what is foremost. They actually have difficulty attending to anything in the classroom for a reasonable period of time. *Distractibility* is also a part of inattention, and it refers to a person who pays attention to everything. Richard Lavoie describes this as "looking at the world through a wide angle lens." *Disorganization* is another component (Hallahan & Kauffman, 1999). Difficulty with attending to a topic can cause a student to be rather disorganized (more about this later). Let's explore these three parts of inattention in more detail.

Short Attention Span

Most students have no difficulty focusing on one topic for 30 to 60 minutes unless they are sick, tired, upset, or faced with some other difficulty in life. However, students with ADHD are usually forced to do battle with their minds on a regular basis if they need to pay attention in class. Their natural tendency will be to attend for the first few minutes, sometimes having very good intentions about doing better today than yesterday. Before one-fourth of the class period has passed, however, their thoughts change. These may include a party this weekend, an unwanted curfew, the passing truck making a strange sound, the papers being moved on another student's desk, and so on. These thoughts all seem to come and go quickly. Even when the student is taking an important test that may mean whether or not the class must be repeated, he finds it difficult to focus. In the middle of a sentence the student finds himself daydreaming. Although he tries as hard as he knows how, he seems to be unable to focus on anything long enough to match his peers. Students with ADHD fail many tests not because they don't know the information, but because they never digest the questions.

Cheryl was referred for testing after she failed the seventh grade. During the testing it was determined that Cheryl had ADHD (without hyperactivity) and that her attention span was usually in the range of 10 to 15 minutes. No wonder that she was having difficulty with her schoolwork! Cheryl said that she really tried to listen to what her teacher was saying (as well as her parents) but that she just couldn't seem to stay with what they were saying. She often found herself thinking about something totally unrelated to the topic at hand. When she tried to pick up on the content, she had already missed too much and couldn't follow.

When I address a group of teachers, I frequently ask this question: "How can you, as a teacher, help this type of student in your classroom?" Let us consider some possibilities for helping Andy and Cheryl, who represent the typical student with ADHD:

1. **Place the student closer to the front of the classroom.** That way, there aren't as many distractors between you and the student, making it easier for you to maintain eye contact. When you think that you have "lost" the student, stand directly in front of him, perhaps touching his desk or book. If this doesn't work, gently put your hand on his shoulder (or his desk). If attention is still a problem, point to the location in the textbook that is being discussed. You might say, "Andy, let me look in your book. Yes, it says here that . . ." This has all been done with no direct criticism of Andy. This is so important because of his already badly bruised self-esteem.

2. **Present the material to the class in several different media.** For example, if you are teaching a lesson in social studies on Napoleon, write on the board, use the overhead projector, show some pictures, refer to the textbook, show a video, have a class discussion, have small group discussions (try using Andy as a leader of the group—sometimes he can concentrate more effectively when he has responsibility for the group). You might also ask the class to try to illustrate the most important battle in which Napoleon was engaged and tell why it was important. Role playing can be an excellent way in which to get Andy's or Cheryl's attention and keep it. Selecting some of the key figures in the life of Napoleon and having students act out their conversations before a battle, and so forth, may help the whole class.

3. **Do not be critical of Andy's behavior in front of his peers.** His self-esteem is quite fragile, and this will only make matters worse. When my children were teenagers, a psychologist gave me some excellent advice that I have tried to remember in all of my dealings with people. He said, "You can never have another person always do exactly what you think is right. Pick your battles, and choose ones that you can win. Try to overlook the other annoying behaviors as much as possible." This works. Try it.

4. **Use the "buddy" system** (Stevens, 1997), which means that another student in the class will help Andy. The student, who is someone whom you feel would be a good influence on Andy, should sit next to him. When he sees that Andy isn't paying attention, he can gently nudge him and try to draw him back into the group. He can make sure that Andy has the homework assignment and can also answer any questions that may arise. It is crucial to discuss with both students that this isn't a license to giggle and chat during class, and emphasize to the "buddy" that he shouldn't do anything to embarrass Andy. Go over the guidelines that you have with them. If any problems arise, talk with both students privately before or after class.

5. Give the student only one assignment at a time. The "buddy" can pass on the next assignment when the appropriate time arrives. This is helpful because sometimes Andy is so overwhelmed with an assignment that he is unable to begin. Instead, his mind wanders whenever he tries to get started.

6. Talk to your school psychologist about teaching Andy how to monitor his attention. First, Andy needs to become aware of when his attention begins to wander. When he does this, it is the first step in learning to monitor his own behavior. I have found it to be helpful to record the sound of a bell on a cassette tape at varying intervals (15, 30, 45, 60 seconds). In the beginning the teacher plays the tape, and Andy (and possibly his classmates as well) notices at the sounding of each bell if attention has been focused. Each student puts a check mark on a grid if attention has not strayed, thereby monitoring himself or herself. The bell is sounded farther and farther apart. When he is at home, Andy plays the tape as he reads a chapter of his textbook. Each time he hears the bell he asks himself if he's paying attention." If he is, he gives himself a check mark on his scorecard. If he has strayed, he uses the bell as a reminder to return to the book. After a varying number of exposures to this experience, students can usually remember to monitor their own attention without the bell, and thus become better students. A good selling approach for this technique is to tell your students, "Are you interested in spending less time on schoolwork? Do you want to learn how to do that? How many of you daydream when you are supposed to be studying?" Students are usually keenly interested in having more phone time and the like, and less time consumed by study.

7. Use computers. The bright colors, frequent rewards, interactive opportunities, etc., make this an ideal avenue for the student who has serious problems with paying attention. Sometimes it helps to tell a student, "If you work on this . . . for 25 minutes, you can use the computer until the end of class." Don't use the computer only as a reward, however, because sometimes the student may need its assistance in just making it through the class period.

8. If problems with attention are severe, try shortening assignments. Sometimes we assign 50 math problems when 25 would be adequate.

9. Give the student extra time to finish an assignment if this seems to be needed.

10. Build as much structure into your classroom as possible. ADHD students seem to perform on a higher level when they add structure to their usually disorganized lives. Have previously agreed-upon procedures for carrying out activities. Here are a few examples:

   a. Have one location for completed papers. That one place (which you should not inadvertently change) is where all completed papers must be placed.
   b. Establish routines for each class period and post them in a prominent location. If a student forgets a rule, it is right in front of him. Be sure that the rules are written in a positive vein. For example, instead of saying, "Do not

speak without raising your hand," say, "Raise your hand before you speak." (I used to jog on an indoor track, and there was a large sign that said, "DO NOT SPIT ON THE FLOOR." Whenever I saw that sign, something within me wanted to spit on the floor, and that is something I never do!)

c. Always post your assignments for the day in the same location. The assignment needs to be in writing so that if a student forgets what you said, it can be read easily without disturbing anyone. When Andy enters your classroom, he should know that he is to look on one chalkboard for today's assignment. If he needs help, he may ask his "buddy" quietly.

d. Distribute and collect papers in the same way. The student who does this for you may vary, but the approach will be the same.

Distractibility

John, a seventh-grader, had an appointment with his physician to discuss ADHD. The doctor was trying to explain ADHD to his young patient and how it affects the lives of many students. When the doctor finished his lengthy explanation, he asked John if he had any questions, and John replied that he certainly did: "Do you know that my dad has a sunfish on his office wall that is exactly like yours?" I hope that the doctor decided to postpone his explanation of ADHD until after John was successfully treated for ADHD because one thing is for certain: it is most unlikely that he will get the message before then!

Solutions

How can you help the distractible student in your classroom (or at home when homework must be completed)?

1. Suggest that the student use earplugs if noises are distracting. Wearing earplugs while taking a test, studying, or doing homework can be a tremendous help. Then others don't need to watch every move, being fearful that they will disturb the distractible student. Some people say that earplugs cause them to hear their body functioning. If this is the case, suggest industrial environmental noise suppressors. They are often available where you rent or buy large or noisy equipment (the type worn by workers who must be outside near the planes at the airport). Although it might appear that any method of isolating oneself from ambient noise would increase realization of sounds of bodily function such as heartbeat, experience has indicated that earplugs seem to produce more of this effect.

2. Seat the student where it will be easy to get his attention to get him back on task. Or use the "buddy system," as described under the section on short attention span.

3. Give the student positive feedback whenever possible. When you see that a student is off task, look at his seat work. Try to find something positive about the work so that you can give positive feedback. This will probably get him back on task much more quickly than a lecture from you.

4. Divide the student's work into 2 to 3 parts. When he finishes the first part, have him show it to you. Give him an opportunity to get a drink of water or something else that will necessitate movement. Then give him the second part.

5. Use attention-getting devices when teaching such as color coding (everything in red pertains to blood, and everything in yellow pertains to the renal system), mapping strategies (illustrating what is being learned in a way that appeals to the student), and silly mnemonic devices (the sillier the better).

6. Seat the student near people who are relatively quiet so that distractions won't occur needlessly.

7. Reward the student for attending. Let the student know privately that when he completes an assignment ahead of time it is acceptable to draw, play tic/tac/toe with himself, use the computer to play a quiet game, or be involved in other activities that are acceptable to you.

8. Assign work that can be done independently. Be certain that the student is capable of doing the seat work that you have assigned. If he isn't, you need to make some changes in the assignment.

9. Encourage leadership as much as possible. For example, when papers need to be passed out, give them to this student. Not only does this involve him in a positive activity; it also gives him an opportunity for "legal movement" (movement approved in advance by you, such as getting a drink of water).

10. Add variety to your teaching techniques. For example, have small groups work at the chalkboard, committees work on more interesting ways to present the topics you are studying, or use an overhead projector. You might also use games to review material (Jeopardy, Hangman, Bingo, etc.). I remember having a review session with a class that took the form of Jeopardy. The class was divided into two teams, and each team was given 15 minutes to write answers. The opposing team, of course, was required to provide the appropriate questions. Score was kept by one of the more hyperactive students, and it was the most exciting, interesting review I have ever seen. The winning team had 15 minutes of quiet free time during class the following Friday.

11. Use nonverbal means to help the student focus. If your student or child doesn't seem to pay attention to you when you are speaking, stand directly in front of the distractible person and put your hand gently on a shoulder. After you have completed your directions or request (make it brief!), ask the student to repeat what you said. Then you will know whether or not you were simply talking to yourself or if the student was listening to you. This can eliminate frustrated moments later for you and the distractible student (as well as his parents).

Disorganization

Sometimes the student with ADHD has even more difficulty with paying attention because of his lack of organizational skills. The older the student becomes, the more crippling disorganization will become.

Cheryl's bedroom is a health hazard, and her mother jokes that if the health department knew about her room, they would condemn it. Cheryl's locker at school is so messy that she can never find what she wants. Her car is full of old drink cups, empty potato chip bags, and old sales receipts that have long since lost their usefulness. Also buried in the car are innumerable completed homework assignments (that she couldn't find in time to turn in to her teachers) and several shoes, blouses, and the like. After viewing Cheryl's car, one gets the feeling that she doesn't care about her belongings or her schoolwork. But that isn't necessarily true. Cheryl cares a great deal. She simply doesn't know how to organize the "things" in her life.

When my cousin was a student in high school, he had a term paper due the following Monday morning. My family and I were visiting for a few days, and I was sitting down in the front seat of the family car on the passenger's side and crumpled some papers with my feet. It was raining hard, and I was concerned about the damage I had done to the partly written term paper. My cousin seemed totally unconcerned. He procrastinated the entire weekend, and late Sunday afternoon he decided to go to the library to do some last-minute research. As you may have guessed, the library was closed. When his paper was finally returned to him (it was turned in three days late), his teacher had written, "This paper needs to improve a great deal before it is even worth an *F!*"

Both of these teenagers want to be good students, but neither one has the organizational skills to "get their act together" enough to realize their dreams. In addition to turning everything in late or not at all, both are often late for class because they can't decide on what to wear to school—or find their homework, and so on.

Solutions

What are some things that can be done by teachers and parents to help teenagers improve their organizational skills?

1. Discuss with the student the lack of organization that you have observed. The first thing that must be done is to talk with the young person privately about how you feel the lack of organization is creating havoc. Explain how you judge that it is interfering with progress in school and in life, and furthermore, that it will probably only get worse.

2. Get the student to admit that the lack of organization is a problem. Ownership of this as a problem is essential if progress is to be made. A few chats may be required before you feel that you have a commitment from the student to want to improve.

3. The teenager will need assistance in putting organization into his life. If you are the parent, help your child to reorganize the bedroom. Purchase closet organizers so that every sweater has its location, every shirt has a hanger, every pair of shoes has its own location. Be certain that a laundry hamper is in the room and within easy reach. I know a young wife who "took the bull by the horns" and told her disorganized husband that she had put the laundry hamper beside the bed on his side. "Then you will have to trip over it to get out of the room. Perhaps now you can get your clothes in the basket!" It worked.

If you don't get along very well with your child during this stage of life, you may need to find someone else to tackle this task (a sibling or an aunt or uncle). Going it alone, you may only make it worse. Try to remind yourself that your child isn't deliberately trying to disobey you. She really doesn't know how to organize her belongings.

4. A planner is a must. The disorganized person needs to have a daily planner and use it every day. Sunday afternoons need to include 30 to 60 minutes when the student plans the week as much as possible. This needs to include all standing appointments such as guitar lessons. As the week progresses, the planner should include homework assignments, studying for tests, free time, time for meals, and so forth.

5. Put a schedule on the disorganized student's closet door. Included should be such topics as laundry, telephone time, dates, homework, bedtime, morning wakeup time, and other items related to his weekly routines. The teenager should be involved in deciding what should be included in the schedule. If a parent is unable to help with this for various reasons, perhaps one of the student's teachers can do so, or maybe a well-organized friend can communicate with the student more effectively to get the job done.

6. Select clothing for the next day before going to bed at night. The student *must* select in advance what is to be worn to school the next day. The clothes should be hung on the closet door or another appropriate place.

7. Put everything going to school at the front door before going to bed. The student *must* collect all books, papers, notebooks, and writing instruments, put them in the book bag, and place them outside the bedroom door or at the front door. If there is a completed homework assignment for the next day, be sure that this is in the book bag. This will eliminate many frantic mornings of last-minute searches.

8. Be very specific. Establish guidelines for neatness and other organizational skills. For example, don't tell a disorganized student to "clean out your desk" or "clean up your room." What you mean by that will puzzle this teenager. Instead, say, "I want you to remove all the crumpled papers from your desk and put them in the trash." When that assignment is completed, say what should be done next.

9. The cause of disorganization may not be apparent. Instead of just looking at the symptoms, try to locate the cause of behavior that is unacceptable, such as disorganization. Students with ADHD are often completely lacking in the ability to insert organizational skills into their lives.

10. Use praise as a reward. When the disorganized student has shown improvement, be sure to compliment generously. All of us enjoy compliments, but for those who rarely receive them, this is even more important.

11. Suggest exercise as a possibility for improvement. When a student finds school work so distasteful that it is avoided at all costs, suggest that the student work out vigorously before school and as often thereafter as needed. This may need to be a recommendation of the placement committee since it will probably involve having the student leave the classroom. If the student can be trusted to behave properly, walking up and down a staircase until exhausted may be beneficial. Walking on a treadmill for 5 minutes may mean the difference between having a good experience in the classroom or being extremely difficult to manage. Sometimes vigorous exercise of this type helps a student pay attention as well as work for a reasonable time before becoming distracted and disorganized.

Impulsivity

A general lack of self-control describes the impulsive teenager best. Or, as a popular comedian recently said, "Ready, fire, aim!" The student finds it all too easy to act first and think later. This can create an unending list of problems, and some of them can be quite serious. The older the person becomes, the more serious the offenses are likely to be. For example, a third-grader may progress from flattening a boy in a softball game when it was thought that the boy had batted out of turn to shooting someone because of an angry exchange of words. Usually, the outcomes are not as serious as causing death, but impulsivity certainly wreaks havoc in many lives. Let's look at a more typical example of impulsivity with teenagers.

Andy has always had a hard time with raising his hand before speaking in class. Each year as he has floundered more and more academically, he has seemed to blurt out comments more easily. By the tenth grade Andy doesn't even make a pretense of raising his hand anymore; he just says what he wants to say when he wants to say it. His teachers are frustrated. They know they can't send him to the office every time he interrupts the class, and usually when they do give him a pink slip he is back in the room in less time than it took to fill out the form for the office. Andy also has problems with written work. Instead of taking his time with an answer, he just writes down the first thing that pops into his head. Controlling his temper has been the most serious problem, however. Andy has few friends because he "flies off the handle" too easily. Anyone who tries to be a friend of his can expect to be involved in quite a few fights instigated by a frustrated, angry Andy. He isn't really angry with his friend, of course; this is only a symptom. The underlying cause of the anger is that Andy is terribly frustrated with his life and finds himself striking out at whomever happens to be in the wrong place at the wrong time.

I'm certain that you can easily see that Andy is upset. If he has an outburst of anger before coming to your class, you will also be a recipient of the continuing effects of anger, frustration, and possibly Andy's disappointment in himself for "losing it." At any rate, Andy will be in no condition to concentrate, to take a test, to participate in a class discussion, or in any other constructive activity. He will first need to have some way of calming down.

If arrangements have been made ahead of time, it may be wise for Andy to go to the gym and hit a punching bag until he gets some of his negative feelings out of his system. If you feel uncomfortable having him go to the gym alone, send his "buddy" with him. This may prevent the occurrence of another traumatic event. It may be helpful for Andy to go to a prearranged "time out" location and remain there until he feels that he is ready to join the class. If there is no location in your school for a "time out" student to sit, make one in your classroom. This should be behind something that will block his view of his classmates and will give him some privacy while he gets his emotions under control. Try having him listen to some calming music through headphones. Baroque classical music is an excellent choice.

There are a variety of other ways to deal with impulsivity in the classroom. Some will be effective with volatile situations, whereas others may be worth trying with students who exhibit their impulsivity in more passive ways, such as writing down an answer on a test before they think it through thoroughly. Let's explore a few of them:

1. **Try role playing.** Have the student role play a situation with you in private. Perhaps when he is in a less volatile environment he can think more clearly, and then perhaps he can see that he made a mistake. He must discover this for himself, however.

2. **Reverse roles.** When #1 doesn't work, try reversing roles. Have Andy be his former friend, and have the other boy be Andy. Tell each boy that he must say or think what the other person said or thought before or during the altercation. As much as possible, each person must use the same body language, and the like.

3. **Describe the role of the other person.** If #2 may be too risky, try this. Each boy must describe what happened through the eyes of a third person. For example, Jamie might say, "Bob was on the playground when Jamie walked up. Bob smiled and said he wanted to play softball. Jamie had a ball in his pocket, and he threw it at Bob. Bob cried because the ball hurt his head so much. Jamie laughed. Then Bob hit Jamie in the nose. Both boys were sent to the office."

4. **Have prearranged hand signals for nonverbal communication.** If there is a danger of speaking out in class without permission, you might select the signal of putting a finger to the lips to indicate quiet. A reminder to read during class time instead of writing notes might include putting a finger to one's eye.

5. **Compliment a student who is following your directions.** If Andy is interested in having your approval, this may serve as a reminder for him to "shape up" without your having to address him directly.

6. **Check with the parent regarding general nutrition habits, sleep patterns, and anything else that may be causing increased impulsivity.** It is impossible to run automotive machinery on water, but sometimes we expect to run our human machinery on little except pizza, soft drinks, and candy. Having the school nurse

conduct a session for your class on nutrition, sleep, and the like, may make an impression on Andy as well as on some of his peers.

7. Be consistent. Have a rule regarding what the consequences are when students speak out in class without permission, and stick to it. Try to consistently ignore those who yell out in class without your permission to speak. Teachers who have the most behavior problems are usually the ones who are strict one day and lenient the next. Students experiment to see how far they can get with these teachers. Inconsistency makes for a long day as a teacher!

8. Use e-mail. If you have frequent problems in your classroom because of impulsivity, arrange to spend 5 minutes two to three nights a week with that student's parents via e-mail. (Today many parents can be expected to have access to e-mail.) This has several benefits. First, it keeps teacher and parent(s) informed about what is going on in the student's life. It is easier to be understanding if you know the reason for a misbehavior. Second, it can be easier to end a conversation on e-mail than it is on the phone. When you write, "Thank you for your understanding. I'll be back in touch with you Thursday night," you can sign off. End of conversation. If you are dealing with a student who is "sneaky," you may wish to agree on a password so that you will be sure that you are communicating with the parent and not the child. For example, have the parent always end the correspondence with "Yours truly" or misspell a word in a prearranged way (appreciate/ apresiate). If the parent has personal access to e-mail at work, this would ensure direct communication with no snooping by the teenager.

9. Send a notebook back and forth. Have a notebook that is used for no other purpose than for parent and teacher(s) to communicate. If the student is unreliable about transporting the notebook, perhaps a sibling or a neighbor will do this. Try to make positive comments whenever possible.

10. Teach the student to use a mnemonic device through a learning strategy. It is possible to achieve success with this without a great deal of effort if the student is generally familiar with the learning strategies approach. Whenever the student realizes that impulsive behavior is on the horizon, having memorized a mnemonic device can prevent disaster. For example, Andy is really upset that John got in line in front of him, and he wants to punch him "good." Instead, he remembers that when he feels this way he is to think of the mnemonic device "SW3." Andy has worked on this with his teacher for some time, of course, and when he feels the urge to be violent he says the mnemonic device to himself: " SW3." Then he goes through each letter of the mnemonic device, taking approximately 30 seconds to do so:

   a. **Stop** and count to 10.
   b. **What** happened?
   c. **What** am I going to do about it?
   d. Is it **Worth** it?

Granted, there are many impulsive teenagers who could not wait 30 seconds before taking action. They are convinced that Ready, fire, aim! is a perfectly good

Title _Leaders of the Civil War_

Subject _Civil War 1861-1865_

Main Heading

President of Confederacy	**Sub-Heading**
	Jefferson Davis
	Detail
	Housed in Richmond, Va.
	Controversial figure
Generals	
	Robert E. Lee
	Offered leadership in S. & North
	Respected by many people
	Outstanding as a general
	Later became president of Wash. & Lee
	Stonewall Jackson
	Given nickname during war
	Died during battle of Chancellorsville
	Shot by one of his own men by accident
	A. P. Hill

Adapted from Language Circle Enterprises,
Project Read, Bloomington, MA

MAIN IDEA
CIVIL WAR LEADERS – SOUTH

	Jefferson Davis	SUPPORTING INFORMATION	Robert E. Lee	Stonewall Jackson	A. P. Hill
	President of Confederacy	DETAIL	Offered Leadership in S. & N.	Given Nickname During War	
	Unpopular		Loved and Revered by Many	Died During Battle of Chancellorsville	
	Office in Richmond		Later President of W. & Lee	Shot by Own Man	

FIGURE 7.2

approach to life. If you are a good salesperson, you may "sell" this idea to some of your students and keep them from doing something they will later regret.

11. Teach active reading to impulsive students. (This is especially important on examinations.) Many impulsive students do not read a test question completely. They often read only part of the narrative and quickly guess at fragments of the four or five choices available. In active reading the student first circles all "signal words," which are words that significantly change the meaning of a sentence (*and, but, however, never, occasionally,* etc.). You can find lists of signal words in many workbooks on study skills or passage comprehension. Next, the student should underline the main idea of the question and then ask himself what the question is asking before he reads the choices. Finally, he reads the choices and goes through the process of eliminating the most obvious ones. It may be necessary to reread the main body of the question. Negative questions are extremely difficult for impulsive students. Have the student read the question as a positive question. For example, "All of the following were Civil War generals for the Union *except:*" The student looks through the choices to find the answer to "All of the following were Civil War generals for the Union," and he circles the four Union generals. He then knows that General Stonewall Jackson is the correct answer because his name was *not circled* and he was *not* a general for the Union.

12. If all else fails, go to your school placement committee and ask for help. Pooling of minds can generate solutions. In serious cases the committee may feel that an alternative placement is wise for a period of time. It is also possible that the committee will need to ask the parent to confer with the student's physician about the problem with impulsivity. Remember that an educator should never refer a student to a physician for a prescription medication. It is perfectly acceptable to make a referral, but the physician will decide on the question of possible medication and will bear the responsibility for whatever is prescribed.

Hyperactivity

Hyperactivity is, without a doubt, the best-known category of ADHD. Some children seem to be hyperactive at birth, and occasionally one meets a mother who reports that her child was even hyperactive during the fetal stage. In these instances it would almost seem that the fetus was preparing the unsuspecting mother for what was to come after birth. Nonstop movement, limited need for sleep, and an aversion to being held or bundled in anything that restricts movement have been characteristic of these children. The parents of a truly hyperactive child lead a life that borders on exhaustion much of the time.

As the child enters adolescence, hyperactivity seems to decrease for many. In some cases the hyperactivity is still there, but it is more socially acceptable. For example, instead of running around an elementary classroom the teenager may tap fingers or swing a foot. To get a clearer picture of a teenager who is obviously hyperactive, let us look at Susan.

Susan's parents are both professional people, and Susan is their only child. Susan was born when her mother was 40 and her father was 45. She was hyperactive at birth and seemed to be very unhappy unless she had freedom of movement. She never took a nap during the day, and at night she rarely slept more than 5 hours. Her parents hired a governess to help them because they were physically unable to cope with Susan's activity. Governesses changed often because Susan wore them out. Her elementary years were good and bad. If she had a teacher who allowed free movement in the classroom with a variety of activities, Susan excelled. If she had a more traditional teacher who expected students to sit at their desks most of the school day, Susan was in agony. She kicked her feet, thumped her hands, and even turned over her desk often when she rocked it back and forth. When she tried to perch her chair on two legs, she sometimes fell on the floor. As a result, Susan was often seen sitting in the principal's office. No one seemed to know what to do with her.

Her secondary years were better because Susan discovered basketball . . . and soccer . . . and volleyball . . . and golf. Actively participating in sports seemed to make it easier for her to remain seated in her classes during the day. When school was over, she could hardly wait to get to the locker room. Susan told me that when she sat in school her limbs often ached with the pain of not being able to move. Her coach told her they were growing pains. Probably as a result of all of her activity, Susan's grades in high school were far superior to her elementary grades.

Then disaster struck. Susan broke her leg in a sporting event. This was no ordinary fracture, and she had many complications. She could not participate in sports for at least six months. She was required to sit from 8 A.M. until 3 P.M. five days a week with little opportunity to move. Earlier she had been able to walk across the rather large campus, but now she was limited to a wheelchair. Susan fidgeted in her seat and kicked her foot until everyone around her complained. Parents even began calling the principal to say that other students couldn't learn because of Susan. Her grades deteriorated, and Susan became depressed. Fortunately for Susan, she had a principal whose daughter had ADHD. One day when the principal had a meeting with Susan, he asked her if anyone had ever treated her for ADHD. When she responded negatively, the principal talked with Susan's parents and suggested that they talk with Susan's physician about the high level of hyperactivity that they had seen at the high school and ask for his advice.

Susan was later diagnosed as having a severe problem with ADHD, and medication was prescribed. For the first time in her life she was able to sit still, she could discuss a problem at length without feeling that she must rush through it, and she could study for longer periods of time without being in agony. Susan also found that she was able to pay attention for much longer periods of time; consequently the information she gleaned from lectures took a decided upswing. Susan told her friends that she felt that the motor that had been driving her relentlessly all of her life had finally slowed down to a normal pace. No longer did Susan dread going to school, and she was actually glad that she broke her leg, because the experience had made it possible for her to learn more about herself. Now she could lead a more normal life.

What are some techniques that can be used with hyperactive teenagers to help them adjust to the limited activity of the regular classroom more easily?

1. Exercise before class. It is helpful to some hyperactive people to engage in vigorous exercise before attempting to sit down for an extended period of time. This recommendation should come from the placement committee so that approved arrangements can be made for the student to exercise in the gym, walk up and down the staircase several times, walk up and down the hall outside the classroom for 5 to 10 minutes, and so on.

2. The student should move around as the need arises. When a student begins to feel fidgety and restless, it may be helpful to allow that student to move around the room or in the immediate vicinity of the room. Activities such as getting a drink of water or going to the rest room, sharpening a pencil, or watering the plants may make the period easier for the ADHD student as well as more pleasant for everyone else.

3. Remember the cause of the hyperactive behavior. If you can force yourself to remember the reason for the hyperactivity instead of merely noticing the symptoms that you see when you are with the teenager, it will make the experience easier to bear. Hyperactivity isn't just a behavior that this young person has developed to send you to an early grave. It is probably as frustrating for the student as it is for you. At least you don't have to be around the hyperactivity 24 hours each day as the student does.

4. Reinforce students' quiet behavior with verbal praise. Most of us enjoy praise, and this may serve as an impetus to help your overly active student observe the rules more often.

5. Encourage cognitive behavior management. When a student is out of her seat without permission, you might say, "And what are you supposed to be doing now?" The purpose of this is to get the student to monitor her own behavior and ask herself what she should be doing at that time.

6. Use movement as a reward. You might have an arrangement with a student whereby being still and quiet for a period of time will be rewarded with going to a specified area of the room and talking quietly, using the computer, or doing something else that interests the student.

7. Rotate active periods of study with inactive periods. For example, have work at the chalkboard followed by quietly reading a passage in the textbook.

8. The right music can have a very calming effect on hyperactive students. A favorite, available on CD, is titled *100 Masterpieces, Vol. 3: Wolfgang Amadeus Mozart*. Included are the following: *Piano Concerto No. 21 in C, The Marriage of Figaro, Flute Concerto No. 2 in D, Don Giovanni*, and other concertos and sonatas. Campbell (1997) reports that those with ADHD who listen to Mozart reduced their theta brain waves in exact rhythm to the underlying beat of the music. They also had better focus and less impulsivity. Apparently, 70% maintained their level of improvement 6 months after the study had concluded.

9. **Allow gum chewing.** You may be shocked and say, "Absolutely not!" Give it a try. You may be surprised at the results. I have found that if the mouth is moving with gum, there is less talking as well as less body movement. You may need to have some guidelines about popping the gum, sticking it under the desk, and so forth, but this has worked with some hyperactive students.

10. **Do some brainstorming with your teenagers to find innovative ways of expelling energy without making noise.** For example, put your hands in front of you parallel to each other with the palm of your right hand near the top of your left hand. Then move your hands around and around in a cylindrical motion, going faster and faster. Leg lifts are also helpful and do not disturb anyone. Fifty leg lifts can deplete one's high energy level for awhile.

There have been a wide variety of suggestions for meeting the educational needs of the adolescent with ADHD. You may be an excellent teacher, but that doesn't mean that the student with whom you wish to use these techniques will be receptive to them. Until the student decides that school is a worthwhile place to be, it will probably be very difficult to experience success with any of the techniques that you try.

A friend of mine once told me that when you are dealing with a student who is ADHD, you need to be fast and you need to be sneaky! In fact, I believe the friend was Suzanne Stevens, the author of the preceding chapter in this book. I have remembered what she told me in jest because it is so true. Sometimes we need to sneak up on them and prove to them that they can be successful in something at school. We all know students who seem to fold their arms in front of them as if to say, "Go on—I dare you—teach me something. You can't!" With this type of student a teacher must find something that really appeals to the student and get the proverbial foot in the door. For example, if a student won't write anything, perhaps he will draw cartoons. Most cartoons need a script, and you have gotten the student to compose on paper without his realizing what you have done. I've known a few students who were willing to write the lyrics to a country music song while a friend worked on the melody. These were boys who would absolutely refuse to do anything in school except sleep. Country music was a first love, and success there led to success elsewhere.

Adolescents without ADHD aren't always the most willing students, but adolescents with ADHD have a "hard row to hoe," as the saying goes. Try some of the strategies in this chapter and see how successful you can be. Add ideas of your own or tips from colleagues. An adolescent who experiences success in your classroom will often be a friend for life. It is what makes teaching the wonderful profession it is, and why I will always be a teacher.

PEANUTS reprinted by permission of United Feature Syndicate, Inc.

FIGURE 7.3   Memories of school aren't always pleasant for the student with ADHD.

References

Campbell, D. (1997). *The Mozart effect: Tapping the power of music to heal the body, strengthen the mind, and unlock the creative spirit.* New York: Avon.

Hallahan, D., & Kauffman, J. (1999). *Introduction to learning disabilities.* Boston: Allyn & Bacon.

Mercer, C., & Mercer, A. (1998). *Teaching students with learning problems* (3rd ed.). New York: Prentice Hall.

Silver, L. B. (1999). *The misunderstood child.* New York: Times Books.

Stevens, S. (1997). *Classroom success for the LD and the ADHD child.* Winston-Salem, NC: Blair.

Chapter 8

The Adult Who Has ADHD: Finding Success in the Workplace or Classroom

BARBARA PRIDDY GUYER

Jerry Browning is one of the world's most likable people. A perpetually moving dynamo who never seems to run out of energy, today he is a much-loved associate dean of a medical school. However, the life he has achieved was anything but a trouble-free climb; in fact, because of his ADHD, he had many obstacles to hurdle to get to his current position. If you need an inspiring story to recount to ADHD students or someone else you know who suffers from this condition, this narrative is made to order.

Jerry's father was the youngest of 21 children, and Jerry was raised on a farm close to his many relatives. At the Browning farm, the adults helped one another with their farm duties while the oldest children baby-sat the younger ones. Jerry vividly remembers being punished daily because of his hyperactivity and impulsivity. His older siblings frequently put him in a corner or else flayed his legs with a switch. But nothing seemed to slow him down. Jerry's mother frequently told him to stop talking and interrupting people. He never did.

In elementary school he always received *C* on conduct and an *A* on everything else. In the fifth grade, Jerry's teacher announced in December that the class would study and then celebrate Christmas in other lands. Jerry became so excited that he literally danced around his desk, and his friends laughed heartily. His teacher ridiculed him. Throughout his growing up years his highs and his lows were always much more extreme than was the case for his peers. When he was in the eighth grade, Jerry got a job after school as a carhop in a drive-in restaurant, and he excelled. The high level of energy that was required for his drive-in job was perfect. Jerry worked on the farm after school, then went to his carhop job, and there was always enough energy to spend time on homework when he got home late at night. In the tenth grade he was placed in a lower level math class although he was an excellent student in mathematics. His behavior seemed to be the main reason for the placement. Jerry's teacher, frustrated with his incessant talking and interruptions, said in the presence of classmates, "Jerry, you may be good in math, but you will fail in life because you keep interrupting everyone all the time. . . . And furthermore, young man, you are spastic!" More than 30 years later, this teacher's words are still etched deeply in Jerry's memory.

Jerry majored in biology and English in college, and he firmly believes that this was the best time of his life. He was the typical hyperactive high achiever. In his junior year, for example, he was

- President of the junior class
- President of his fraternity
- President of the German Club
- President of the biology honorary fraternity
- Laboratory assistant

Needless to say, he slept little, and he began a pattern that continued until ADHD was diagnosed later. He ran nonstop until he finally collapsed from complete exhaustion. He had to be hospitalized to be revived.

As a professor and associate dean of a medical school, he is outstanding. He has won the most outstanding professor award innumerable times although the students have teased him about his hyperactive behavior during lectures.

Three years ago Jerry and I were invited speakers at a national conference about medical students who have LD/ADHD. (Some time ago I began a program called Medical H.E.L.P., which is a remedial program for medical students and physicians who have been unable to pass Board examinations.) Jerry had everyone's undivided attention as he spoke of the capable young people with whom he has worked who happen to have LD and/or ADHD. He emphasized how important it is that we make medical education possible for them because they have so much to offer. Afterwards, a conference attendee approached Jerry and asked him how his ADHD was treated. Jerry responded that he didn't take anything; in fact, he didn't have ADHD! The woman suggested that he read a book by Edward Hallowell titled *Driven to Distraction*. While he was still at the conference, Jerry purchased the book, and it changed his life from that day forward. Jerry saw himself on every page of the book and approached me with the list of characteristics that he saw in himself. I was so relieved because I had wanted to tell him of my suspicions several times, only to lose my nerve. I've spoken to other adults, and some of them have become very angry with me. I didn't want to say the wrong thing to the associate dean, with whom I had to work frequently. After we discussed this revelation at length, I suggested that he see a psychiatrist who treats many adults with ADHD.

Today Jerry takes medication, and his life is totally different. He can sleep. He is no longer a tornado on the move, and he interrupts others less often. Life is much more enjoyable for Jerry today, and best of all, he can stop to smell an occasional rose along the way.

Reaching and Teaching the Adult with ADHD

It can be very difficult to spot the adult who has ADHD because by adulthood the person may have learned to compensate and "cover up" so well that only the skilled observer will notice the symptoms. In my college classes I usually watch my students, ever being on the lookout for a constantly swinging foot, tapping fingers, moving pencils, or eyes that are seldom focused on one object for very long at a time. It is not unusual for one or more of my graduate students to come to me each semester stating that they think they have a learning disability and/or a problem with ADHD. For example, this semester two graduate students who are also teachers approached me to say that they think they need to be tested. I referred both of them for testing, and both were diagnosed as having ADHD. One also has a learning disability that was originally diagnosed in elementary school. Both were failing their graduate classes because they had reached an academic level where they could no longer compensate for their deficiencies with their good intelligence and survival skills. Medication and a review of study skills and test-taking strategies have changed these two students from failing to making excellent grades. However, it should be noted that some adults require more remedial help than the two students I just mentioned. For example, they may need assistance in areas such as learning to organize their lives, set goals, monitor their own behavior, plan for adequate physical activity, etc.

There are specific techniques that are effective with adults who are in college as well as those who are in the workplace, and we will discuss those in this chapter. We will also address the typical characteristics that may be present in the adult in each area of ADHD. Some of the characteristics are the same as we find with the child or adolescent, but other characteristics are specific to the adult. Although there may be some overlap, the primary characteristics will be presented.

Difficulty in Accepting Existence of Symptoms or Diagnosis

Some adults are relieved when ADHD is finally diagnosed because they can find some reason for the many difficulties they have experienced throughout their lives. However, others refuse to admit that they have difficulty focusing, that they are impulsive, etc. Some seem to be in denial and make statements such as "I may have a few symptoms, but I don't really have what you would call ADHD." I will never forget the college student who had been a borderline failure in college for two years although his IQ was superior. His tutors, as well as the psychologists who had tested him, all felt that his problems with ADHD were the cause of his poor grades, but he refused to admit that he had any of the symptoms. Whenever he and I went through an ADHD checklist together (and we did this every semester when I received his poor grades), he said "no" to every question. When it became apparent that he could go no further in school until he had some assistance with ADHD, I had him come to my office for another conference. I decided to be more assertive with him this time, and I said, "Tell me, Mark, do you really believe that you have been honest with yourself when you and I have talked about ADHD?" He hung his head and said, "No, I haven't. What do you want me to do? I tell you what—you ask me those questions again, and I'll tell you the truth this time." I did, and he did. He responded "yes" to almost every question on every checklist. Later I asked Mark why he hadn't answered the questions honestly at other times, and he gave me a very interesting response: "There is no way that I can hide my learning disability from you, but I can hide the ADHD. I decided that one handicap was all I wanted. I didn't want to be saddled with two handicaps in my records. So I just decided that I'd keep that little secret to myself. Wasn't very smart, was it?"

This scenario has occurred with a number of other students and with parents as well. Occasionally, we test children and young adults whose parents find it impossible to accept the fact that their child may have a problem. They either refuse to acknowledge characteristics that are present, or they refuse to talk about them. It isn't unusual for parents to change their minds later, when their child continues to have problems in school or at work. Later can be too late, however, because the young person may have been totally turned off by school or become deeply involved with a group that is involved in drugs, theft, and the like.

Categories of ADHD for the Adult

We will discuss the following areas of ADHD as they pertain to the adult: inattention, impulsivity, hyperactivity, and executive function. Descriptive information and suggested activities for remediating the problems will be presented.

Inattention

Teachers' comments: "I don't understand it. He seems so bright in class discussions, but on quizzes or tests he fails miserably."

"If he interrupts my history class one more time when I'm lecturing, I believe that I shall lose my temper completely!"

Spouses' comments: "Yes, our marriage is in trouble. And do you know why? He never listens to what I'm trying to say. He may listen for 5 minutes, and then he is thinking about something else!"

In the preceding chapter we discussed the characteristics of short attention span, distractibility, and disorganization as they apply to the teenager. These characteristics are also relevant to adults. That information will not be repeated at this time. Please refer to the preceding chapter.

Short Attention Span

Adults with a short attention span become more and more handicapped as they see their peers become more skilled in focusing their attention. Textbooks become more complex, passages become longer, and students are expected to learn more information on their own (Nadeau, 1995). It is especially common in upper-level classes for a professor to assign material to be read. That material is not discussed in class, and instead the professor uses class time to cover important topics not found in the textbook. Some professors will very quickly review a chapter and indicate what is most important. If the ADHD student (or employee in training) is not paying attention, the material may be completely missed.

Adults who have a short attention span usually find that this directly affects reading comprehension. When one's mind flits in and out, it is extremely difficult to comprehend what is being read. We should mention *selective attention* here because this is sometimes a confusing factor in the diagnosis of ADHD. When an adult is asked if he has difficulty focusing on one thing for any period of time, he may think of the hours he spends on the Internet engaged in a chat room. He may play a game for hours on the computer, overjoyed with the rapid movement, frequent rewards, vivid color, and so on. The problems begin when he must read a chapter in a textbook on the Revolutionary War or, if he is employed, a chapter on some aspect of company policy. He first finds it easy to procrastinate, putting off reading until the last minute. When he finally sits down with the book, he reads for 5 minutes before he begins thinking about going to do the laundry, buying groceries, calling his mother, making up with his wife, and so on. The chapter is never read. He ends the attempt at reading, feeling a little more inferior than he did before he began.

Impulsivity

A person who is impulsive usually acts first and thinks later (Lerner, 1996). As someone once said, the general approach is "Ready, Fire, Aim!" Impulsivity is somewhat different in the adult from what we see in the child. The adult is more likely to interrupt conversations than the average person is, but he will not be as rude in doing it as the ADHD child usually is. The adult may find it difficult to wait his turn in line and try to find a loophole so that he can gain admittance sooner. My husband and I were in a crowded restaurant recently when a man I know who has ADHD entered with his son. When he saw the length of the line, he immediately went to the kitchen and spoke to the owner about getting in ahead of others. He didn't get in any sooner than he would have, and he annoyed everyone in the restaurant with his poor social skills. Every word that he spoke embarrassed his son, and I'm sure he gave no thought to his words before he uttered them.

The typical impulsive adult also shifts from one uncompleted activity to another, seldom finishing anything. He rarely gives any thought to what he is doing before he changes activities; he just does it. The adult who is prone to violence may engage in a fight without giving any serious thought to the consequences of his actions. For example, Karl, a 19-year-old I knew, was leaving a bar when two boys began yelling obscenities. Karl ignored what they said, but when he got in his new sports car, which was a gift for his high school graduation, one of the boys threw a soda bottle from his car window at Karl's car. Although the aim was poor and the bottle missed the car, Karl was furious. He began chasing the boys in his car down the main street of town. The vandals headed for a deserted marina, with Karl in hot pursuit. When Karl got out of his car at the boat ramp, one of the boys stabbed him. He died a few hours later. He lost his life because of a soda bottle that didn't hit his car. If Karl had not been so impulsive, he would probably be alive today.

Although impulsivity usually doesn't result in anything as serious as death, it can significantly complicate one's life. A thoughtless response to a spouse or an employer can have devastating effects. Uncompleted projects at work can cost a person his job. Andrew, a very attractive man in his thirties, approached me one day. He had been a very successful employee in a computer laboratory until he was promoted. At the time of our meeting he was in charge of assigning projects to employees and seeing that time was well spent. Andrew was unable to do this. He repeatedly pulled employees from tasks before they felt they were ready, which was exactly the problem he had in his personal life. He had been successful at work previously because he had someone to tell him when to begin and when to stop. Andrew found that he was making decisions on the spur of the moment, and he was paying dearly for this. He was afraid he was going to be fired. A diagnosis of ADHD, a trip to a physician, a prescription for medication, and Andrew changed his life. Today he has been promoted again, and is again successful. With medication, impulsivity is no longer a problem for him.

Hyperactivity

Most adults who have been hyperactive as children exhibit different behaviors as they grow older. Only individuals with the most severe cases of hyperactivity are obviously hyperactive. Connie, a skilled oncological surgeon, was referred to our center because she was so hyperactive that her colleagues had difficulty being around her. She could not seem to sit still. During grand rounds at the hospital she paced up and down, distracting others who wanted to hear the lecture. A definite advantage of her hyperactivity was that she could operate twice as long as her peers without becoming tired. She usually had two separate teams assist her. No one could function successfully in the operating room as long as Connie could. A diagnosis of ADHD with prescribed medication changed her life. Previously, she had not been able to maintain a relationship with anyone because she couldn't sit still long enough to carry on a conversation, much less get to know someone well. How she survived as long as she did is amazing to me. Her mother told me that she was never referred for help because she always did so well in school. Connie thought that everyone felt as "antsy" as she did. It wasn't until she began taking medication that she was at last able to relax and lead a more normal life.

Most adults aren't as extreme as Connie, fortunately. The typical hyperactive adult may do one or more of the following: tap or snap fingers, swing a foot, or chew gum almost constantly. He or she may find it hard not to "fiddle" with something such as a pencil or strands of hair. ADHD adults are also prone to interrupt another's speech during a conversation. Whatever the ADHD person is thinking must be said at that moment; it can't wait. I am always amused when I see an ADHD student pacing outside my office door, constantly looking through the small pane of glass to see if I have seen him. It makes no difference if I have six people in my office for an important conference—the student still paces outside my door. It is only when I interrupt the conference and go to the door to tell the student that I am involved in a conference that the pacing ceases. Often the student will try to quickly tell me what is needed, and it seems that almost invariably it is something that could have waited an hour—or even a week.

Executive Function

Executive function refers to one's ability to sequence cognitive processes that will be performed. It is the organizational directive for short-term and long-term memory (Bender 1993). Those who experience difficulty with executive function may find that they cannot successfully sequence activities when they are attempting to solve a problem. Nor can they discern whether the type of processing required is verbal or nonverbal. They also have difficulty monitoring behavior in action, reorganizing sequences of activities, or evaluating the results of activities or projects (Pressley, Scruggs, & Mastropieri, 1989; Bos & Anders, 1990).

Dennis is a whirlwind writer and editor in his fifties. His early professional life was spent as a news service correspondent in major cities, at home and abroad. Bouncing from one story to the next, often under intense deadline pressure, suited

PEANUTS reprinted by permission of United Feature Syndicate, Inc.

FIGURE 8.1 With ADHD many things are hard to do.

his ADHD tendencies well. In recent years he has taken up a lifestyle as an independent editor, specializing in helping professionals draft and publish books and articles. Sometimes he revises manuscripts the professionals have already written, and at other times he gets involved in the process of creating the first draft.

Though he enjoys his work, Dennis has found it excruciatingly difficult to schedule his time well, send out bills, collect monies owed, and ensure that the accounting function is properly handled. He frequently loses track of receipts and even of important files he needs to complete the projects he has undertaken. A good assistant or secretary would help, but thus far he has not found anyone he could afford who would actually stick with the work and keep him on track.

It should also be mentioned that Dennis has had trouble in marriage and has already gone through two divorces. Medication and counseling and his current, more understanding spouse have all helped, but Dennis would be the first to tell you that the battle has not yet been won.

Techniques for Working with Adults Who Have ADHD

How can you, as a teacher or employer, help the adult who has a short attention span, is impulsive, hyperactive, and/or has problems with executive function? Here are a few suggestions:

Give shorter reading assignments. The length of the assignment is often completely overwhelming to those who have short attention spans. Assign a few pages, and when they are completed, assign a few more pages.

Teach the adult how to become involved in active learning. Active learning means that you can't just read the passages. This makes it too easy to daydream. Instead, read aloud if the person is an auditory learner. Highlight only the *main idea and supporting information* in each paragraph. This often includes the first sentence. (If you can get the person to read the first sentence of each paragraph, it is better than not reading at all.)

Encourage the adult to use a structured outline to aid in organizing the material that has been read. Students have told me that this has helped them more than anything else they have attempted. Then teach the adult how to use *mapping strategies*. There are many books that describe this process, but in brief this is an illustration of what has been read and needs to be learned.

Encourage the adult to become involved in a study group. If there isn't one, encourage the class to organize one. The person who is easily distracted may find that a study group is just what the doctor ordered, but some people may find this distracting as well. One must consider the individual's learning style.

Develop an informal screening test to determine which sensory channels seem to be of the greatest assistance in enabling students to recall information when needed. Students need to know how they learn best. Which sensory channel is their strongest, or do they need a multi-sensory approach in order to perform on a higher level? To administer this informal test, you will need an overhead projector or a chalkboard. Make a chain of numbers beginning with 3 in the chain such as 793. Give two or three with three numbers in the chain. Then increase the length of the chain gradually, always giving two or three opportunities in each chain. For example, you might use these numbers:

368	942	702		4631	7639	9513		68429	86319	80513
7905418	5316962	0813662			80914226	77549013		75130806
1085312793	2417508590	8632509127						

Be careful not to chunk (group) the numbers when you say them aloud. First, you say the numbers aloud and have students write the numbers after you complete the chain, allowing a 15 to 30-second pause before they write. Be sure to explain that you want to help them determine how they learn best through their sensory channels. Do they perform best when they depend on auditory or visual channels, or do they learn best when they employ a multi-sensory approach? Ensure that they write *auditory* above the numbers for the auditory evaluation, and so on. The visual testing is very important because so much of what we learn is presented to us visually. Write the numbers on the chalkboard in advance, and cover them. Uncover each chain of numbers one at a time, or use an overhead projector. This is especially helpful if you have a limited amount of space, and it is also easier to cover the numbers. Give the students 15 seconds to look at the chain of numbers. Then have them write what they saw after you cover the numbers. Wait 15 seconds after covering the numbers before students are allowed to write. Go through each chain in this manner. When the multi-sensory informal test is administered, make the numbers visible, probably using the overhead projector. Have the students say the numbers aloud softly as they look at them. Simultaneously have them trace the numbers on their desk tops. Then give them 15 to 30 seconds after you cover the numbers so that memory may also be a small part of the picture. Since visualization is such an important part of learning for this population, I prefer to include this in the testing. To do this, show the class a sequence of numbers; have them say the numbers silently as they visualize them. It is important not to use the same sequence of numbers for each informal test. Change the sequence for the evaluation of each sensory channel. Each student can correct his or her own paper, unless there is a problem with transposing numbers. Have students tally how many are correct for each sensory channel. Each student needs to determine if it appears that one sensory channel is superior to another when information is presented and retention and recall are required.

   Next, discuss what the results mean. For example, if some students seem to be visual learners, they need to outline material they read, use color coding, use mapping strategies, and look carefully at graphs, charts, illustrations, and so on.

   After students understand which sensory channels may be the best avenues for learning, be certain that this is followed with the specific study techniques that seem to work best. Which specific techniques seem to help those with ADHD the most? Auditory learners should investigate the following and determine which seem to be the most effective: reading aloud, taping lectures, listening to textbooks on tape, taping individual and group study sessions, and listening to tapes while driving to and from class and on any other drives when there will be no auditory interruptions (unless this creates a driving hazard). Visual learners should try the following to determine their effectiveness: using color coding, outlining so that the structure is more visible, visualizing structure of what was read, and reproducing charts and graphs so that they will have more meaning. Tactile/kinesthetic learners should write information on the desk with a fingertip, write large on a dry-erase board, build models when appropriate, draw a flow chart and use a finger to trace the pattern, or act out a scene using role playing. Multi-sensory learners should try to integrate all of the above. For example, when studying, students should remember to read aloud, using color coding on outlines and mapping strategies, write information on a desk top with a fingertip, and visualize the structure of what has been learned. As the student visualizes, it is crucial to verbalize the information as well.

Help students realize that they control their success in learning. It is not unusual for students to begin to feel (after many failure experiences) that they must take whatever happens to them and that they cannot significantly influence their future. This is what absolutely needs to change. Teachers have a responsibility to help their students discover for themselves that "I am responsible for what happens to me. Blaming other people for my failures only hurts me, and it doesn't help me to become a successful person. I need to use the energy that I have previously devoted to blaming others for what has happened to me to spending time learning exactly what I need to do so that I can be successful." The wise teacher will devote a small amount of time each day to this philosophy.

I have found the following books helpful in working with college students: *Learning to Live between Office Visits* (Siegel, 1993); *Peak Performance* (Ferrett, 1994); *The Wilson Reading System* (Wilson, 1996); *Essential Study Skills* (Wong, 1991); *The Joy of Failure* (Root, 1996); *Learning to Learn* (Frender, 1990); *Way of the Peaceful Warrior* (Millan, 1984), to name a few.

As a teacher, you need to develop motivational strategies that will be of benefit to your students. Probably the most important one is to teach your students to accentuate the positive. Your students come to you with many disappointments and failures behind them. Many have developed poor survival skills. Today we are beginning to realize that those who succeed believe in themselves. First of all, you need to learn how to think more positively. Only then can you pass this skill on to your students. Take a few minutes each day to read something positive. *Chicken Soup for the Soul* has many editions popular today, and the stories they contain offer great encouragement. Help your students learn to substitute positive thoughts for negative thoughts. It is wise to plan strategies in advance. For example, if my English professor tells me that I don't belong in college, what will I do? Will I go into a deep depression that lasts for days and get myself into an even deeper hole than I was in previously? Or will I give myself time—say, 12 hours—to mourn, to make myself as miserable as I possibly can? Then after 12 hours, I'll plan my line of attack. I'll list my pros and cons of remaining in college. Next, I'll talk with my favorite professor and ask if he or she agrees with Prof. English. I'll talk with my tutor in the college support program and ask for advice and help. What else can I do to make the professor think more highly of me? It may be that the professor is biased against all handicapped students and that there is nothing I could do to change his mind. If this is true, I may need to drop his class and enroll in someone else's class next semester. We all know professors who feel that students who have handicapping conditions seldom belong in college. A recent letter to the editor in the *Chronicle of Higher Education* actually expressed this misinformed viewpoint.

Other motivational strategies that need to be addressed are developing self-esteem, focusing on goals, staying healthy, building a support group, improving basic skills, leading a balanced life, and planning rewards for a job well done.

As a teacher, help your students reduce their stress levels while in class. Some students are so anxious about being called on in class to answer a question that they are unable to attend to anything that occurs. Rick Lavoie suggests telling such a student privately that you won't call on him in class unless you are standing directly in front of him. This enables the anxious student to be more relaxed (and you hope to attend to the lecture and discussion) until the professor stands in front of him.

When you see that a student is becoming inattentive, give the student an opportunity to move around. Discuss the situation privately with the student, and say that if restlessness is going to prevent the student's paying attention, it is acceptable to sharpen a pencil or unobtrusively leave the room to get a drink of water or run up and down the stairs a few times. Let the student be the monitor of his or her own behavior and determine when movement is appropriate.

If nothing that you try with a student seems to work, you may want to suggest that the student confer with his or her physician. If medication has been prescribed, perhaps the physician will want to reconsider or change the type of current medication or the dosage. Always remember that as a layperson, you should never tell a student anything like "What you need is medication for ADHD; please get your doctor to prescribe something for you."

Techniques for Adults Who Have ADHD

If you are a student, you must become aware of your legal rights. (See Chapter 10, on legal rights.) The following are accommodations that you should request through your support service: time extensions on tests, placement in a separate room to avoid distractions while taking a test, the option to take tests while using a computer (some students with ADHD think more rapidly than they can write by hand, and they can more accurately express what they know when typing the information), priority registration for classes, or, possibly, course substitutions.

Talk to your tutor or the person who diagnosed your ADHD about how you seem to learn best. (See pp. 106–107.) When you discover how you learn most effectively, be sure that you use this approach when you study.

Before school begins, write down your strengths in one column and your weaknesses in another. Talk with someone you respect, such as your tutor, about how you can use your strengths to help you overcome your weaknesses. For example, if you have excellent visual memory and poor auditory memory, when you are studying for a test, develop a mapping strategy and verbalize the contents. In this way, you are using your visual strength to help you strengthen your auditory weakness.

Use cognitive behavior management to improve your ability to stay on task when you are studying or taking a test. Make an audiotape with some type of noise on it. Each 15 seconds, 30 seconds, 45 seconds, 1 minute, and so forth, have a bell or a beeper sound. Play the tape as you study. When you hear the noise, it is your cue to ask yourself, "Am I paying attention now?" If you are, give yourself a check on a card. When you get a certain number of checks, give yourself a prearranged reward, such as going for ice cream or another treat. After a time of doing this while reading or studying, you will no longer need the tape to ask you if you are studying. Instead, you will be able to monitor yourself without the use of a tape and bring your mind back to where it should be.

Sit near the front of the classroom so that you will have few distractions between you and the professor. When dealing with entertainment such as concerts, plays, or athletic events, we are often willing to pay more to obtain choice seats enabling us to see (and perhaps hear) better. Only in college lectures or religious services do people consciously gravitate toward the rear of the room (with no break in price!).

Purchase a daily planner so that you will not waste time and will organize your time carefully. A planner will also give you confidence that you are probably expending your time wisely and meeting all appointments. When all due dates, appointments, and the like are included in a planner, the person may relax and stop worrying that important dates will be overlooked.

Get someone to proofread your papers before you turn in anything. A person with ADHD has a tendency toward being sloppy because one must usually be in a hurry. The reader should evaluate your work for neatness, form, spelling, grammar, and the like.

Learn how to keep yourself from procrastinating. Ask a friend or tutor to remind you when papers are due or when extra-credit assignments must be turned in. Set an alarm reminder on your electronic planner to give you an adequate warning regarding the due dates of important papers, tests, and the like.

Don't be embarrassed to ask for help. Professors or employers are usually pleased that a person cares enough to ask questions. Many students don't want the professor to know that they don't know something, but in reality, most professors respect you more when you care enough to ask questions.

Be honest with your professors or employers. If a topic has just been explained in detail and you found your mind wandering, go to the professor or employer and say that you were thinking about something else that was discussed earlier. You failed to listen when the second topic was explained. Would the person mind telling you once more? (Promise to listen carefully this time.) When my students have done this, I appreciated their caring enough to ask me to repeat important information.

If you are easily distracted, in addition to the suggestions previously given, begin to use as many techniques as possible that will help you to keep on task. Such techniques may include the following: (1) writing key words in the margins as you read; (2) reading aloud if you are an auditory learner; (3) making up games such as Jeopardy to play with a classmate that will aid in reinforcing the material to be learned; (4) paraphrasing the material that you are reading—if an auditory learner, paraphrase aloud; otherwise, write the paraphrase on paper or on a dry-erase board; (5) outline the steps that you will follow in completing a complex task; and (6) play classical music that seems to help you focus more easily.

Do not attempt to study or plan when you have the TV or radio on. If you feel a need to have noise of some kind, turn on the electric fan or play music that is not distracting. If you play a cassette tape or a CD, you have control that you do not have with the radio. The TV is especially unwise because you will be tempted to watch what is on the screen.

Summary

The adult with ADHD has characteristics that make it quite possible to be successful in school and in life. The high energy level enables the adult to work longer hours than others can. The verbal skills and empathy that are often present make it possible for some adults with ADHD to be very effective professionals, especially in service areas.

In order to be successful, however, it is crucial that the adult carefully plan exactly how the problems presented by ADHD will be dealt with. How will the adult remain on task when tempted to engage in mind racing or wandering? How will the adult develop adequate reading comprehension skills so that material may be learned more easily and test questions may be answered correctly? How will the adult avoid procrastinating? How will the adult explain to professors or employers how ADHD affects him or her? How will the adult deal with interpersonal communication so that long-term relationships may be maintained successfully? These are only a few of the areas that must be carefully explored by the adult with ADHD if success is to be possible in school and in life.

References

Bos, C., & Anders, P. (1990). Toward an interactive model: Teaching test-based concepts to learning disabled students. In H. L. Swanson & B. Koegh (Eds.), *Learning disabilities: Theoretical and research issues*. Hillsdale, NJ: Erlbaum.

Fenett, S. (1994). *Peak performance*. Burr Ridge, IL: Irwin Mirror.

Frender, G. (1990). *Learning to learn: Strengthening study skills and brain power*. Nashville: Incentive.

Lerner, J. (1996). *Learning disabilities: Theories, diagnosis, and teaching strategies* (6th ed.). Boston: Houghton Mifflin.

Millan, D. (1984). *Way of the peaceful warrior: A book that changes lives*. Tiburon, CA: Kramer.

Nadeau, K. (1995). *A comprehensive guide to attention deficit disorder in adults.* New York: Brunner-Mazel.

Pressly, M., Scruggs, T. E., & Mastropieri, M. (1989). Memory strategy research in learning disabilities: Present and future directions. *Learning Disabilities Research, 4,* 68–77.

Root, W. (1996). *The joy of failure.* Arlington, TX: Summit.

Siegel, B. (1993). *How to live between office visits.* New York: HarperCollins.

Wilson, B. (1996). *The Wilson reading system.* Millbury, MA: Wilson Language Training.

Wong, L. (1991). *Essential study skills* (2nd ed.). New York: Houghton Mifflin.

Recommended References and Materials

Bell, N. (1991). *Visualizing and verbalizing: For language comprehension and thinking.* Paso Robles, CA: Academy of Reading Publishers.

Ferrett, S. (1994). *Peak performance.* Burr Ridge, IL: Irwin Mirror.

Frender, G. (1990). *Learning to learn: Strengthening study skills and brain power.* Nashville: Incentive.

Guyer, B. (1997). *The pretenders: Gifted people who have difficulty learning.* Homewood, IL: High Tide.

Parker, H. (1996). *The ADD hyperactivity handbook for schools.* Plantation, FL: Specialty.

Sack, A. (1985). *The 90% solution.* Baltimore: College Skills Center.

Sack, A., & Yourman, J. (1983). *100 passages to develop reading comprehension.* Circle Pines, MN: American Guidance Service.

Wilson, B. (1996). *The Wilson reading system.* Millbury, MA: Wilson Language Training.

Wong, L. (1991). *Essential study skills* (2nd ed.). New York: Houghton Mifflin.

Social Interactions and Family Relationships

JOHN MACCALLUM

Dr. John MacCallum is a child psychiatrist who specializes in working with children and adults with ADHD. Although Dr. MacCallum is a "child" psychiatrist, he ultimately spends more time speaking with adults than children about these problems, educating teachers and parents by providing them with interventions and methods for supporting offspring and students with ADHD. Although he employs pharmacological and other medicinal interventions, Dr. MacCallum feels that a multidisciplinary approach to attention deficit hyperactivity disorder (ADHD) is important and says that individual, family, and parent counseling are all critical to the success of a broad-based treatment program that should include parents, teachers, extended family members, and other appropriate adults and peers. He suggests that the process of supporting a person with ADHD is like getting a degree in higher education in a subject not previously studied: you must take a little at a time and build on the knowledge as you become more experienced. Dr. MacCallum frequently addresses the issue of ADHD with school audiences. The following is a compilation of questions and answers often discussed during these sessions.

Question: I'm a teacher without any special training in ADHD. Suddenly, I have a child with ADHD in my classroom, and the parents are asking me to "fix him." What do I tell them?

Answer: You don't have to be an expert to be helpful. As a teacher, you can explain to parents that they also have to be students. If parents and teachers are willing to accept the student role and learn a little bit at a time, as we all do when we go to school, they can be eminently successful. Dealing with a child with ADHD can present challenges, but information, support from others, and patience all combine to create a path toward successful intervention. An ongoing holistic or multifaceted approach makes for greatest success, and treatment should not be limited to childhood or adolescence, because the problems associated with ADHD are lifelong and often require intervention during adulthood.

Question: This is so new to me. Where do I start?

Answer: You have to know what you're dealing with first. Talk with other teachers and parents who know about ADHD. Do some research in the library or bookstore. Then begin to apply what you learn, slowly and one step at a time. Most importantly, don't respond with judgment toward children. Don't use labels carelessly, and avoid creating the notion that the child has some kind of ominous medical or psychiatric problem. As you work through one issue, you will see measurable gains which can serve as a foundation for the next step. Break goals down into manageable chunks that you and the child can work effectively with, and take care not to flood the child with overwhelming expectations which cannot reasonably be met.

Question: But isn't the child with ADHD different from other children?

Answer: Yes, but the difference may be more the extent of your response. With the normal child, you may say something once. With the child who has ADHD, you might have to say it several times. Or you may have to switch to a behavioral intervention from a verbal intervention much earlier than you would otherwise. However, that doesn't mean the child is "bad" or beyond help. It means that more intense or prolonged interventions may be necessary, or that the usual interventions will need to be applied more consistently. The child has the same problems that many other children have, but they are more prominent, more challenging, for the ADHD child than for others. These children *are* different in some ways from other children, but they are similar in many more ways. We need to emphasize their similarities and work with their differences.

Question: Are children with ADHD treated differently in the classroom?

Answer: School systems and teachers do treat children differently, depending on many factors. Teachers invariably tend to pick out the students who are more articulate, and usually spend more time with them. They're more excited to be around them. Likewise, teachers avoid certain other students based on their behavior and classroom performance. They don't do this maliciously. They are individuals who have individual preferences, and they naturally gravitate toward certain personalities more than others. This is not a judgment against either teachers or students. It is simply an ongoing expression of personal interests, tolerances, and goals. Every teacher and parent has experienced these forces at work. Generally, they cause no major problems for the classroom or the home, but taken to extremes such differences can create challenges for the child with ADHD, teachers, and school administrators. *All* children are subject to being "treated differently" at times. Our task as parents and teachers is to be sensitive to these differences and individualize our responses in whatever ways necessary to benefit each child.

Question: Is there any way I, as a teacher, can avoid reacting adversely to children with ADHD?

Answer: Yes. First, you need to recognize that your personality is one of your greatest teaching tools. You can use your relationship with a child to enhance trust, foster effective modeling, and develop commitment to the learning process. You can demonstrate, inspire, and motivate through this relationship. It is perhaps your strongest teaching tool. It offers additional opportunity for influence because you can change *your* behavior to create change in a child's behavior. ADHD children do not differ greatly in substance from their peers with regard to basic learning problems and strengths, but their expressions of problems are usually greater in intensity than those same problems are with other children. If you realize that intensity and frequency of a problem are the major variables, then you can make your responses more frequent and intense as necessary to communicate effectively and intervene successfully with the ADHD child. The regular classroom teacher is well equipped to manage most problems exhibited by ADHD children, but the intensity and frequency of interventions must match the needs of each child. Once teachers and parents understand this fact, they can be very effective dealing with ADHD problems at school and home.

Also, it is important to understand that your reactions as a teacher always reflect information about your own unfinished psychological business. If you find yourself very aggravated by a particular individual, then it is likely that you yourself are struggling with some of the same issues that the other individual's behavior is exhibiting or reminding you of. The more we become aware that we project our anger and frustration onto others, the more we come to be in control of our emotions and reactions to others. When we exercise mastery in our own lives, we pass it on to those around us. This principle is nowhere more evident than in our relationships with children.

Paradoxically, the answer to the question is that we need to learn about ourselves before we can teach the lesson to others. A student with poor impulse control is a great teacher for those of us who have problems with impulse control ourselves! This does not mean that we are not able to set limits, express anger, or communicate the need for change. But it does underscore the necessity for self-awareness and self-exploration, as we encounter others who seem to illicit anger or disdain from us. When we acknowledge the anger, we can then explore our own psychological circumstances, make changes as necessary regarding our own feelings and attitudes, and then be in a better position to help children in the classroom who try our patience or test our limits.

Question: Parents say to me, "I have two other kids, a job, and a house to run. *You* have to understand that I just don't have time." Is it realistic to expect a parent to even have the time to participate in the education of their children, and what do I tell them?

Answer: Hundreds of parents have told me how tough it is. Nobody has said this was going to be easy, not for a moment. I don't want people to believe having a child with a learning disability or ADHD is the same as having a child without these problems. However, it's not necessarily negative. It taxes a parent in different ways, and expands the parenting role. You don't have to be a special parent to be successful. You do need information, and you do have to work diligently at it, and sometimes work a little harder. But any parent can do that.

If you are the teacher, you are a primary source of information for parents. You need to serve as advisor and teacher to parents, to encourage them to be actively involved with their children's school activities and progress, and emphasize to them how important it is for them to be committed to their children, even though it takes time away from other activities. There are few subjects that rank as more important than a child's education, and parents who are involved with their kids see the results in academic performance and psychosocial maturation. Even parents with busy workdays and heavy vocational commitments can find some time each day to work on the educational growth of their children. If parents tell you that only teachers are responsible for the education of their children, firmly but kindly tell them that this is simply not true. Educate *them* about their roles and potential, and to whatever extent you can, encourage their participation and involvement. Don't accept total responsibility for the education of their children, but embrace every opportunity to model and teach both parents and children.

Question: What kind of training or education do teachers need to deal with children who have ADHD?

Answer: Many teachers say, "I've never been trained to deal with an ADHD child. My colleague next door has had twenty years of special reading experience for dyslexics, but I've never had any of that." However, teachers don't need a lot of additional training. They need additional awareness and knowledge. Any teacher can be a good teacher for ADHD students, because what they do with them is the same as what they do with other kids, except they may have to do more of it or may have to do it more intensively. There is nothing per se "special" about being a teacher for a child with ADHD except the need for more consistent and often more intense application of the techniques and principles used in a regular classroom environment. Yes, it is more challenging, but the basic tools are the same.

Question: What about support groups?

Answer: Support groups can be dangerous because they can end up as mutual story-telling sessions where people recount their miseries and misconstrue such sharing as productive or beneficial when it is actually a way of rehearsing pain and suffering. However, support groups *can* be tremendously helpful, especially if they function as an information source and forum for the exchange of healing experiences. Sympathy is not all we need to solve a problem. We need to know first that the other person's problem is similar to our own, and then we need to hear how that person used his or her inner and other resources to solve the problem. Support groups function best when their purpose is not to gain sympathy, but to say, "You know what? This is what happened to me, and this is how I faced the problem."

Question: What about the Alcoholics Anonymous model?

Answer: While the twelve-step model is a stronghold for addiction recovery and support, it can also create some strong dependencies. I directed an inpatient substance abuse and addictions program for several years, and am a strong supporter of the AA principles and community, but I worry about extremes. These support groups are really helpful if they serve an educational and experiential role, but if they create dependencies and pathology rather than looking at wellness, they can also send a person down the wrong path. With alcohol and drugs, there is a place for the concept of powerlessness, but with regard to ADHD, I would prefer to lead people in the direction of empowerment and mastery.

Question: Is private, personal psychiatric help a better approach?

Answer: I'm concerned about myself and the helping professions. We often give too much emphasis to the victim role. I don't believe there are any victims. I think we are here to learn about ourselves and teach others as they learn. We are all ultimately teachers *and* students. To fall into a victim perspective is to give up your controls. If a person with ADHD sees himself as a victim, then that person is setting himself up for a lot of tough times, because he will expect solutions from others and fail to realize that the solutions arise from self-awareness and transformation. Regarding psychiatric help, I think most children and adults who have ADHD need to be assessed by a physician (a child psychiatrist or other physician who has extensive experience with ADHD). There are medical and psychiatric disorders that can be present with many of the symptoms of ADHD but which require diagnostic and treatment interventions that can only be undertaken in a medical environment.

This medical evaluation should be undertaken early on in the intervention process so that any medically remediable problems can be effectively addressed before other interventions are pursued or implemented. As I have mentioned earlier, the treatment process needs to be multidisciplinary—and psychologists, educators, family therapists, and other professionals need to be involved. I believe a psychiatrist is usually the best person to choreograph the diagnosis and treatment process as a whole, but many other variations on this theme can be successful. Regardless of the leadership, psychiatric involvement is a necessary component of the assessment and treatment process.

Question: Should I dodge the issue of ADHD with the child completely?

Answer: No. When we are born with and grow up with a problem, we usually don't think we have a problem. We learn to live with what we have and who we are. A person who is born with a handicap often does not view his limitation as a "deficit," but attempts to accomplish what he wants by adapting to his circumstances. For example, the person who is born with one foot doesn't see the problem, because he grew up learning how to move around even with this deficiency. But when a person loses a foot at age fifteen, he begins to feel sorry for himself.

Children with ADHD need to be told, for example, that they have problems attending, but that is only the first step. They need to understand that *every* person has unique talents and challenges, and that their challenges can be successfully addressed with appropriate training and information. They do not need to be repeatedly criticized, because they likely already recognize that they are different from their peers. But they need to gain the insight that whatever their problems, there are resources and concerned adults who will help them learn how to succeed with their particular skills and struggles.

If we as therapists or teachers encourage people to listen to us because they are victims, we are being misleading. If we think we have all of the answers for them, we are also being misleading. But if we believe we can provide helpful information that can assist an individual with the challenges of life, and if we do so in a way that does not perpetuate or encourage the victimization role, then we have an opportunity to lead that person to a new level of awareness, to participate in a paradigm shift. We should never dodge such an opportunity. As teachers, parents, and counselors, we need to embrace this challenge with great enthusiasm and dedication.

This challenge requires us to see each child as a unique individual, and demands that we find individualized approaches for every occasion we have the opportunity to influence a child's education and maturation. To avoid individualizing an approach to a child because he has ADHD is akin to avoiding a child because of his facial expressions or skin color. It simply is not appropriate to keep our heads in the sand because the problem seems perplexing or overwhelming. As parents, teachers, and counselors, we also must be students. When we face a problem that requires additional knowledge, we must follow our own advice and learn new information. If you have a student with ADHD, then you will need to learn about ADHD. Don't avoid it; embrace it. The information you gain will assist with every student.

Question: What should I say to the parent who resists counseling or therapy?

Answer: Everyone needs information—teachers, children, parents, and even "counselors." The more information someone has about a problem, the more likely that person is to find solutions and answers. When we have problems with our cars, we seek advice from a mechanic. When we are sick, we seek the advice of a medical provider. When we have need for economic advice, we speak with an accountant or financial consultant. It follows that when we have a problem with a child's learning or behavior, we need the support of a professional who can guide us to solutions, just as we would do in any other similar situation. Resisting counseling or therapy will only delay the process of problem solving and bring additional stress to everyone involved. Some people still see psychiatric and psychological counseling as embarrassing or stigmatizing, but it is time for us to all get past such uninformed prejudices and face the reality that education really does provide the tools for solving problems, whether they are academic, psychological, or psychiatric. Parents who do not feel comfortable with this notion need support and advice from you to help them do what is best for their children and themselves.

Question: If ADHD can't be cured by therapy, isn't it self-indulgent to seek it?

Answer: No. The word cured is not appropriate. The child who is born with only one foot cannot be "cured" of that circumstance, but much can be done to help. An artificial limb can replace the missing foot. Physical therapy and training can teach the child how to function well with the resources available to him so that a productive and happy life can follow.

Therapy is education and information, not self-indulgence. However, if therapy does not lead to growth and change, then perhaps it *is* self-indulgent. If the therapist sees the individual as a victim, then therapy may be self-indulgent for the therapist. But if therapy is what it should be, then a child or family will benefit visibly, and therapy will not be self-indulgent at all. Also, it is important to remember that any approach to an attention deficit disorder needs to be multidisciplinary and multifocal. The most effective interventions will involve teachers, parents, counselors, psychiatrists, or psychologists and perhaps others, working in concert to provide information and support for change. Therapy is an important part of the formulas for success.

Question: How long does therapy take?

Answer: Therapy is education, and the length of the lesson depends on many factors. If a family needs only a push in the right direction, is generally open to suggestions, and practices actively, then therapy will not need to be frequent or extensive. On the other hand, if a family needs lots of information and coaching and practice, then the process may take longer.

I generally work from the first meeting to teach people how *not* to come and see me. I suggest development of some treatment goals and a general time line for accomplishing these goals. I generally do not see people weekly or bi-monthly, but try to space appointments as far apart as possible without losing track of issues and need for new information or redirection. As an example, I might see a 12-year-old child and family initially for 1 or 2 hours during the assessment phase, and follow with an appointment in 4 to 6 weeks, anticipating 6 to 8 visits during the first year, and maintenance appointments every 3 or 4 months thereafter for medication review and progress assessment. As the educational and behavioral needs became more effectively met by parents and teachers, my role might shift to exploration of nonprescription agents to replace stimulant drugs, and if we could find success with these or other alternative treatments, I would then remove myself from the treatment team, unless a new need for additional information were to arise.

If I make someone addicted to, or dependent on, the therapy process, I have done that person a disservice. My best role is to teach people the information they need to open up their ability to heal themselves. If I am successful, then eventually people will outgrow me and will no longer need my services. That is the result of effective therapy.

The medical profession and healing arts have become fixated on the victim role and often view their clients as victims and not as sojourners. We figure out ways, not maliciously, to get people to keep coming back. We say, "Here's your blood pressure pill; come back next month." Or "Come back in a month, every month, for the next twenty years." Often, consumer demands and legal hurdles influence the frequency and content of visits. There is the tendency to apply the same model to the educational environment. Once people get "pathologized," they seem to need help forever. I would rather see people get help when they need it intermittently, but not necessarily say they will need it forever. There are enough exceptions to all of these rules to show that not everybody needs the same treatment. The more control we give back, ultimately the happier people are. We're happiest when we're in charge of ourselves, whether we are patients or students.

Question: I can teach a child, but I can't nurture him. What can I say to a parent about the best way to nurture a child with ADHD? What tools can we together give him?

Answer: The experience that creates self-esteem more than anything else is unconditional acceptance. Most children in healthy homes receive more than a fair share of that for the first year or so. But at a later age, earning this unconditional regard may be more difficult, especially for the impulsive or inattentive child, whose ability to please parents or teachers is often inhibited by disorganized or scattered efforts and accomplishments. When a child does not meet performance expectations, there is less unconditional acceptance by parents and teachers.

We often fall into the habit of making acceptance dependent on performance, so the unconditional regard occurs as a result of meeting expectations. That's not pathological; it just happens to be the way most of us are wired. We begin to reinforce others with our affection when they accomplish what we want; we withhold it, or share it, based on the other person's behavior. But it is more appropriate for us to grant affection and acceptance regardless of performance or behavior. We are all entitled to basic respect and consideration. We must earn other measures of accomplishment with performance, but we are all entitled to love and compassion.

I believe teachers *can* be nurturing. In fact, the best teachers are always nurturing in many different ways. Parents are not the only ones to nurture a growing child. All of us who participate in the treatment and education of a child have nurturing opportunities and responsibilities. As a teacher, you can serve as a great example to parents by the way you respond to a child's failures and success, by talking with parents about self-esteem issues and emphasizing positive reinforcement, and by individually supporting each child with your praise and personal recognition. Like it or not, as teachers you are very powerful influences on your students, and you have a great opportunity to nurture them along the way.

Question: What do I say to the parent who says, "I can't parent my child; he seems to hate me?"

Answer: Unfortunately, kids who have ADHD will test limits more than those who do not, so their parents come to regard them with more conditions than the average child. Those conditions usually relate to their inability to conform to their environment, to pay attention to it, or to conform to the rules of the environment. By the time the preschool years have passed, children with ADHD have been negatively reinforced more than most other children, so they have developed low self-esteem and a high consciousness for failure. As the elementary school years pass, more rules bring more failures, and the low esteem blossoms into self-contempt (for failing so often) and maybe "self-hate" at some levels.

Children do what we adults do with their self-judgments: they project them onto others. In this case, they project their self-anger onto parents or others in authority. The anger that often accompanies such expressions is usually sufficient to impair communication or even sometimes stop it altogether. Parents who become discouraged with this predicament need to be given information about how to set firm and effective limits without breaking the spirits of their children. They need to be told *not* to give in or give up. They need to know that many children feel uncertain about themselves and express their insecurities in responses to parents. They need to know that it is appropriate to keep communication open between parents and children, even when there seems to be a major impediment to clear exchanges. They need to be shown that their unconditional commitment to the child's best interests is foremost, regardless of the communication problems. Most of all, parents need to know never, never to give up.

Question: How do children with ADHD deal with failure in the face of their limitations?

Answer: They can overcompensate and be aggressive toward the external world. Or they can be passive, in which case they often become more depressed. At the point of graduating high school, an ADHD individual will have a more compromised self-esteem than most other children. It is a fair assumption to say that he has not succeeded in most of the ways other children are allowed to succeed, although there are a lot of exceptions. When he looks at his life to that point, he searches for anchors of success. He'll have a lot more trouble finding those anchors than most of his peers. His self-esteem may be lower, his confidence less, and his ability to succeed in the usual work or educational environment may be limited.

Question: Aren't there exceptions to that? My student with ADHD is clumsy but creative. Aren't there some compensations there, and peer-level trade-offs?

Answer: Children instinctively find their strongest assets to counterbalance experiences that might otherwise cause loss of self-esteem or autonomy. Those who either have a brighter intellect or other skills to negotiate with may be less ultimately affected by such impediments to usual development. Often, children with ADHD are very creative. In fact, it may be their ADHD characteristics that manifest such creativity. The ability to juggle several thoughts at once or bring together several seemingly disconnected concepts into one coherent whole is often exhibited by children with ADHD. While the trade-off in the classroom may be limited ability to focus and achieve high academic performance, the social and interpersonal assets may provide compensatory success in other areas of life, including social, artistic, and intellectually creative activities.

Question: If a child has ADHD, does that mean that he is destined to a life of failure?

Answer: There are some kids who have fairly severe symptoms but excel in so many different areas that the symptoms may not even be detected, Some go all the way through high school and are the class clowns. They are very distractible, yet get straight *A*'s. They can tame any teacher, so their self-esteem survives pretty well. These children are uncommon, but not rare. They fall among the top 5% or 10% of children intellectually, but are also often gifted athletically, artistically, musically, or socially.

A lot of impulsivity can be channeled into creative activity on the basketball court or in an art class, and never be detected for what it actually is. Some of the best athletes in high school achieve their performance excellence because they learn intuitively to channel their energies into areas that provide the greatest return. They may not excel academically, but they possess other areas of strength, including their ability to multi-task and integrate well. The very limitations imposed by ADHD symptoms in one area can offer an opportunity to excel in another. Examples exist in other arenas as well, including music, art, dance and movement, creative writing and literature, architecture—in fact, in almost any area of achievement that allows for individuality and creativity (and that could be *any* field of accomplishment). The presence of ADHD does not forecast a life of underachievement or failure. For many, it can be the unique collection of talents and skills that earns success and recognition in any area of creativity.

Question: Do ADHD symptoms disappear with adolescence, or can they extend into adulthood?

Answer: ADHD is lifelong, but the symptoms may change with age. In the past we thought that most people "outgrew" ADHD by the late teen years. Now we know that this is not the case. Rather, we have learned that, as the years pass, an individual with ADHD often develops specific coping strategies which allow for compensation and adjustment to the symptoms of the disorder. When children reach the teen years, they develop abstract reasoning skills and are able to "think about thinking." As they mature, they discover ways of compensating for problems that are the result of ADHD. For example, they may learn that keeping note cards of school assignments helps them to turn in those assignments on time, or that daily task lists facilitate timely completion of work and other responsibilities. Additionally, experience is a great teacher, and as ADHD children find ways of being successful in one environment (e.g., the classroom), they often generalize those successful lessons to other settings such as the workplace. Most adults with ADHD retain some symptoms lifelong, but learn to live with these symptoms and often transform them into creative and stimulating strategies for success and wisdom.

Question: How does labeling a child with ADHD affect his self-image and his life?

Answer: On the one hand, we have to honor the notion that he has a problem which has potential for affecting all aspects of his life, but at the same time, to make him "disabled" as a result of his symptoms of ADHD is a dangerous assumption. While labeling is often a problem, there is a more important process at work that affects self-esteem from an early age. Preschool children with ADHD experience a pattern of recurrent failure. They find difficulty following instructions and are negatively reinforced more than peers, because their capacity for remembering and following instructions is limited. While their behavior may indeed warrant more frequent intervention, the nature of that intervention is more often negative, and the result is an increased tendency toward compromised self-esteem. That tendency is magnified when a pathological label is attached to the intervention. When the ADHD child receives frequent negative verbal interventions, and when his behavior becomes characterized by a negative name, then certainly there are detrimental effects on self-esteem.

Question: Then why do we use labels such as ADHD?

Answer: Diagnostic labels have evolved out of a traditional medical model of diagnosis and treatment that emphasizes looking at symptoms and searching for their root causes. Collections of symptoms represent a specific diagnosis, and a specific diagnosis demands a specific treatment. The assumption is that once you have labeled the problem, you then know the treatment. In a strictly medical setting, this model has merit, but in an educational environment it can create problems, because it causes teachers and other students to have fixed expectations of anyone who has the label. The diagnostic label often predisposes teachers to expect inattentive and distracting behavior from such children. Peers often associate the label with taking medicines or being difficult to get along with. Because the labeling process often takes on "public" proportions, it is often punitive or limiting to the student with ADHD and can create barriers in the classroom and elsewhere. The term has a stigmatizing effect that is sometimes difficult to avoid. One way of combating the negative connotations of the label is to help children see the positive characteristics that are associated with ADHD.

Question: Is keeping quiet about ADHD the best way for a parent to handle the problem? Or doesn't that leave the teacher in the dark?

Answer: Generally, it is not wise to "keep quiet" about any information that would help a teacher understand the needs of, or provide more educational opportunities for, a child in the classroom. First, if the teacher is aware of a problem, then more attention and support can be focused on the child and the problem. Second, it is not healthy to model deception or avoidance to the child. If we want our children to be open and honest with their problems to us, then we must be the same with our (or their) problems when we discuss them with the teacher.

Occasionally, there may be need for exception to this view, if a teacher is particularly vituperous or prejudiced toward children with ADHD. If we could be assured that all teachers would be accepting and appropriate with their reactions to the label, then we would have no need to protect the child by withholding information from a teacher. Sadly, there are times when such behavior seems warranted. If the child is viewed as "difficult" by the teacher because of the label, then often the label is passed along as the child proceeds through the grades. It precedes him as he travels to the next year. Teachers know "so-and-so is coming and he has this problem"—as opposed to the notion that these children are creative, multi-talented, and flexible in ways that other people can't be. For example, often they are good at abstract reasoning and creative thinking. When we can say, "Here comes one of my gifted, creative, inspiring kids, who happens to bounce off the walls occasionally," we can use the term ADHD more positively. This is the direction we must work toward.

Question: I have 30 kids in my classroom. Should I be required to sacrifice the needs of all the others for one child with ADHD?

Answer: No. Nearly all of the problems ADHD children have can be addressed effectively in a regular classroom and without sacrificing the needs of other students. Extra effort may be required sometimes, but the strategies and interventions that help ADHD children also are applicable to other students. Usually when a teacher makes this complaint, it is because he or she has not developed strategies at all to deal with the challenges of the ADHD child and feels overwhelmed. Once that teacher has been equipped with effective interventions, the presence of a child with ADHD is not intimidating or frustrating, and the teacher can manage the classroom with less difficulty.

Question: Weighing both sides of the problem, which is best for the child, labeling or not?

Answer: There is a definite need to recognize the problem, and you can't recognize it without labeling it. On the other hand, we have sometimes used labels punitively, to the disadvantage of lots of kids who have this problem. We stereotype them and don't allow them to be who they are, or who they can be. We look at them as a label, rather than as the individuals they are. Labels used in this fashion lead to problems for teachers, students, and parents. We are all familiar with the concept of an individualized education plan, and the concept has been effectively implemented in some segments of the educational world. The principle of individual attention based on individual needs is becoming a more generalized trend in every sector of society, as we become more aware that attention to individual needs results in better outcomes (whether they be educational, consumer oriented, or even political). Despite this growing respect for individual needs, we have not yet been successful at addressing many of the individual needs in the classroom environment. Diagnostic labels are a necessary component of this process, but I believe their future importance lies in the realm of accurate and clinically individualized application which serves the best interests of the patient, rather than simply as a diagnostic, planning, or billing tool. Finally, labels serve an educational purpose by serving as names and definitions for the problems we are dealing with, and they offer educators, parents, and patients a framework for understanding ADHD and the interventions they precipitate. Rather than shy away from them, we need to understand them and then make certain that they are not carelessly or irresponsibly used.

Question: What about medications? Do they help? Are they appropriate?

Answer: I am perhaps more conservative with medicines than many child psychiatrists, but I certainly feel medicines have been lifesaving to many kids who have this problem. I appreciate the numerous other ways of dealing with ADHD, but often nothing will work as well as stimulant medications.

We live in a culture that has a strong interest in immediate gratification. We are looking for a "quick fix," and pharmaceutical interventions are often seen in this way. We get angry at people who use street drugs, marijuana, and alcohol excessively, but if we're taking Valium or Librium for our "nerves," we think this is acceptable. We protest the use of medications to help ADHD children in the classroom, but we condone our own daily use of Excedrin, Tylenol PM, and NyQuil. We're hypocritical about the whole issue of medicines. Politically we take a stand against drug trafficking and drug abuse, yet we sanction use of other drugs to treat ADHD and other learning disabilities. We have for decades waged a war on drugs, yet we are a medicine-oriented society with a high reliance on pills and medicines, both prescription and over-the-counter. To complicate matters further, the symptoms of ADHD are often not really visible. These kids look "normal," so why should they take medicines? Critics say, "All they need is a swift kick in the behind, and they will be fine." We have an inconsistent view of these things, and there is great need for education and information.

Regarding the issue of medications, there is no question that stimulants are the cornerstone of treatment for many who have ADHD, both child and adult. Physician experience, classroom observation, and numerous clinical studies have shown without question the effectiveness of these drugs, and no responsible clinician will overlook their use. However, medicines must be used carefully, conservatively, and within the context of a broad treatment program that takes an integrated view of the person and his/her total life circumstances.

Question: But aren't there side-effects from these drugs that I might see in the classroom?

Answer: Misuse of stimulants occurs fairly frequently because people don't know how to use stimulants effectively, or don't monitor their use appropriately. There are kids who go to the classroom totally over-dosed or over-medicated, and others who are mis-medicated. These criticisms arouse public attention enough to make many of us wonder whether medicines are a good idea at all. That's an overreaction. Most medicines can have side-effects—including those used to treat ADHD. But proper management can usually minimize untoward effects while at the same time providing effective symptom control. If you observe adverse reactions to medicines in the classroom, you need to notify parents and the treating physician so the problem can be corrected and the child can obtain optimal benefit from the medicine. Side-effects alone do not constitute a reason to avoid medicines, because they can usually be eliminated with adjustments in dosage or other changes.

Question: How do medicines help a child with ADHD in school?

Answer: Ultimately the medicines, or any of the interventions we use, are not aimed only at helping someone succeed academically. They're aimed first at improving self-esteem. If the medicines help someone to achieve more in the classroom, then he will feel better about himself. It isn't only the grade on the report card that counts; it's what the person feels about himself after he finishes that year. The major disadvantage of having ADHD is what it does to your self-esteem. We don't give pills to kids simply to help them perform better, although that is hopefully a result and certainly a most important contributing factor toward improved self-esteem. Also, there are many alternatives to medicine. There are interpersonal and behavioral interventions. Even if you take medicines, you need someone who loves you and respects you and who praises you and gives you the psychological side of things. This is equally important to wholesome self-esteem.

Question: Why is self-esteem so vital to a child with ADHD?

Answer: To function well, a person must have self-esteem and autonomy (or a sense of self-control). Any experience that takes away either of these resources impairs function. If you are depressed and have lowered self-esteem, you may be less independent. You certainly will not function as well as usual. If the psychiatrist can help you re-create self-esteem, and restore self-control—even if you haven't addressed the real reason that relates to depression—he has succeeded in treating you effectively.

The same is true for people who have ADHD. If we encourage self-esteem and independence, then the person will find ways to make himself happy and successful. Without those basic ingredients, it's very difficult to be successful, no matter what else is happening. If we consider the issue of failure, we can see how an individual with ADHD often creates a legacy of failure because he cannot keep up with peers or cannot perform according to the demands of his environment. Obviously, his self-esteem will be compromised under such circumstances. Often, depression and behavior disorders will follow, and this constellation of symptoms will eventually produce self-fulfilling drops in self-esteem and more consciousness of failure. Anything we can do to raise self-esteem under these or similar circumstances will obviously greatly benefit the person with an attention deficit disorder.

Question: Do you think that ADHD is "disabling"?

Answer: I think it is dangerous to label ADHD per se as disabling. Just as it is with other psychological and psychiatric problems, there are many variations on the theme, and each individual must be considered on the basis of his particular symptoms. Generally, I do not consider the problem to be "disabling," but severe expressions of the disorder can prevent a person from succeeding in certain arenas of life, especially academically and vocationally. Further, I think it is important to recall what we said earlier about self-esteem. We know that telling someone he is disabled is a limiting view which can severely curtail a person's opportunities for success. It is better to begin by defining the problem, acknowledge its presence, and then provide ways to manage the problem so that a person can still feel mastery even if he finds answers in an unconventional way or requires problem-solving strategies beyond the conventional (including medicines).

Actually, there may be advantages associated with ADHD. People with ADHD often excel in creativity and imagination, and have the ability to find solutions to problems that other people would not think of, simply because they are able to view a problem from several different perspectives at the same time. This ability to multi-task can be a strong asset for a person with ADHD, one which is often unrecognized because the other symptoms that stand out to the rest of the world are irritating and frustrating. We tend to see the negatives rather than the strengths of people who have this problem.

Question: Do you choose not to label the person with ADHD at all?

Answer: I emphasize the need not to over-pathologize the whole area. People need to understand what the problems are, but not to focus excessively on them.

Question: Yet you maintain there may actually be advantages for persons with ADHD, particularly with regard to intelligence.

Answer: This issue of creative thinking is important. There are a lot of opinions about IQ. Some people think IQ is emotional; other people view it from a social perspective, or an artistic, even specifically a musical or rhythmic perspective. I think this more-encompassing view of intelligence makes more sense to me than simply focusing on an IQ score. From that perspective, it may be that people who have ADHD may be geniuses in some ways and that their particular genius contributes a lot to their work scene, or the social or educational scene. Regarding IQ, we must choose if we want what is traditional and comfortable, or what is true.

Question: I assume there is a natural chronology of ADHD from birth to adulthood.

Answer: Infants are totally helpless. The world around them is their servant for at least the first year. Until locomotion is adequately developed, they are extremely dependent on their surroundings. Virtually everything that happens to them doesn't happen at their request, but because people anticipate their needs and give up whatever necessary to serve them and to meet their needs. So the agreement that parents at first have is that "No matter what you do as a child, as an infant, I accept you, I love you unconditionally."

Question: Do parents make no distinction at this age?

Answer: There is a very unconditional quality to initial parent/child relationships in normal and healthy circumstances, and that fosters in the child a high level of acceptance without restraints, so that even if the child could conceive of deficiencies, it would not be an issue at this point. In the natural course of things, once children learn how to walk, they escape the controlled environment of this first year. They also become potentially harmful to themselves, and at the same time they become verbally engaged with their parents (rather than just behaviorally engaged), so parents begin to issue commands, especially in dangerous situations.

Question: Is initial discipline different for a child with ADHD than for other children? If so, does this account for some of the problems teachers see later on?

Answer: The first thing that usually happens is that a child steps into or touches something that is risky, and parents at that point begin exercising discipline. Assuming that these problems with ADHD began at birth, or before, and that they exist during the pre- or para-verbal phase of development then those initial efforts to discipline, to set limits, are affected by the inattentiveness, and an inability to focus. This is a delicate time, because if the first responses to discipline are not what the parent expects, then the parent will over-modulate with future responses. If the child has an ability to perceive or respond appropriately to these initial interventions, then this process of growing awareness to danger and response to authority will be much smoother. But I believe that for kids who have ADHD, even from the early interactions there is an imbalance, and that imbalance affects the child, the parents, and the parents' style of intervening. At the next level, the child develops some verbal skills and the lessons of the first couple of years become solidified in habit. At that point the child is faced with debating authority. All children do this, but if this imbalance persists (and it does), then the child has to deal with this verbal debate and wrestling with a different perspective than the normal child would.

Question: How is verbal communication different for a child with ADHD than for other children?

Answer: First, the child has trouble listening or focusing—but also trouble understanding the nuances of communication. What would normally be registered as something of high importance in the normal child may be minimized or ignored by the child who isn't picking up on the cues. That intensifies the parents' response. It makes the parent feel the need for more assertive intervention, and sometimes more abrupt intervention. Teachers easily recognize this problem because of their (usually) more objective position in relation to the child.

Question: How does this trouble recognizing nuances of communication manifest itself?

Answer: By preschool, most children have grown to respect verbal intervention and have learned to appreciate the emotional message that comes along with it. The ADHD child has not learned to do this. At this point we see aggressive behavior, rebellious behavior, defiant and authoritarian acting out, all of which are traceable back to these original imbalances in communication between parent and child. Once the relationship is a little off balance early on, each phase of development magnifies the imbalance. By the time the child is at the preschool age, things are already fairly distorted. If you ask parents, most will say, "He was manageable.

Even during those early years we could handle it. But by the time he was ready to go to preschool, he was very difficult for us." What they don't realize is that each year has added to the problem, but the full force of the challenge is not evident until the early school years.

Question: This is a child who majors in hyperactivity. What about the other side, the child lost in the woods?

Answer: An inattentive child will have similar academic problems, but he will be behaviorally different. He will still have difficulty responding to his parents' emotional messages, and will often be lost among his peers in the classroom. He may be more compliant behaviorally, but he will be more detached intellectually, and more likely not to hear what's going on, even though he might be there in his body. Many of these children don't get identified at all during school years. They get to high school and appear to be either lazy, shy, or socially backward—but they're just detached, not picking up on the cues, dreaming, and missing out on their education. Teachers and parents need to watch more carefully for these children, because they don't ask for help or exhibit challenging behaviors that will draw attention from adults.

Question: How does school affect a child with ADHD?

Answer: School is the first external representation of authority beyond home and parents. Initially, most ADHD children will follow the crowd and conform to the ways of the classroom. But because the classroom environment demands more restraint than they were accustomed to at home, most ADHD children will experience only a brief honeymoon before they begin to test the limits of the classroom just as they have done at home. However, there are some important differences between these two environments that may support the ADHD child. First, the classroom is usually more consistent with limits and rules, and added structure may offer opportunities for self-control. Second, this is a new and different experience, which can offer opportunities to learn from peers and teachers. Third, the learning process can be exciting and stimulating, and interest may provoke social and educational progress.

On the other hand, school can create problems for the ADHD child. Those children who do not adapt socially may be isolated by both students and teachers, and their repeated failures academically and interpersonally may create lowered self-esteem, acting out, and expressions of aggression. Missed social cues may provide cause for conflict with peers and authority figures. Without appropriate classroom practices and individualized educational interventions, ADHD children can be harmed by the school experience.

Question: Does ADHD stay with a child forever?

Answer: Most agree that ADHD is a disorder that is present at birth and remains with a person lifelong. However, the symptoms may change from one age to the next, and numerous factors can influence the ultimate expression of symptoms or their apparent disappearance. For example, an ADHD child who grows up in a chaotic family system may be exceedingly distractible and disorganized compared with an ADHD child who is raised in a very consistent and predictable setting. A child with high intellectual abilities may not be identified as having ADHD until his grades fall to failing levels. This may not occur until the later high school years. As children enter adolescence, they develop abstract reasoning skills and have the chance to "study" their thinking habits and skills. Given the opportunity, many ADHD children can develop coping strategies to better deal with the classroom or social challenges that come their way. Often it appears that ADHD symptoms wane as a person enters adulthood. This apparent resolution of symptoms is more likely the result of having learned more elegant and effective strategies for dealing with ADHD symptoms, rather than resolution of the disorder. Or symptoms may appear to be quiescent for years, only to be exposed by major change or distress. For example, promotion, marriage, or serious illness may bring to the surface ADHD symptoms that had previously been little noted.

Question: What typically happens in the classroom to the "daydreamer" or the inattentive child?

Answer: Again, the inattentive child will go for several years in the school setting before he is detected, making it to the seventh or eighth grade. When he shifts to middle school and the high school academic pressures are too great for him, the teacher or the parent will notice and say, "We've got to take a look at this and see what's going on." Ultimately, most of the ADHD problems have surfaced by the time the child reaches the seventh or eighth grades. Before, when I was growing up, ADHD was probably frequently missed. I had classmates who probably fell into all these categories. In some cases I'm not sure it was unhealthy that they were not singled out, because they maintained some sense of normalcy. On the other hand, most would have greatly benefited from individualized educational plans that included measures specifically addressing their ADHD symptoms and supporting them more effectively in the classroom.

Question: What if ADHD is not identified? How does that affect the child's school years?

Answer: Children who go untreated beyond grade school into junior high and high school settings will often end up as academic failures, or at least poor achievers. Those who are more impulsive will be identified first for their behaviors. They usually get attention from the system, but it is not always positive. The other group, those who are inattentive but do not stand out because of their conduct, end up being school dropouts and passive victims to the system.

Question: Is there a good chance ADHD will be overlooked so late?

Answer: One of the virtues of our current educational process is that we have provided vocational education that is supportive to some of these children. It may not be all they deserve or need, but before, there wasn't even that net to catch them. We do a better job of identifying these people at the end of eighth or ninth grade, and often the vocational setting allows them to be successful in ways that could not be accomplished in the regular classroom environment.

Question: Then should parents trust the system to catch ADHD in their child?

Answer: By and large, our school systems have not handled the problem of ADHD well. Many teachers still don't recognize the problem exists, or even know what the term means. For years I have visited classrooms to inform teachers about ADHD. I have often returned to the same schools later to discover many teachers who have never heard of the term. The frequent mention of ADHD on television and radio, and in newspapers and magazines, has improved name recognition of the problem at least, but the schools still do not serve the needs of the children who have ADHD. So parents should not expect the school system to diagnose the problem—but we hope that teachers and school administrators will become more adept at seeing the problem and referring children to appropriate resources for help.

Question: Then where will the help for the children come from, if not from schools?

Answer: The children who do best are those whose parents have identified the problem and who are advocates for their children—advocates not in a negative way, but parents who see that their children are appropriately assessed and who build on their strengths by working with them at home, and giving them the extra educational opportunities they might not otherwise get in the school system alone.

Question: What percentage of parents are doing this?

Answer: A fairly small percentage, maybe 25%–30% of the parents of children who have this problem, work with their children. It is amazing what extra support kids can get from their parents, especially if the parents get involved. I know of a child who has Down's Syndrome. Her parents were told not to expect much from their daughter, but they chose to work extensively with her from infancy into early adulthood. She was given multisensory physical training and patterning from infancy, and during school years her mother attended school with her every day through the eighth grade. This was required by the school system, because the parents elected not to follow school recommendations to place their daughter in special education, but chose instead to have her mainstreamed in a regular classroom, and the school permitted this only if the mother agreed to be present every day (and all day) in the presence of her child.

As a result of parental involvement and dedication to this child's education, she was able to keep up with her peers in most subjects, and now as a young adult works as a secretary in her father's office. Her skills far exceed the expectations for an individual with Down's Syndrome. Similar opportunities exist for most children, regardless of limitations or impairments. Intimate parental connections with children always enhance outcomes and often enable children to excel beyond their usual expectations.

If parents really want their children to become the most they can become, then they need to be involved and share the responsibilities of the educational process with teachers and schools. The rewards will be higher academic performance, increased self-esteem, more intimate connections with their children—priceless gifts that cannot be purchased except with involvement.

Question: I have seen the system work with some learning disorders. Are there any examples of extra work paying off with ADHD children?

Answer: I know a child who had some developmental delays but who also had ADHD. His mother is a special education teacher who began working with him in the preschool years. At the end of the second year of high school, his parents arranged for him to attend a school in New Jersey that specializes in the education of children who have learning disabilities and ADHD. He and his parents have high expectations that he will attend college and become self-supporting as an adult. He has far exceeded the expectations of most who have worked with him over the years, but his parents have always somehow believed that their intimate involvement with him would allow him to achieve his greatest potential, and their faith has been confirmed by his numerous successes.

Question: What about those parents who can't afford a specialized school in New Jersey? Shouldn't we use public funds to support these educational efforts? Don't these children deserve, or are they not entitled to, the additional expense required to upgrade them in their educational skills and their experiences?

Answer: Some kids need specialized education that community schools can't provide. The parents of the child I just mentioned are struggling with that issue. The board of education in their school district has so far declined to absorb the cost of this special environment, and they are faced with the question of whether or not to bring legal action against the school system. On the other hand, most school systems simply do not have the resources to afford such specialized education for all who might need it.

However, there are other possibilities that need to be explored. If more parents took a greater interest in their children's education, and if they were willing to devote some time and energy to the educational needs of the community at large, then perhaps most students would not have to leave their home states to receive specialized services. If children received more support and involvement from parents at home, then perhaps teachers would be able to accomplish more with children in school.

As a society, we have come to assume that education of our children is the responsibility of the school system and that we as parents have little to do with the activities in the classroom. This assumption is simply not accurate. If children have learning disabilities or ADHD, parental involvement and encouragement is even more important. We *are* entitled to a public education, but that does not abolish our responsibility to be committed parents who are willing to demonstrate our interest in our children by giving time and energy to their academic progress and accomplishments.

Question: Do you endorse only self-financing special education?

Answer: No. I think public funds must be dedicated to specialized educational services. But I believe that money alone is not the answer. With motivated and involved parents, I think many educational challenges could be met locally, and such community support would allow for reallocation of funds to meet specific extra needs.

Question: Then it's actually cost-effective to give ADHD children special education?

Answer: Yes. If you pay later, the cost can be a lot higher. The quick fix is not the cheapest. But I am not certain that "special" education is the right term. Perhaps it is more appropriate to say that ADHD children need additional support both in and out of the classroom, and that support can often come from parents.

Question: Is there a connection between ADHD and antisocial behavior? Obviously, some of the kids who are not dealt with adequately never have an understanding of their own ADHD and just drift off into games. Do they need some validation?

Answer: There is data to support the notion that ADHD is a precursor to delinquency. I hesitate to make that conclusion directly, but I certainly agree that if you go through grade school and high school without actually knowing that you have ADHD, and if by that time you have failed academically, have been ostracized, have failed socially, have trouble at home, and exhibit conduct difficulties, then your best opportunities for self-esteem lie beyond the classroom. Under such circumstances, delinquency and conduct disorders can often appear. People normally seek the lowest common denominator of behavior that will allow them to be acceptable, or the one that requires the least work on their part to maintain social importance. So it is very important for us to identify problems early if we are to successfully intervene and prevent them. I suspect also that absence of intimate parental involvement contributes to lack of timely recognition and inadequate responses to such children's needs—underscoring again the need for parents to be active participants in the education and nurturing of their offspring.

Question: Should I be concerned if I see a child in my class who is a social failure, a loner, or a bully?

Answer: Kids who have failed to satisfy usual societal expectations—including school performance, the usual age-appropriate social graces and norms—are at high risk for becoming delinquent and for ultimately becoming so angry and frustrated with themselves that they project all of those feelings on a more general plane to society at large. They become burdens to themselves and ultimately burdens to all of us if that process is not interrupted. It is therefore very important to investigate and evaluate the circumstances of any child who appears to be lagging behind socially or is exhibiting unsuccessful behaviors. These students need to be academically, medically, and psychologically assessed, and parents need to be involved and informed about the evaluations and findings.

Question: What about adults who learn that they have ADHD? Should they be assessed and treated?

Answer: One adult who comes to mind is an older gentleman who had been fairly successful as an assembly line worker in an automobile factory all of his life. While he had supported himself and his family over the years, he realized that he had to work harder and often take longer performing tasks than his peers. He decided that he would get a college education and become an alcohol rehabilitation counselor. For several years he pursued this goal, and at age 62 he received the Master's degree and found employment. In the classroom he had studied learning disabilities and come to the conclusion that he had ADHD. He decided to seek a professional assessment, at which time the diagnosis was confirmed and treatment initiated.

At this point in his life, he didn't need to work for economic reasons; he made the choice because he had always wanted to be a counselor. The decision to obtain treatment for his ADHD symptoms was another choice, an effort to improve the quality of his life. He had already shown himself that he could be academically successful, even though it had taken him longer than others. When he came to my office, he already had a job and was functioning adequately in his role as a counselor. But he knew there was more, and he wanted to give himself every opportunity to find the best for himself in his older years.

His story is very powerful because he had a lot of options at this point. He didn't have to do any work; he didn't have to seek treatment for his problem either, because he had gone through school, gotten degrees, and had a job. But this was a gift he was giving to himself—a form of fine tuning, after almost a full life, with the idea that he could probably live a long time and have a second life or career basically free from the problems of ADHD.

Anyone who demonstrates signs of a problem such as ADHD should be evaluated and treated if there is a chance that perception and quality of life can be improved. Of course, the earlier in life that we can become aware of, and rectify, problems, the better. But it is never too late, and one is never too old, to learn more and accomplish more.

Recommended Readings

Barkley, R. A. (1998). *Attention-Deficit Hyperactivity Disorder: A handbook for diagnosis and treatment.* New York: Guilford.

Goldstein, S., & Goldstein, M. (1992). *Hyperactivity: Why won't my child pay attention?* Salt Lake City, UT: Neurology, Learning and Behavior Center.

Hallowell, E. M., & Ratey, J. (1994). *Driven to distraction: Recognizing and coping with Attention Deficit Disorder from childhood through adulthood.* New York: Pantheon.

Ingersoll, B., & Goldstein, M. (1993). *Attention deficit disorder and learning disabilities: Realities, myths and controversial treatments.* New York: Doubleday.

Johnson, D. (1992). *I can't sit still: Educating and affirming inattentive and hyperactive children.* Santa Cruz, CA: ETR Associates.

Levine, M. (1991). *Keeping ahead in school.* Cambridge, MA: Educators Publishing Service.

Silver, L. (1999). *Attention-Deficit Hyperactivity Disorder: A clinical guide to diagnosis and treatment for health and mental health professionals.* Washington, DC: American Psychiatric Association.

Silver, L. (1998). *The misunderstood child: Understanding and coping with your child's learning disabilities.* New York: Times Books.

Vail, P. (1987). *Smart kids with school problems: Things to know and ways to help.* New York: Dutton.

Weiss, L. (1996). *Give your ADD teen a chance: A guide for parents of teenagers with attention deficit disorder.* Colorado Springs, CO: Pinon.

Weiss, L. (1997). *Attention Deficit Disorder in adults.* Dallas: Taylor.

Wender, P. H. (1987). *The hyperactive child, adolescent, and adult: Attention Deficit Disorder through the lifespan.* New York: Oxford University Press.

Wender, P. H. (1998). *Attention Deficit Disorder in adults.* New York: Oxford University Press.

Wodrich, D. (1994). *What every parent wants to know: Attention Deficit Hyperactivity Disorder.* Baltimore: Brookes.

Dr. MacCallum and Dr. Guyer wish to thank Sal Norris for her editing of transcripts that produced this chapter.

Chapter 10

A Coaching Model for the Management of ADHD Behaviors in the Classroom

PEGGY E. RAMUNDO

The bell had already rung. As I had a lot of important material to cover in an hour, I was anxious to get started. Unfortunately, the vast majority of my students were not in their seats when they were supposed to be. Most did eventually arrive, reluctantly straggling in and settling down. This happened neither quickly nor quietly, I might add. Some entered whispering, "This class is a waste of time." Others rearranged chairs to optimize comfort: one chair for sitting and the other for stretching out legs. With the exception of a few muttered "Let's get this show on the road . . . I want to get out of here's," most voices were engaged in various, small-group conversations. Chatter stopped only after my second or third request for everyone's attention. After the last two of my students raced into the room, one apologizing that he was late because he had to call the mechanic about his car and the other that she'd misplaced her notebook, I finally began my presentation. For the remaining 45 minutes, as I talked to the students, a number of them made comments about my lecture. Not all chatted when they were supposed to be listening because some were engaged in other, more interesting pursuits. One was reading a book and another writing a letter, both glancing up every now and then. Two students in the back compared their schedules. Others worked on homework assignments. One enterprising young lady sat quietly in the back row doing needlepoint. I should mention that some students were actively involved in the subject at hand, taking notes on the lecture, sharing insights and answering questions.

Most would say that arriving late, not paying attention, and coming to class unprepared are behaviors not conducive to learning. Beyond this majority viewpoint, though, there are undoubtedly observations and judgments born of the disparate paradigms unique to each reader. If the reader "sees" this situation as one in which students are way out of line, he or she would judge them in need of a swift *attitude adjustment*. If cease-and-desist warnings went ignored, some punishment would definitely be in order. Or perhaps the consequences of individual student behavioral contracts would be invoked instead. Other readers might view the situation from a different perspective—that the teacher is woefully deficient in her classroom management skills and therefore needs additional training and/or a mentor.

So who were these inattentive students? They happened to be the teaching staff of a local elementary school. And my class was an after-school in-service training session titled, "Understanding and Managing ADHD Behaviors in the Classroom." The reader should know that far from being unusual, this scenario is representative of virtually every workshop or in-service training I have ever conducted, and they number in the hundreds. And although my attendees don't know it, I would be disappointed if it weren't. An educator can never have too many such wonderful teachable moments. So I "call" my teacher–students on their respective inappropriate behaviors. I receive a variety of reactions, explanations, and apologies:

- I didn't realize I was talking so loud/so much.
- These in-services shouldn't be held after school—it's hard to listen when you're so tired.
- I just have so many other things on my mind.
- I have to get this homework checked, so I figured I'd listen while I worked on it.
- If I don't do something with my hands, I'll fall asleep.
- These chairs are so blasted uncomfortable.
- I wanted to share an insight I just had with my colleague; that's why we were talking.
- I'm sorry I came in late; I just remembered that I needed to schedule my dentist appointment—if I don't do something as soon as I think of it, I totally forget about it.
- I already know about ADHD, and frankly, I don't understand why my principal said attendance was mandatory.
- This is boring; I don't find this information useful because I already use behavior contracts with students.
- I am not a child and resent being treated like one. . . .

Variations on this last statement are expressed by one or two teachers in every group, angry at being targeted for what they assume is going to be a moralistic diatribe: "Do as I say and not as I do, huh? Well, ha . . . gotcha!" Fortunately, these teachers are few in number; as they are unwilling to study their own behavior, chances are nil that they will be capable of guiding an ADHD student to examine and understand his. As reflected by the foregoing comments, however, the emotional response of most

teachers typically runs the gamut from embarrassment to remorse to a new awareness—the Aha! of a paradigm shift. When the classroom is experienced from the
other side of the desk, so to speak, it looks and feels much different. From this perspective, the picture of the ADHD student is enlarged and new insights can
emerge, clarifying some of the troublesome misconceptions—like the following—
that otherwise get in the way of our using behavior management effectively with
ADHD students.

Excuse . . . Explanation

I was late because—I forgot my notebook. . . . I was talking because—I had to tell
my friend something. . . . I was tapping my pencil because—it gave me something
to do. These are among the explanations my teachers provided. When ADHD students offer similar ones, they are admonished to *stop making excuses*. It would do
well for the reader to keep firmly in mind the powerful influence of the personal
paradigm. Same scenario. Different perceptual viewpoint and far different outcome for the student.

In this writer's experience, the word *excuse* is used regularly in the same sentence as AD(H)D.* Admittedly, ADHD students are incredibly resourceful at
inventing stories to wriggle out from under their various transgressions. Undoubtedly these elaborately concocted and preposterous tales give rise to honest skepti-
cism—at the very least! It is conceivable that on the heels of such farfetched
confabulations, the run-of-the-mill "I forgot's and I didn't hear you's" might be
assumed to be equally unbelievable. After all, they come from the same source. As
if this weren't bad enough, their parents seem to be co-conspirators: "He has
ADHD and can't complete so many arithmetic problems; she misunderstood the
directions because she has ADHD and was distracted by the gerbils." With the
excuse assumption operational, vital information is left out of the picture, rendering
behavior management useless.

In recent years, behavior management has become nearly synonymous with
Attention Deficit Hyperactivity Disorder, in that when asked in my workshops

---

*This writer generally prefers to refer to the learning disability treated here as AD(H)D, as
in Attention Deficit (Hyperactivity) Disorder. In the interests of a uniform style for this text,
the writer has agreed to use ADHD—that is, without putting the *H* in parentheses. Using
parentheses around *hyperactivity* is a personal invention, included as a reminder to readers
that the official diagnostic label, ADHD, does not reflect the reality for the many diagnosed
ADDers who do not manifest symptoms of hyperactivity. The issues problematic for these
non-hyperactive children, adolescents, and adults are uniquely different from those of their
hyperactive peers. They do indeed have poorly regulated activity levels, typically manifested as hypoactivity (under-activity) or swings between the two, rather than the characteristic over-activity. Frequently associated with the low energy of these non-hyperactives
are symptoms of severe disorganization and distractibility. Since these children, adolescents, and adults have symptoms less readily observable than those of impulsivity and
hyperactivity, their unique needs go quietly unmet far too often.

about behavior management, many educators and non-educators alike reply that it is a method used with ADHD students to control inappropriate behavior. *Controlling inappropriate behavior* is actually a misrepresentation, and not an insignificant one either. It implies, first, that it is the teacher who assumes the active role and, second, that the emphasis is on the unwanted behaviors. If controlling inappropriate behavior were the primary goal, the practical application of behavior management would be an exercise in futility. Rather, it is to facilitate the learning of skills, the active role being assumed by the student. Further, the emphasis is on increasing the incidence of appropriate behaviors and decreasing that of inappropriate ones.

Drew's teacher, for example, was at her wit's end when I first observed him in her classroom. Mrs. F. was a caring, dedicated teacher who welcomed both the parents' and my input. Her general classroom management was effective, and she had good rapport with her students, including Drew. She used positive behavior management techniques, ignoring inappropriate behavior when possible, praising individual students in private. With Drew, she had been using an individualized management plan that included, among other things, daily home–school notes to monitor behavior, the current day's schedule taped to the desktop, and a positive behavior star chart updated throughout the day. In spite of these strategies, Drew's behavior continued to be disruptive.

Work completion was not a problem except that he rushed through it, and his writing was always messy. Grades were also not a problem as Drew was a straight-*A* student, except for an *F* in citizenship/conduct. However, his acting out and clowning around were definitely problems. It seems that Drew would race through his work not caring what the product looked like, get finished long before his classmates, and then start disrupting the class. One of his personal favorite diversions was to get up on his chair and wriggle around until he'd lose his balance and tumble off it to the raucous laughter of his audience. He played aquarium-bowl-ball, tossing crumpled papers over the heads of two rows of students in an attempt to sink a shot. (Based upon the results noted on the tally sheets he kept of these games, he was an incredibly good shot.) None of this was performed quietly, of course. A running dialogue with no one in particular typically accompanied these various endeavors. Mrs. F. confessed to me that she was just plain tired of hearing Drew's excuse that he behaved like this because he was bored.

Drew's behavior management plan had been only marginally successful because it targeted the disruptive behavior as if it operated in a vacuum. Drew's claim of boredom actually held important clues about the larger context in which the behaviors were occurring. In other words, it could have been an enlightening explanation, but it was missed because the excuse assumption was operational.

There were two reasons for this student's boredom. First, Drew had ADHD with serious impulse-control problems and hyperactivity, his brain demanding novelty and highly intense stimulation. When the environment did not provide this motivation, he created it, behaving inappropriately to keep things interesting, as it were. This second-grader needed intense stimulation for another reason. In addition to having ADHD, he was highly gifted, speaking in complete sentences when he was only eight months old. His IQ tested at 155-plus, and his achievement levels as of mid-first grade ranged between the ninth and eleventh grades.

Mrs. F. agreed to try the new management plan I subsequently developed for Drew, and was pleased with the results. Drew did not magically become a perfect student, nor did the episodes of misbehavior disappear. However, the frequency with which they occurred was reduced. The plan included far too many components to describe in their entirety, but a few of the highlights were as follows:

1. With Drew's permission and at his request, the class was briefed on the new plan. Classmates were given ideas about how to remain unresponsive to Drew's antics when they occurred.
2. The parents were asked to refrain from becoming enmeshed in Drew's after-school complaints and were coached to "hang in" throughout the predictable ups and downs.
3. The upper-school teachers' help was enlisted in sharing study guides and projects that were put together in a binder for Drew. These became his "busy work" when his regular work was finished.
4. Drew became a peer-teacher to other primary children. These sessions were regularly scheduled and took place in another classroom.
5. Recess privileges were not to be revoked for misbehavior. Natural and logical consequences were to be used in place of punishment. For example, Drew earned points towards spending time in the upper-level science lab; conversely, points were lost as a consequence of a particular misbehavior.

Fairness . . . Equality

"It isn't fair!" might well be the most common phrase in the English language. It reverberates through the home of every parent who has more than one child. "Why does he get to stay up until ten o'clock but I have to go to bed at eight-thirty? It isn't fair." "Why does she get to wear makeup but I can't? It isn't fair." Parents know the answers to these questions and do their best to impart the wisdom to their offspring—the rules are different because the children are of different ages. Different factors . . . different rules. This makes sense, does it not?

Something seems to get lost in the translation, though, when the question of fairness surfaces in the classroom. Somehow, the word undergoes a transformation in meaning, taking on a new one in this setting. Judge for yourself—Stewart has ADHD and a hard time writing creative stories because his brain goes way too fast to get the thoughts written on paper. His teacher refuses Mom's request that Stewart be allowed to tape-record his stories on the basis that "It wouldn't be fair to the other children."

Strange, isn't it? Different factors . . . yet the same rules. Per the dictionary definition, the teacher should say, "It wouldn't be *equal* to the other children [in regards to assignment format]." Not every student uses glasses to see the board, but those who need them are always permitted—rather, urged and reminded—to wear them. Most students can write their creative stories on paper, but some, like Stewart, cannot. He needs the help of a tape recorder. With it, he can complete the assignment. Without it, he can't—which brings us to the closely related Can't/ Won't assumption.

Can't . . . Won't

Every morning the teacher distributes seat work assignments to the class. Since there are four different reading groups, four different explanations follow, as directions are given to each of the respective groups. No sooner is the first one called for their lesson than Josh is up out of his seat seeking out a fellow group member's assistance in figuring out what he's supposed to be working on. Josh just *won't* pay attention. Or Josh *refuses* to listen when directions are given. At least, these could be the assumptions of the teacher observing Josh's behavior day after day. If they were, punishment or negative consequences typically would be the behavior management strategy of choice. What if this assumption is faulty, despite how things appear to be? What if Josh is confused about his assignments every day because he can't filter out the extraneous noise competing for his sensory attention—papers are being shuffled around, textbook pages are being turned, questions are being asked and answered, and the principal's voice is coming over the intercom as it does each morning, announcing the events of the day? If this were the case, punishment couldn't "cure" the behavior, and all the star charts in the world accompanied by the most coveted of all rewards couldn't bring about significant change.

It would seem, then, that the first to-do of behavior management is the analysis and adjustment of assumptions. The rationale for this is best explained by these guiding principles of behavior management:

1. Behavior management does not/cannot work in isolation.
2. Behavior management must be viewed within the larger context of the interplay of *learning, behavior, and the environment.*
3. Behavior management must include modifications to the specific learning environment.

Although behavior management as a specific method was quantified in a science laboratory, it is not an invention of humans, but rather a component of the complex behavior known as learning. It is part and parcel of our daily lives. We go to work and collect a paycheck for our efforts. There are exceptions to this depending upon specific situations, like paid leave after childbirth or personal leave days. We drive 50 miles an hour on a street within a 30-mile-an-hour speed limit, and we get a speeding ticket and fine, unless of course, the vehicle we are driving is an ambulance rushing an accident victim to the hospital.

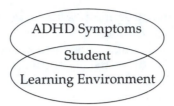

FIGURE 10.1

Whether called rights and responsibilities, or rewards and consequences, the system creates a checks and balances within the larger society. Likewise within the classroom, a collective unit of individual students, rules are established for the "good of the whole," and general behavior management techniques, like those of the larger society, are indigenous to its operations.

We already have firsthand knowledge about the mechanisms of behavior management by virtue of experiencing it in our own daily lives. There is no great mystery about it in a general sense. When it comes to applying it, however, we often forget that it is part of a much larger framework. It does not work effectively in isolation because learning and behavior do not "work" independently of each other. They function interactively within the larger context of the classroom environment. And as we saw in the vignette about Josh, when the dynamics of ADHD are added to the mix, this functional interaction becomes even more complex.

In working with the ADHD student, then, it is essential that a teacher look closely at the various elements of this interaction, gathering relevant information from observations over a period of several weeks about the interplay of behavior, antecedents, and consequences.

This process is called functional analysis, and it results in a *contextual blueprint* that can be used to tailor the best possible environment–student fit. The reader should note that the operative principle here is to *fit the education to the student*, not the other way around.

Functional Analysis: B(ehavior) A(ntecedent) C(onsequence)

- describe the problem behavior in objective, nonjudgmental terms
- identify the antecedents—the prompts or cues that seem to "set the stage"
- identify the consequences—how they follow the behavior and on what schedule
- analyze how antecedents and consequences affect the behavior

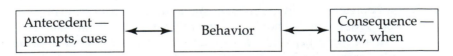

FIGURE 10.2

What about Responsibility and Personal Accountability?

That modifications to the learning environment are essential to behavior management should not be taken to mean that inappropriate behavior is the teacher's fault—"If only Mrs. F. had taken a different approach, Drew's behavior would not have gotten out of control. . . ." Now, that would be one gigantic leap of a (il)logic! If Drew's behavior were not disruptive in the first place, Mrs. F. would not need to modify an environment that was effective in facilitating learning for the majority of her students.

A circular argument in logic? It could be viewed that way if it weren't for the equality/fairness and can't/won't puzzle pieces. If given the choice, Josh, Drew, Stewart, Suzy Q, and most other ADHD individuals most assuredly would not want to be the identifiably lazy, noncompliant, impertinent, underachieving students in their respective classrooms, disappointing themselves, their families, their teachers, and their peers. After years of failure, defense mechanisms become learned and protective walls of "I don't care" are erected, but in the beginning, and later under the suits of armor, are children, adolescents, and adults yearning to be happy and successful and anguishing that they are not. The neurological disorder of ADHD is central to their respective problems, and their behaviors are manifestations of its associated symptoms. No one is to blame for the inappropriate behaviors, but everyone, teachers and ADHD students alike, have responsibilities in their regard.

It is the teacher's responsibility to create a classroom environment conducive to learning. As a matter of fact, if it weren't for linguistic awkwardness, the word *teacher* would be replaced throughout this chapter with the phrase *one who facilitates learning and the acquisition of skills*. Our job is to teach math facts, science lab procedures, concepts in political science, and the like—the learning is the student's responsibility. An adolescent I know was repeatedly sent to the office by his student teacher. Totally confused about algebraic formulas, he had already failed the first three quarters, so knew he couldn't pass for the year. Every day he went to class, quietly sitting with his head in his hand, and most days he ended up finishing class in the counselor's office. The offense noted on the referral forms was not his head-in-hand behavior, but rather his disrespectful comments—she would insist that he sit up and try harder because she had to teach him this information. And he would reply that she had the right to teach him, but she could not make him understand and learn.

All a teacher can do is facilitate learning; he or she cannot *make it* happen. Our examination of assumptions and paradigms and the imperative that they be scrutinized for fallacies was not a collective criticism about the shortcomings of teachers. It was to raise awareness about how faulty assumptions can sabotage our efforts to use behavior management effectively. This awareness and a concomitant knowledge about Attention Deficit Hyperactivity Disorder are tools that can help the teacher address the unique needs of these students. Therefore, the educator's responsibility is to establish a management framework within which the individual ADHD student has a chance of experiencing success. This environment is one that has been modified to: optimize learning—minimize weaknesses—maximize strengths. Within this structure, the ADHD student is responsible for self-management, with ongoing support, of course. In this safe environment that makes success possible, he or she has the opportunity to make mistakes and the responsibility to learn from them, thereby adding new ways of behaving to his or her repertoire.

Personal accountability is then an essential part of this assumption of responsibility. Although the balance of a behavior management plan is weighted toward positive reinforcement, how does negative reinforcement, or accountability, fit into the picture?

Let's assume for the moment that you have to go to work every day with no expectation of receiving a paycheck. Granted, many do this in volunteer work, but it is by choice—although there are no financial rewards, there are many emotional ones. In your situation, however, there are few non-financial rewards for you at your job either, save the occasional pat on the back. Instead, your boss routinely berates you for your poor performance, forbids you to take any breaks until the quality of your work improves, and threatens even harsher reprisals for your continued refusal to "shape up." What effect do you suppose this would have on your motivation? This would never happen in the society of the workplace—at least the part about not being paid. The rest of the scenario certainly can, and does, happen.

Regrettably, this is not unlike the way school is experienced by far too many ADHD students. Reacting to various behaviors without understanding that they are symptomatic of an underlying disorder, teachers frequently use punishment in an attempt to control them. Punishment is given for all sorts of reasons—missing homework and classwork assignments, messy desks, poor attitude, talking. Punishment doesn't work and, in some cases, paradoxically makes things worse. An ADHD student expends an incredible amount of energy "willing" his brain to stay focused. In spite of these efforts, however, most work is not completed, and that which is completed is rejected for its poor quality. Punishing this child for not *trying hard enough* is a virtual guarantee that he or she will stop trying altogether because personal efforts have been judged insufficient and unacceptable. If failure is a given, what motivation could there possibly be to attempt the impossible?

Accountability, Punishment, and Consequences

I have a cartoon I use in my workshops of an unfortunate young miscreant awaiting execution. As he stands on the gallows, neck in the noose, he suggests, "Instead of this, could we try behavior modification?" The transparency always evokes laughter from the audience, and humor, as readers are undoubtedly aware, is a highly useful teaching tool.

Although the precise nature of this young man's unacceptable behavior is a mystery, one cannot assume that it was necessarily reprehensible or unforgivable. The crime and punishment cycle is often far from logical and objective. During the 1920s, for example, my mother was repeatedly and soundly whacked on the left hand with a branch each time she made the grievous mistake of writing with it instead of the correct one. Never mind that her left hand was her dominant one.

Instead of this, could we
try behavior modification?

FIGURE 10.3

The raised and reddened welts she sported on it for much of first grade were, according to her teacher's explanation, "for her own good." At some point, the branch was replaced by a more modern and civilized device: the paddle. Many of my colleagues had one at the ready at all times. One never knew when a youngster would fail to return his homework or throw a chair at a classmate. There's that crime and punishment problem again. A "swat-able" offense in one classroom could be simply a reprimand in another.

The arbitrary nature of punishment is really a small part of the problem. After all, the alternative would be an operating manual of universally codified classroom rules and mandatory "sentencing" procedures. Now that's a frightening thought! No, the notable problem with any form of punishment is that it doesn't work with anyone except someone who doesn't need it. This is not a play on words or a brain teaser to get the reader's attention. It is a fact that requires examination because it has important relevance to the subject of behavior management.

Punishment is aversive. It is something done to someone by someone else. Its goal is to stop the recurrence of an act judged to be inappropriate or unacceptable. To accomplish this, it has concomitant objectives, such as to cause humiliation, unpleasantness, or even pain (as in the practice of swatting); to withdraw acceptance or even affection; or to remove assorted privileges. Is its use ever justified? Yes, of course. A toddler should be physically grabbed and subdued to prevent his or her running into the street. Physical assaultive behavior requires immediate and unequivocal intervention, short of matching it in kind. The issue for us, however, is not its justification, or lack thereof, but its effectiveness—or, as we should say, ineffectiveness.

Let's try a little experiment. For the next ten minutes, stop reading and do not think of pink elephants. Under no circumstances are visual learners to see them in their mind's eye, painted in various shades of mauve or cotton-candy pastels, auditory learners to imagine the sounds of trumpeting or pounding hoofs or "read/spell" the letters of the words *pink elephant,* and kinesthetic/tactile learners to sense their movement, shape, or texture. Now do what you were told not to do. By the way, the sentence "I will not be distracted by pink elephants" is to be written 100 times by those who are noncompliant.

Admittedly, this may be slightly off center regarding the subject at hand, but not as far afield as it may initially appear. The specific point here is that in the absence of an alternative, forgoing a specific behavior is well-nigh impossible to accomplish. This is the mechanism at work, for example, when weight loss is attempted. The goal of weight loss programs is to assist the client in breaking a learned behavior—the habit of overeating—not simply by stopping it, but by substituting another behavior in its place. The underlying principle is that learning is easier than unlearning. The harder we try to break a bad habit—i.e., try to unlearn an inappropriate behavior—the more deeply entrenched the learning becomes, because we are inadvertently reinforcing it in the thinking about it. Or in other words, if one is to get out of a hole, one must stop digging, or the hole will just keep getting deeper.

The shortcoming of punishment, then, is its emphasis on *what not to do.* It is left to the student's imagination and resourcefulness to figure out what to do instead. Clearly, this is not the teacher's intention. Rules are posted and reviewed. Children who are behaving appropriately are identified as models of good behavior. Reminders are given. *I-messages* are shared, as in, "I need for you to use a quieter voice." These strategies are so effective, in fact, that they make punishment virtually a non-issue for the so-called "normal" child. Following those occasions that this child is punished, a repeat performance is unlikely as the lesson has been learned fairly effortlessly. The child knows the rules, clearly understands how personal actions are at odds with those rules, and has the skills to behave in accordance with them. Punishment works for this someone who doesn't need it.

For anyone else—individuals with ADHD, for example—it doesn't work well at all. They also know the rules. Just ask them. Sometimes they hear the reminders, observe the modeling of appropriate behavior in action, and acknowledge the *I-messages.* With faulty sensory filtering systems, though, they may miss them entirely because their brains are engaged in counting thumbtacks on the bulletin board, hearing cars whooshing by and contemplating their destinations, and keenly feeling the discomfort of clothing rubbing against their skin. When the teacher, in exasperation, takes away recess privileges, they are abruptly pulled back from their respective distractions, none too happily either. Angry outbursts are not uncommon when realization dawns that they are in trouble again. They are instructed to think about what they did wrong while they sit out recess in the classroom so that next time they will remember how they are to behave correctly.

There are readily apparent problems with this process. The first is that knowing the rules—that is, having the ability to recite the list—does not equate with having the requisite skill to stop and think first, and act later. Second, these students are not entirely sure what it is they did wrong in the first place since they weren't "there" when the infraction occurred. Third, for the concrete thinking, *now is the only moment* for the student with ADHD, there is little to relate the act of sitting in the classroom and thinking with future events. Fourth, as was previously noted, unlearning a behavior by thinking about not doing it is counterproductive, strengthening and reinforcing the unwanted behavior that led to the punishment. Fourth, the *what not to do* factor is simply fuel for the fire of an ADHD student's expansive imagination: "I'm not supposed to run in the classroom? OK, I'll skip, leap, gallop. . . . I'm not supposed to talk so loud? How loud is loud? Loud like a radio? Loud like a wailing firetruck siren? I could maybe sing loud instead." Finally, there is the negative impact of repeated failure that is insidiously hazardous to motivation, wreaking havoc on the learning process. Is it any wonder that many ADHD students simply give up? Punishment certainly does have a learning outcome, but often not the one a teacher desires nor intends.

Logical and Natural Consequences

There is a better way. *Instead of this, could we try behavior (modification) management?* Yes, we could and we should. Do not infer from this, however, that behavior management's primary role is as an alternative to punishment; this is the "spin" put on it by far too many. It should be clear by this point in the chapter that the issue of accountability is integrated into the whole of behavior management and is addressed specifically with logical and natural consequences.

When each of my children attended a Montessori preschool, parents were forewarned that *natural consequences* would be a way of life for youngsters. Rain, for instance, was considered an opportunity for wonderful, hands-on learning experiences and would not deter the class from using the outdoor environment. Parents were advised to dress children appropriately and to expect offspring to arrive home with wet shirt sleeves and dampened pants. We were also told to expect some of our children to arrive home completely soaked to the skin—those who chose to ignore the teacher's instructions to put on their raingear before going out. This natural consequence was experienced up close and personal, so to speak. It eventually made an impression on even the most contrary preschooler, like this writer's son with ADHD, who stopped coming home soaked after the fourth or fifth rainstorm. Care must be taken, however, that natural consequences are used to facilitate experiential learning and not to sugar-coat what is in reality punishment intended "to teach that kid a lesson."

Natural consequences cannot be used in every situation. Using the natural consequence of standing barefooted in the snow because boots are refused is most assuredly not an option, for example. The best alternative in these situations is the application of a predetermined *logical consequence.* Like punishment, it is invoked as a result of misbehavior. Unlike punishment, the focus is not on the misdeed but on the behavioral skill the student is learning as an alternative and more acceptable response. In most cases, then, a logical consequence is the flip side of a corresponding reward, as we saw in Drew's behavior management plan highlights. The advantage of logical consequences is that they make responsibility and accountability largely the province of the student. The privilege of spending time in the science lab Drew so dearly loves is his for the taking . . . or for the losing. There are a variety of ways the logical consequence/reward process can be applied using the strategies of response–cost and token economy reinforcement, signed teacher–student contracts, and self-monitoring formats. Their specifics will be left to the reader to pursue through other avenues, however.

The Teacher's Role as Coach

In recent years, a new approach has become part of the ADHD treatment protocol. It is called Coaching. Although originally targeted for the ADDult population, its basic philosophy and objectives are, in this writer's opinion, well-suited for adolescents and, with adaptations, for younger children as well. In fact, when it comes to the behavior management paradigm suggested throughout these pages, the teacher's role is that of Coach. As the word *coach* may conjure images of the one running up and down the sidelines of a football field, shouting at players and referees, it would do well to clarify what ADHD Coaching is all about and how it dovetails with behavior management.

The goal of Coaching is to improve the life "fit" across the spectrum of activities: work, school, recreation, self-care, relationships, etc. The essence of its philosophy, captured in the proverb "If the shoe doesn't fit, don't blame the foot," is but a variation of that of fitting the education to the child, rather than trying to fit the child into the education. Coaching, like behavior management, is client-based, the "practices" evolving from identified goals. If an adult client, for example, is in danger of being fired due to repeated missed project completion deadlines, the Coach would facilitate an analysis of the situation. Through this process of problem solving, the Coach would help the client to identify strengths and weaknesses, the factors contributing to the problem, and the client's larger goals, among other things. If the client's goal was to keep the current job, the Coach and client would work together to design systems such as time management tracking forms. Depending on the particular client, a schedule of check-in phone calls might be established wherein the coach and client would have periodic discussions about where a current project was in relation to the long-range plan that they had developed. On the other hand, during the process of problem solving, the client might become aware that the responsibilities of this particular job overtax his or her weakest skills and that the "fit" really doesn't work well. The Coach would in this case help the client zero in on what would be a better setting, one in which he or she would be better able to capitalize on strengths.

Is this not much like the role a teacher plays with students with ADHD—problem solving, goal setting, developing systems, periodically evaluating how things are going, and the like? In this role the teacher can use techniques similar to those used by the professional ADHD Coach: interviewing, observing, overseeing, supporting, cheerleading, nudging, and, yes, even nagging sometimes. The goals that are set must be meaningful to the student/client, and they must be achievable. With students, this means teachers need to be aware of individual learning styles and unique strengths that can be used to bypass weaknesses. Teachers need to consider the classroom fit regarding not only the student's style but also their own. Sometimes a "change in venue" could be the best behavior management plan possible; this would not be an admission of failure but a recognition of the importance of "fit."

Part detective, part systems analyst, the teacher as Coach gathers evidence, views the whole of the captured image through a wide-angle perceptual lens, and analyzes how and why the parts operate as they do within the larger environment. His or her observation that a student doesn't turn in homework assignments is not used as a conclusion but as the catalyst for a series of relevant questions. Is homework completed in some subjects but not in others, suggesting the need for skill remediation in a particular content area rather than a rewards–consequences contract? Is homework that is turned in typically incomplete? This could reflect lack of skills, assignments too lengthy or complex for the students with ADHD attentional stamina, or simply an overly busy after-school regimen of sports and work. For a 14-year-old boy I was Coaching, the general source of his homework problem turned out to be disorganization.

Tim had done relatively well in school until he started seventh grade. This is not atypical of students with ADHD. In fact, the diagnosis of ADHD occurs commonly during the first, fourth, and seventh grades as the transition into these grade levels is accompanied by significant changes in teacher expectations and performance standards. Seventh-graders should already know how to study and organize themselves and their materials so that they have what they need when they need it. Like many students with ADHD, these "shoulds" were his undoing. He was too old to need help organizing his notebook and study guides, or so the thinking went, despite the fact that many disorganized adults could not function effectively without their secretaries and personal organizers.

By mid-eighth grade, Tim's grades had fallen significantly in large part due to the zeroes accumulated as a result of his not turning in homework assignments. He was doing particularly poorly in science, his average a 62% when I first interviewed him. As Tim's Coach, my objective was to figure out the *why* of the behavior. Tim knew the answer, telling me within the first 15 minutes of our meeting that he actually did his homework most of the time but never had it on hand to turn in on time—it was always in the *other* notebook in his locker or somewhere in his backpack. He had told his teachers the same thing, but with the mind-set that these were excuses, they missed the explanation entirely, thereby responding to the problem by taking points off Tim's overall grade in the respective courses. I met with Tim's mother for the second half of our session, and her perception of the situation bore out what Tim had explained to me. At home, his room was in a constant state of disarray, his clothes a rumpled pile on the floor, his desk covered with the debris of books, outdated assignment lists, and last year's quiz papers. Needless to say, punishment would not address Tim's real problem.

For our second meeting, Tim was to bring his backpack and current science study guide, latest test paper, textbook, and notes so we could get a handle on why he was repeatedly failing tests in this subject despite the fact that his teacher was tutoring him for an hour, once a week after school. Predictably, Tim's study guide was nowhere to be found in the depths of the black hole that was his backpack. Neither was the test nor the notes. He did manage to locate his textbook.

He agreed that keeping all materials in one binder would address the messy locker and backpack problem. Often, organizing by color is helpful for students with ADHD since many are strong visual learners, but not for Tim, whom I had identified as an auditory learner through a simple set of preference questions. Tim didn't like the option of an alphabetical system, choosing instead to organize his binder according to his daily schedule of class periods. The first page of each subject division was a pocket folder to hold the current homework assignment. The second page was a back-to-back manila folder so current study guides, teacher handouts, etc., could be put in the front and then moved to the back when a new topic of study was started in class. The remainder of the section was for Tim's notes. His assignment book was at the front of the binder, and Tim was to begin not only writing down assignments, but also listing the specific supplies he would need to complete each one. After school, a quick glance at the supply lists would help him grab the correct textbook from his locker, which was to be specially organized with morning books on the top shelf and afternoon ones on the bottom.

I saw Tim twice more at two-week intervals. It was clear that the system was working because his backpack contained nothing but his lunch bag, textbooks, and binder. He had also raised his science grade eighteen points by using the flashcards I suggested he make for each chapter—terms/concepts on one side, definition/description on the back. Tim had been doing beautifully in English, getting A's on book reports, so poor comprehension skills were ruled out as a factor. As had been guessed, Tim understood what had been read, but had no system for committing that information to memory. Through a process of listening to the student client and blending the answers with the observations, I was able to design a relatively simple yet effective behavior management plan to provide the organizational systems Tim needed to manage what had appeared to be a problem with homework completion.

It is undoubtedly clear that the general elements of the Coaching process described and used by this writer are similar and directly applicable—with slight modifications—to the behavior management paradigm proposed in this chapter:

1. information gathering and brainstorming
   - review of relevant school history, testing, work samples
   - multiple classroom observations of the student in different settings at different times of day, to include transition times

- interview with parent(s), teachers, and other school personnel, including but not limited to the principal, instructional assistants, and counselor
2. identification of short-term and long-term goals
3. record keeping and compliance system design
4. specific monitoring and feedback schedule: frequency, duration, and method—i.e., phone check-ins, face-to-face meetings, or both
5. team approach—sharing resources, information, plans, progress, etc., with parents and appropriate school personnel

A Reality Check

Needless to say, the professional Coach has the luxury of working with only one client at a time. Time, in such short supply for the classroom teacher, is not an issue in one-on-one Coaching. Complete attention can be devoted to individualizing a behavior management plan for one student. How then can one use a Coaching/behavior management model with individual ADHD students when 25 or more other students need attention? In the words of Theodore Roosevelt, the answer is just to "Do what you can, with what you have, with where you are."

First and foremost, this means to do an expectations self-check. How realistic is each expectation? The caveats below may prove helpful:

- **Caveat One**—Behavior management, like medicine, is not a magical cure for the behavioral symptoms of ADHD because the disorder cannot be cured, only managed. Guard against personal feelings of failure by having realistic expectations about outcome.
- **Caveat Two**—Individual accommodations and modifications must fit not only the student but also the personal and professional realities of the teacher. They must be time- and cost-effective and doable in regards to one's personality and unique teaching style. They must be doable given the available resources of a particular school.
- **Caveat Three**—The concept of *available resources* and the roles they play must be enlarged. If on-site counseling is available, the teacher can enlist the counselor's help with some of the Coaching tasks, the two professionals sharing responsibility for developing a behavior management plan. Teachers work in their classrooms, and counselors work in their offices. How much more effective it would be for the two roles to mesh into a joint effort. Individual teachers would do well to work towards a greater team effort. Colleagues can help by doing observations during their planning periods with a mutual agreement of reciprocity. Instructional assistants can be called on to take over the class for 15-minute periodic intervals to afford one-on-one time between student and teacher. Special arrangements can be made with the principal or assistant principal for some time-out so the teacher–coach could work with an individual student. Let's especially not forget the contributions that parents can make to the process and the input the student himself/herself can provide. Finally, at the very least, teachers can link the family with community resources, such as

local ADHD support groups, which often maintain referral lists of local professional Coaches and other ADHD-informed educational professionals, tutors, and therapists.

Conclusion

The behavior management-Coaching model presented in this chapter suggests a more complex and larger view of the subject than that of reward-and-consequence strategies. It challenges the teacher to examine his or her role and to question a number of sometimes long-held assumptions about behavior and how it should be managed. It also requires a personal commitment to professional growth and a substantial investment of personal time and energy. This initial commitment and investment, however, pays enormous dividends later.

Teachers have the responsibility for and the privilege of helping ADHD students reach their full potential. Many ADDults, this writer included, would not opt for a "cure" even if one existed because many of the ADHD characteristics so problematic in childhood become assets in adulthood. In general, ADHD kids make terrific adults! It's the getting there that's so tricky. Let me leave readers with the following. I hope you find it inspiring. When asked to identify what helped them the most, the majority of successful ADDults say that it was having one person who truly believed in them. The person mentioned most often? A teacher.

Suggested Readings

Gordon, M. (1993). *I would if I could: A teenager's guide to ADHD*. New York: G.S.I.

Hallowell, E. M., & Ratey, J. J. (1994). *Driven to distraction: Recognizing and coping with Attention Deficit Disorder from childhood through adulthood*. New York: Fireside.

Kelly, K., & Ramundo, P. (1995). *You mean I'm not lazy, stupid or crazy?! A self-help book for adults with Attention Deficit Disorder*. New York: Fireside, 1995.

Setley, S. (1995). *Taming the Dragons: Real help for real school problems*. St. Louis: Starfish.

Silver, L. B. (1992). *The misunderstood child: A guide for parents of children with learning disabilities* (2nd ed.). Blue Ridge Summit, PA: Tab.

Solden, S. (1995). *Women with Attention Deficit Disorder: Embracing disorganization at home and in the workplace*. Grass Valley, CA: Underwood.

Chapter *11*

Legal Rights of People Who Have ADHD

PATRICIA H. LATHAM   *PETER S. LATHAM*

Statutory Overview and Basic Information

The Fifth and Fourteenth Amendments to the United States Constitution are the most important source of constitutional rights for individuals with disabilities, including those with ADHD. In order to ensure that employment, education, and access to public accommodations are open to all individuals with disabilities, Congress enacted three key federal statutes.

The Rehabilitation Act of 1973

The Rehabilitation Act of 1973 (RA), 29 U.S.C.A. §701 et seq., made discrimination against individuals with disabilities unlawful in three areas: employment by the executive branch of the federal government, employment by most federal government contractors, and activities funded by federal subsidies or grants. This third category includes all public elementary and secondary schools and most postsecondary institutions. The statutory section that prohibits discrimination in grants was numbered §504 in the original legislation and is often referred to simply as "Section 504." Under Section 504, individuals with impairments that substantially limit a major life activity, such as learning, are entitled to academic adjustments and auxiliary aids and services so that courses, examinations, and services will be accessible to them.

The Individuals with Disabilities Education Act

In 1975, Congress enacted a statute titled the Education for All Handicapped Children Act. That statute, now called the Individuals with Disabilities Education Act

(IDEA), 20 U.S.C.A. §1400 et seq., which was reauthorized in June 1997, provides funds to state and local elementary and secondary schools for public education, including the education of children with disabilities. It provides for a free appropriate public education (FAPE) and represents a unique approach to civil rights in that the IDEA provides at least a part of the funds that enable these school systems to comply with federal disability-based civil rights laws. Comparable financing does not exist for compliance with race- and gender-based civil rights laws. Under the IDEA, the school is responsible for identifying and evaluating students with disabilities who by reason thereof need special education.

The Americans with Disabilities Act of 1990

In 1990, Congress enacted the Americans with Disabilities Act (ADA), 42 U.S.C.A. §12101 et seq. This act extended the concepts of "Section 504" to (1) employers with 15 or more employees (Title I); (2) all activities of state and local governments, including but not limited to employment and education (Title II); and (3) virtually all places that offer goods and services to the public—termed "places of public accommodation" (Title III). In addition, ADA standards apply to employment by Congress.

Elementary and Secondary Schools

Public elementary and secondary schools are governed by the IDEA, the RA, and the ADA. Private, nonsectarian elementary and secondary schools are governed by the ADA. All private schools that receive federal funding are subject to the RA. Only those religiously controlled schools that receive no federal funds are exempt, and many of these opt to pursue a policy of nondiscrimination towards those with disabilities.

IDEA (Individuals with Disabilities Education Act)

The IDEA has been the most important influence shaping public policy towards those children and adolescents with disabilities. The overall goal of the IDEA is to "ensure equality of opportunity, full participation, independent living, and economic self-sufficiency for individuals with disabilities." To put over 100 pages of fine print in a nutshell, the IDEA provides that each child with a disability shall have available to him or her a free appropriate public education that provides special education and related services by means of an individualized education program designed to meet the unique needs of that child and prepare him or her for employment and independent living. Each area is the subject of extensive implementing of regulations and court decisions.

Special education and related services are, according to the Department of Education, delivered in several basic modes ranging from regular classes (which represent the greatest inclusion) through the resource room and separate classes to home-bound/hospital environments (which represent the least inclusion). In general, students with ADHD are served in the environments with fewer restrictions.

In *Commonwealth of Virginia Department of Education v. Richard W. Riley, United States Secretary of Education* (1996.C04.1659), the Fourth Circuit considered the obligations that a state accepts as a condition of federal funding. Virginia had a policy under which a child with a disability could be deprived of all educational services by way of expulsion or long-term suspension if that child misbehaved in a manner unrelated to his or her disability. Following a hearing, the U.S. Department of Education ruled that the Virginia policy was contrary to the IDEA and that all of Virginia's IDEA-B funds should be withheld unless and until the state amended that policy to provide that expelled or suspended children with disabilities could receive educational services in an alternative setting.

Duty to Identify

Central to the IDEA is the duty of every school district to identify students with disabilities. Under the IDEA, the school is responsible for identifying students with disabilities who by reason thereof need special education and related services and for providing to them such special education and services. The IDEA (20 U.S.C. §1413 (a)(1)) requires that state or local educational agencies "shall conduct a full and individual initial evaluation" in order "(i) to determine whether a child is a child with a disability (as defined in [the IDEA]); and (ii) to determine the educational needs of such child." The IDEA is quite specific about the methods by which evaluations are to be conducted. These methods are required by 20 U.S.C. §1413 in all evaluations, re-evaluations, and IEP preparations. The educational agency must, under these detailed requirements, perform assessment that is both comprehensive and objective.

In a letter of findings issued to Camdenton (MO) Parish R-III School District, OCR Docket No. 07931031, 20 IDELR 197 (Apr. 30, 1993), the Office for Civil Rights of the U.S. Department of Education ruled that ADHD is covered by the definition of disability and required a school district "to evaluate a student who may need special education or related aids and services because of any disability, including ADHD, which substantially limits a major life activity."

A school district may not evade its responsibilities. In *Pasatiempo v. Aizawa* (1996.C09.930), the Ninth Circuit struck down a school district's scheme to avoid compliance with the IDEA. There, a Hawaiian school district created a special class of assessments for students whom it did not suspect of having a disability, but who exhibited "achievement delays or adjustment difficulties, which may require alternative teaching strategies." The scope of these evaluations was approximately as extensive as those contemplated for students with "suspected" disabilities, with one critical difference: the district's due process procedures did not apply to disputes concerning these evaluations. The district's assessment method would have permitted it to meet every parent's request for evaluation with a determination that the district did not "suspect" the existence of a disability, to be followed by its own assessment and placement, neither of which could be contested in a due process hearing or in court. The court enjoined the use of this procedure, stating that it would give the school district "almost absolute control over whether parents and students may avail themselves of the procedural protections offered under the IDEA and §504."

Informed parental consent is required for evaluation. Disagreements between parents and school authorities concerning evaluations are to be resolved through mediation and due process hearings.

Child with a Disability

A child must (1) have a listed disability and (2) "by reason thereof need special education and related services." The IDEA applies to every "child with a disability," which 20 U.S.C.A. §1401(3)(A) defines this way: "The term 'child with a disability' means a child . . . with . . . serious emotional disturbance (hereinafter referred to as 'emotional disturbance' . . . other health impairments, or specific learning disabilities; and . . . who, by reason thereof, needs special education and related services." The IDEA further defines a "specific learning disability" as "a disorder in one or more of the basic psychological processes involved in understanding or in using language, spoken or written, which disorder may manifest itself in imperfect ability to listen, think, speak, read, write, spell, or do mathematical calculations." Examples of specific learning disabilities given by the IDEA are "perceptual disabilities, brain injury, minimal brain dysfunction and dyslexia." ADHD is not expressly mentioned by the IDEA but is mentioned in the regulations as an "other health impairment." In addition, the Department of Education has ruled that children with ADHD may receive services under the categories of "other health impairment," "specific learning disability," or "serious emotional disturbance" if they meet the statutory criteria for those conditions. Those rulings are set forth in two Department of Education memoranda dated September 16, 1991, and April 29, 1993. Moreover, numerous cases recognize ADHD as a condition covered by the IDEA when it requires special education and related services. (See, for example, *Capistrano Unified School District v. Wartenberg*, 59 F.3d 884, 9th Cir. 1995.) Others clearly hold that it is an impairment within the meaning of the RA and the ADA. (See, for example, *Bercovitch v. Baldwin School, Inc.*, Docket No. 97-1739, 1st Cir. Jan. 12, 1998, and *Davidson v. Midelfort Clinic, Ltd.*, Docket No. 96-28.)

Needs for Special Education and Related Services

To be covered by the IDEA, the child's disability must be such that the child needs special education and related services. Special education is "specially designed instruction (including physical education), at no cost to parents, to meet the unique needs of a child with a disability" whereas related services are "such developmental, corrective, and other supportive services as may be required to assist a child with a disability to benefit from special education." They include transportation and psychological services, but not medical services other than those undertaken for diagnostic and evaluation purposes.

The I.E.P. (Individualized Education Program)

Special education and related services are delivered by means of an "individualized education program" (IEP) that reflects agreement between the school district and the parents regarding the placement and the specific services that will be delivered. Failure to agree triggers a right to a due process hearing, whose purpose is to create an IEP based on evidence to be supplied from a variety of sources, including classroom teachers, parents, and professionals. The IDEA does not require any particular method for delivering special education and related services. Rather, it provides a procedure for the development of an IEP that is intended to consider all factors relevant to the education of the child with a disability.

The IDEA requires that an IEP "team" be assembled and that the "team" prepare an IEP by considering various factors listed in the statute. Each IEP team member ideally brings a different perspective to the process of creating an IEP. In general, the team is intended to possess knowledge concerning (1) the child, (2) the child's disabilities, and (3) the school's resources from which the special education and related services will be provided. The parents are also to be included. The IEP is intended to provide a detailed statement of the special education and related services to be provided, and to this end, the IDEA requires that the IEP address a series of listed factors. Collectively, these provide a description of the child's educational and related service needs and a plan for meeting them.

An item of key importance to many parents whose children have ADHD is the following IEP requirement: "The IEP Team shall—(i) in the case of a child whose behavior impedes his or her learning or that of others, consider, when appropriate, strategies, including positive behavioral interventions, strategies, and supports to address that behavior . . ." (20 U.S.C. §§1413(d)(3)). This provision then ties into the procedures for disciplining a child and for creating an alternative educational placement. In essence, the IDEA requires that all children with disabilities receive education. The question, where discipline is involved, is where that education should take place.

The preparation of the IEP is the most important point at which the parent can help his or her child. It is the time at which the team of experts will have the opportunity to structure a program for him or her. Time, effort, and money are generally far more effective when spent here than anyplace else. However, note that whereas an attorney's presence may be helpful at the IEP meeting, attorneys' "fees may not be awarded relating to any meeting of the IEP Team unless such meeting is convened as a result of an administrative proceeding or judicial action. . . ."

Procedural Protections

An additional federal requirement imposed on the states is the availability of procedural safeguards to protect the rights of children with disabilities and their parents in the special education process. The procedures generally consist of (1) notice to parents, (2) access to school records, (3) the right to participate in the IEP process, (4) voluntary mediation, (5) an administrative (due process) hearing, (6) appeal within the state educational system, and (7) suit in state or federal court.

Inclusion

The new IDEA is based on the fundamental premise that its ultimate goal is to educate children with disabilities in as integrated a setting as is appropriate. The congressional findings embraced the proposition that "Special education should be a service for children with disabilities, not a place where they are sent." The Department of Education's Q&A on the IDEA note that "The new law is designed to remove financial incentives for placing children in more separate settings. . . ."

The requirement for inclusion is a presumption, not a mandate. What this means is that the parent or school district that seeks to deny a child with a disability full inclusion in the school's mainstream educational program must prove that the more limited environment is required (*Hartmann. v. Loudoun County Board of Education*, Docket No. 96-2809, 4th Cir. July 8, 1997.)

Private School Placements

Where no free appropriate public education is available, private schools may be used and the cost should be defrayed at public expense (*Florence County School District Four v. Carter*, 114 S. Ct. 361, 126 L. Ed. 2d 284, 1993). Private education at public expense may become increasingly hard to justify under the new IDEA, especially in cases of mild to moderate impairment; even before the new law, in such cases, courts often denied private school placement. For example, in *Monticello School District No. 25 v. George L. and Carolyn L. et al.* (1996 CO7.794), the Seventh Circuit considered the issue of inclusion in a case involving mild to moderate impairment. There, the parents of a child with mild to moderate ADHD sought placement in a private school for him on the grounds that the public school failed to provide him with a "free appropriate public education" ("FAPE") under the IDEA. The court ruled against the parents.

Student Discipline

The IDEA provides for the use of an "alternative educational setting" as a means of ensuring safety in the schools. The IDEA's new language is set forth at 20 U.S.C. §§1414(k). Basically, the IDEA provides that schools can remove students for up to 10 days for disciplinary purposes without restriction and remove students with guns for an additional 45 days to an interim alternative placement (IAP). The IEP team is required to determine if any of the acts in question are related to the student's disability. If they are not, the school will be permitted to discipline the student with a disability as it would any other student. If they are related, the selection of an appropriate placement is undertaken. The IDEA provides that an assessment of the student's relevant behaviors and reasons for it be on file (20 U.S.C. §§1414(k)(1)(B)).

The new IDEA represents a compromise among many views and states an apparently fair set of principles. Whether it is a satisfactory approach will depend on how it is implemented.

The RA/ADA

The ADA and the RA are civil rights statutes that outlaw discrimination but do not provide funds for the activities mandated by them. Collectively, these statutes created the right to be free from discrimination based on one's disability, and together they apply to virtually every educational institution; most state, local, and federal governmental entities (including professional licensing boards and excepting the federal judiciary); and all private employers with 15 or more employees. Although the coverage differs, the elements to be proven under these statutes are the same.

In order to obtain the protections of the ADA/RA, it must be established that (1) one is an "individual with a disability"; (2) one is "otherwise qualified"; (3) one was denied a job, education, or other benefit by reason of the disability; and (4) the ADA or RA applies to the case. It should be noted that it is not necessary to prove that the individual in question is "otherwise qualified" to receive public elementary or secondary education. All states require that elementary and secondary education be provided to everybody. Everyone, therefore, is qualified to receive public education at these levels. (See the letter of findings issued to Susquehanna Community School District, Docket No. 03931473, Oct. 18, 1993.)

The RA and the ADA are more general in nature than the IDEA and employ a definition of disability that is broader than that found in the IDEA. The IDEA applies only to those disabilities that are specifically enumerated in the statute and regulations and for which "special education" and "related services" are the remedies. Therefore, it is possible for a school district to violate the RA by discriminating against a child with a disability even though the child was not entitled to special education under the IDEA. (See the letter of findings issued to Conejo Valley Unified School District, OCR Docket No. 09-92-1062, Apr. 21, 1992.)

In order to ensure a common approach to individuals with disabilities, all three statutes use the same definition of "specific learning disability" (*Argen v. New York State Bd. of Law Examiners*, 860 F. Supp. 84, W.D.N.Y. 1994; and *Lyons v. Smith*, 829 F. Supp. 414, D.D.C. 1993.) Further, an IEP issued properly under the IDEA complies, as a matter of law, with the RA/ADA. 34 C.F.R. §104.33(b)(2) provided that "Implementation of an individualized education program developed in accordance with [the IDEA] is one means of meeting the standard" of compliance required by the RA.

Failure to comply with disciplinary codes may be treated differently under the RA/ADA where private schools are concerned. Instead of creating the need for an alternative placement, repeated code violations may result in expulsion from a private school, even if the code violations are the product of a disability. That is because compliance with disciplinary codes is an essential element of a private school education under the RA/ADA. In *Bercovitch v. Baldwin School, Inc.*, Docket No. 97-1739 (1st Cir. Jan. 12, 1998), the court held that a student with ADHD was not qualified to attend a college preparatory private school because he was unable to conform in important and basic ways to the school's behavior code. The school was not required to modify its behavior code as an accommodation. To do so, the court found, would, in effect, make it a "special needs" school.

Postsecondary Education

In general, postsecondary education includes college, graduate school, and professional school. These educational programs are not subject to the IDEA but only to the RA and ADA. As noted above, there are four elements that an individual must establish in order to show that he or she is an individual with a disability and entitled to the protection of these laws. Specifically, in order to obtain the protections of the RA/ADA, a person will be required to establish that (1) he or she is an "individual with a disability," (2) he or she is "otherwise qualified," (3) he or she was denied access to the educational program in question "by reason" of the disability, and (4) the postsecondary program is governed by the RA or the ADA.

Postsecondary institutions are affected by the RA and the ADA in three principal areas: (1) testing (for admissions, evaluation of academic performance, and graduation); (2) the delivery of course materials, and (3) nonacademic benefits of campus life—e.g., sports and dormitory living. In the case of ADHD, the first two are the important ones.

Individual with a Disability

The RA/ADA covers three categories of disabilities: (1) a physical or mental impairment that substantially limits one or more of the major life activities of such individual, (2) a record of such impairment, and (3) being regarded as having such an impairment (42 U.S.C. §12102(2)). The first—"physical or mental impairment" that "substantially limits" one or more of a person's "major life activities"—is the most important. There are three prongs to this definition.

Physical or Mental Impairment
"Physical or mental impairment" is the easy one. ADHD is widely recognized as an "impairment" under this definition. (See *Bercovitch v. Baldwin School, Inc.*, Docket No. 97-1739, 1st Cir. Jan. 12, 1998; and *Davidson v. Midelfort Clinic, Ltd.*, Docket No. 96-2860, 7th Cir. Jan. 7, 1998.) In the latter case, the court found that ADHD is an "impairment" within the meaning of the ADA: "There is no dispute that ADHD qualifies as an impairment for purposes of the statute. See 29 C.F.R. sec. 1630.2(H)(2)." Implementing regulations further provide that the term "physical or mental impairment" includes "any mental or psychological disorder, such as mental retardation, organic brain syndrome, emotional or mental illness, and specific learning disabilities" (29 C.F.R. §1613.702(b)).

But the existence of an impairment is not enough. The impairment must be serious enough to "substantially limit" a "major life activity."

Major Life Activity
The major life activities that have been generally recognized are "caring for oneself, performing manual tasks, walking, seeing, hearing, speaking, breathing, learning, and working."

Included in the list of major life activities that the investigators from the Equal Employment Opportunity Commission (EEOC) will recognize are "thinking, concentrating and interacting with others as well as sleeping." The EEOC's emphasis on emotional processes, such as thinking, concentrating, and interacting with other people, confirms more clearly than ever before that the RA and the ADA protect individuals with mental as well as physical impairments.

Substantially Limits

Mild interference with one's life is not considered a disability under the RA/ADA. In *Davidson v. Midelfort Clinic, Ltd.*, Docket No. 96-2860 (7th Cir. Jan. 7, 1998), the court, summarizing applicable regulations, ruled that the term "substantially limits" means that the individual is either unable to perform, or significantly restricted as to the condition, manner or duration under which the individual can perform, a major life activity as compared to an average person in the general population. In the context of postsecondary education, learning is the major life activity most often alleged to have been limited substantially. A limitation of a major life activity must be substantial, compared to most people.

A limitation may be substantial in one context and not another. In *Davidson v. Midelfort Clinic, Ltd.*, Docket No. 96-2860 (7th Cir. Jan. 7, 1998), the court recognized that an individual with ADHD might be limited substantially in learning in an educational setting but not in employment. Therefore, an individual would have to establish that he or she is substantially limited in learning in the workplace environment in order to obtain accommodations there.

Otherwise Qualified

An "otherwise qualified" individual is one who, though possessed of a disability, would be qualified for the education with or without a reasonable accommodation. (See *Wynne v. Tufts Univ. School of Medicine*, 932 F. 2d 19, 1st Cir. 1991, aff'd. 976 F. 2d 791, 1st Cir. 1992, cert. denied, 507 U.S. 1030 (1993); *Pandazides v. Virginia Bd. of Educ.*; 946 F. 2d 345, 4th Cir. 1991, rev'd, 13 F. 3d 823, 4th Cir. 1994; and Letter of Findings Issued to Florida Department of Education, OCR Docket No. 04931399, Region IV 1993.)

In *Ellis v. Morehouse School of Medicine* (925 F. Supp. 1529, N.D. Ga. 1996), Ellis, an individual with dyslexia, requested and received a decelerated first-year curriculum and double time within which to complete his examinations. The medical school refused to provide a decelerated program for the third and fourth years, which consisted of clinical rather than classroom programs, on the grounds that the accommodations would require modification of the essential nature of the clinical programs. Ellis was found to lack the ability to understand patients, to formulate a diagnosis, to follow protocols for patient care, and to integrate and process information accurately and promptly in a clinical setting. He was disenrolled from the medical school, he brought suit under the RA/ADA, and he lost. The court ruled that Ellis was not otherwise qualified to be a doctor and that medical school accommodations are required only for individuals with disabilities who request them.

In a letter of findings issued to St. Louis Community College at Meramec (OCR Docket No. 07912049, Jan. 16, 1992), the Department of Education held that a student with ADHD who met admissions criteria was a qualified individual with a disability. When the student requested additional time for tests but not the right to use looseleaf sheets for laboratory notetaking and the right to transcribe those notes into the lab book, the educational institution was permitted to lower his laboratory grades for failure to comply with the requirement that all notes be entered directly during the laboratory session. Remember: no institution is obligated to provide assistance that has not been requested. (Accord: Letter of Findings issued to Almont Community Sch. Dist., OCR Docket No. 15-96-1140, Oct. 11, 1996.)

Applicants and students who are seeking to obtain accommodations must present reasonable documentation to support the requested accommodations. In *Dubois v. Alderson-Broaddus College, Inc.* (950 F. Supp. 754, N.D. W. Va. 1997), the court considered the case of a student who was extended accommodations (oral rather than written exams), but was required to give 48-hour notice of his need for these accommodations. This was not satisfactory, and the student sued under the ADA. The court held that the student had not established that he was an individual with a disability because his only documentation consisted of a psychologist's report stating that he "might suffer from a specific learning disability." The student had also refused to take a WAIS to confirm the diagnosis.

Reasonable Accommodations

Postsecondary institutions are affected by the RA and the ADA in three principal areas: (1) testing (for admissions, evaluation of academic performance, and graduation), (2) the delivery of course materials, and (3) nonacademic benefits of campus life—e.g., sports and dormitory living. In the case of ADHD, the first two are the important ones. In each of these areas, the institution must provide reasonable accommodations. It should be noted that these are often called auxiliary aids and services, or academic adjustments.

Testing

In general, postsecondary institutions are required to provide nondiscriminatory tests and reasonable accommodations in testing for admissions, evaluation of academic performance, and graduation. Discriminatory testing is prohibited. Examinations must be structured in such a way that their results "accurately reflect the individual's aptitude or achievement level or whatever other factor the examination purports to measure" (28 C.F.R. §36.309(b)). In general, entrance and other examinations may not reflect "the individual's impaired sensory, manual, or speaking skills" unless (1) the purpose of the test is to measure those factors and (2) the measurement of those factors has a valid educational purpose. Testing that relies on a single criterion is unlawful where that criterion can be shown to be an inaccurate predictor of performance and the use of that criterion has no compelling justification. (See *Stutts v. Freeman*, 694 F. 2d. 666, 11th Cir. 1983.)

The examinations are generally required to be modified "in the length of time permitted for completion" and in the "manner in which the examination is given" (28 C.F.R. §36.309(b)(2)). Auxiliary aids and services must be provided. Testing modifications are required if they will not alter the fundamental nature of the instruction being offered or create an undue hardship. Typical modifications include taped examinations, interpreters, Brailled or large-print examinations, Brailled or large-print answer sheets, qualified readers for individuals with visual impairments or learning disabilities, and transcribers. Alternative accessible arrangements including "provision of an examination at an individual's home with a proctor" may be employed if accessible facilities are not available (28 C.F.R. §36.309).

Delivery of Course Materials

Course accommodations include taped texts, interpreters, and other effective methods of making orally delivered materials available to individuals with hearing impairments. Brailled or large-print examinations, Brailled or large-print answer sheets, qualified readers for individuals with visual impairments or learning disabilities, classroom equipment adapted for use by individuals with disabilities, and alternative accessible arrangements, including videotaped lectures, cassettes, and prepared notes, may also be employed (28 C.F.R. §36.309(b)(3)). The accommodations must "recognize individual communications needs" and must provide "contemporaneous communication" of the entire educational experience—including class participation—being offered (*United States v. Becker C.P.A. Review,* CV 92-2879 (TFH) (D.D.C. 1994)). Their selection is to be primarily guided by the student's needs and recommendations by qualified professionals.

Course Substitutions

Postsecondary institutions are not required to permit course substitutions where the required course is considered essential. The letter of findings issued to Wingate University, OCR Docket No. 04962051.RES, Apr. 11, 1996, reflects an important case. In that case, a student with a learning disability that "limits his ability to be successful in foreign language courses" was unable to pass the Spanish courses required as a prerequisite for obtaining a Bachelor of Arts degree in English. The university, believing a threshold mastery of foreign language to be an essential requirement for its English B.A. degree, refused to permit a course substitution. Indeed, the record showed that the university had never waived this requirement. The student filed a complaint with OCR, which upheld the university's position, stating that "Section 504 and Title II impose no requirements upon an educational institution to lower or to effect substantial modifications of standards to accommodate a person with a disability. It is the prerogative of an educational institution to decide what requirements are essential so long as each requirement has a rational relationship to the program of instruction and, therefore, is not a pretext for discrimination."

In general, a postsecondary institution may decide for itself which course features are essential to the educational program offered and which are not, which ones can be modified and which ones cannot. However, the institution must use a rational, deliberative process in doing so. In *Guckenberger v. Boston University* (C.A. No. 96-11426-PBS; 1997 WL 523931, D. Mass. Aug. 15, 1997), the court ordered Boston University to consider in an orderly, professional, and unbiased manner the question of whether the foreign language requirement is and should continue to be a mandatory one for a liberal arts degree from Boston University, with no course substitutions permitted. Specifically, Boston University was directed to propose to the court "a deliberative procedure for considering whether modification of its degree requirement in foreign language would fundamentally alter the nature of its liberal arts program." Reconsideration of Boston University's foreign language policy was mandated because "the weight of the evidence supports plaintiffs' arguments that students with learning disorders such as dyslexia have a significantly more difficult challenge in becoming proficient in a foreign language than students without such an impairment." Because that was found to be so, the court considered that, in general, "requesting a course substitution in foreign language for students with demonstrated language disabilities is a reasonable modification." In the court's view, it must be permitted, unless the results of Boston University's "deliberative procedure" indicate otherwise.

The court also ruled that Boston University had no obligation to consider whether to insist on its no-math substitution policy. The court found that "there was no scientific evidence introduced at trial to support plaintiffs' claim that a course substitution is a plausible alternative for a learning disability in mathematics (i.e., dyscalculia)." The standard for deciding whether a particular accommodation poses an undue hardship is different from the standard used to determine whether a testing or course requirement is fundamental. The U.S. Department of Education has stated that, in making undue hardship determinations, the primary consideration will be the size and budget of the institution, compared with the cost of the requested aids and not the amount of tuition paid by the student (letter from W. Smith, Acting Assistant Secretary for Civil Rights, U.S. Department of Education, to Neill Stern, Executive Vice President, Parker College of Chiropractic, March 6, 1990, at 3–4). Auxiliary aids and services, like all reasonable accommodations required by law, must be provided at no additional expense to the student. The obligation of postsecondary institutions to provide to qualified students with disabilities needed academic adjustments and auxiliary aids and services, at no additional charge, has been confirmed in regulations that implement the ADA (28 C.F.R. §35,130(f) and 28 C.F.R. §36.301(c)). The only exception to this rule is that surcharges may be permissible for programs intended to increase the skill level of students who are not qualified for admission to a regular program offered by the institution (*Halasz v. University of New England*, 816 F. Supp. 37, D. Me. 1993).

Professional Licensing

In general, American society in the final years of the twentieth century is deeply committed to academic and professional excellence. Unlike prior times, which relied heavily on apprenticeship, achievement today is often measured by standardized testing. Most applicants for college-level education are tested by administering the SAT or ACT. Admission to graduate school generally requires a favorable score on the GRE, whereas prospective doctors and lawyers must take the MCAT and LSAT, respectively. To become a licensed doctor, one must pass the medical licensing examination (USMLE), Steps 1, 2, and 3, whereas a license to practice law requires successful passage of the bar examination. These tests are primarily multiple-choice examinations, but the bar examination is supplemented by essay portions.

Title II of the ADA

Title II of the ADA prohibits disability-based discrimination by state and local governments (42 U.S.C. §12132). 28 C.F.R. §35.130(b)(6) governs licensing and provides that a state or local government agency "may not administer a licensing or certification program in a manner that subjects qualified individuals with disabilities to discrimination on the basis of disability, nor may a public entity establish requirements for the programs or activities of licensees or certified entities that subject qualified individuals with disabilities to discrimination on the basis of disability. . . ."

Testing may be done directly by a state licensing board or by private firms on behalf of licensing boards. The National Board of Medical Examiners (NBME), for example, is a private entity that administers the United States Medical Licensing Examinations (USMLE) that are used by all state medical licensing boards. Private testing entities and test preparation courses are governed by Title III of the ADA.

The ADA Applies to Licensing

The ADA applies to licensing in the same way that it applies to postsecondary education. To invoke its protections, an individual with a disability must show that he or she has a physical or mental impairment that substantially limits a major life activity. As before, ADHD is a recognized impairment. (See *Soigner v. American Bd. of Plastic Surgery,* 92 F.3d 547, 7th Cir. 1996, cert. denied, 117 S. Ct. 771, 1997.) ADHD must be severe enough to limit substantially a major life activity. Substantial limitation may be measured by comparing the individual's limitation against the achievements of the average person (*Price et al. v. the National Board of Medical Examiners,* 966 F. Supp. 419, S.D. W.Va. 1997). It may also be measured by "the condition, manner or duration under which the individual can perform, a major life activity as compared to an average person in the general population."

What Questions May a Licensing Board Ask?

Controversy has centered around the means by which licensing boards acquire disability-related information about applicants. Information concerning ADHD and other impairments might be elicited in response to questions asking: "Have you ever received treatment for emotional or mental illness, or received treatment by a psychologist, psychiatrist, or other mental health professional?" "Have you ever had a mental illness or emotional disorder?" In general, questions this sweeping and intrusive have been held to violate the ADA (*Doe v. the Judicial Nominating Commission for the Fifteenth Judicial Circuit of Florida*, 5. Am. Disabilities Case (BNA) 1, Docket No. 95-8625-CIV-Hurley, S.D. Fla. 9 Nov. 1995). The courts have reached various results as to the breadth of questions permitted. (See *Applicants v. Texas State Board of Law Examiners*, 5 Am. Disabilities Cas. (BNA) 1, Docket No. 95-86.)

As a result, some licensing boards have narrowed the disability-related questions they ask. There are fewer "have you ever . . . ?" inquiries. Some simply inquire: "Do you have any condition which might prevent you from practicing your profession with reasonable skill and safety?" At the same time, there is a greater reliance on conduct-related questions. For example, one board asks whether the applicant has ever been convicted of any misdemeanor or felony, had a civil judgment entered, had employment terminated, been treated for an illness that affected ability to function in any education or practice setting, or discontinued practice for a period of one month or longer. These conduct-related questions are both effective and permissible.

Employment

The rights of individuals with disabilities in the workplace are created by two key federal statutes, the RA and the ADA. State laws must provide at least these levels of protection. Between them, the RA and the ADA apply to virtually all employers. In many cases, employers are covered by both laws. The simplest way to think of these two laws is to consider what they do not cover. The principal employers and employees not covered are (1) active duty armed forces personnel, (2) the federal judiciary, and (3) private employers with fewer than 15 employees. Finally, an individual with a disability must show that the ADA or the RA is applicable not only to himself or herself but also to the entity with which he or she is dealing.

To invoke the protection of these statutes, (1) the individual must have a disability; (2) the individual must be otherwise qualified for the job, with or without reasonable accommodations; (3) the alleged act of discrimination must be by reason of the disability; and (4) the laws must apply in the particular case. If otherwise qualified for the job, individuals with disabilities are entitled to be free from discrimination in all phases of employment: recruitment, testing, hiring, promotion, termination, rehiring, and be granted reasonable accommodations where necessary.

The Major Life Activity of Working

Individuals with impairments such as ADHD that substantially limit a major life activity are individuals with disabilities. We have discussed these requirements at length in this chapter in the context of education and professional licensing. The employment setting, of course, involves the major life activity of working, which is treated differently from all other major life activities for purposes of considering whether an individual with an impairment is substantially limited. In order to determine whether a substantial limitation on working exists, the individual's impairment must bar him or her from significant classes of jobs, not just a particular job. Only disabilities with the former (and broader) impact are considered substantially to limit working. *Davidson v. Midelfort Clinic, Ltd.* (Docket No. 96-2860, 7th Cir. Jan. 7, 1998) concerned an individual with late-diagnosed ADHD who had struggled through school, including graduate school, and obtained a professional license as a psychotherapist. She was found not to be limited substantially in working. Her ADHD presented in such a manner that she did not qualify for accommodations.

Essential Job Requirements

An individual with a disability must show that he or she is otherwise qualified to do the work required by a job but for the effects of that disability, and that those effects are either irrelevant to job performance or may be handled by a reasonable accommodation. A reasonable accommodation is a modification to the job requirements that neither alters the essential features of the job nor imposes an undue burden on the employer. Reasonable accommodations include anything necessary for the affected individual with a disability to do the work on equal terms with individuals who have no disabilities. The essential requirements of a job include competence in the central job tasks. In *City of Columbus v. Lowe* (1995 WL 390925, Ohio App. 1995), the court held that a police department was justified in refusing to hire a hostage negotiator with depression because she was not otherwise qualified. She did not always remain calm or reason well in stressful situations, was combative with co-workers, and became too emotionally involved in her cases. Additionally, employers may require that employees obtain necessary degrees, security clearances and licenses. In *McDaniel v. Allied Signal, Inc.* (896 F. Supp. 1482, W.D. Mo. 1995), the court found that an individual with mental illness was properly terminated because, as a result of that illness, he was no longer able to have a security clearance required for his job. He was not a qualified individual with a disability. Similarly, in *Despears v. Milwaukee County* (63 F. 3d 635, 7th Cir. 1995), the court upheld the demotion of an employee to a position not requiring a driver's license, after his license was revoked for a fourth DUI conviction. The court found that the demotion did not violate the ADA and that persons with alcoholism, a disability under the ADA, may not avoid the consequences of their criminal activity. Performing one's job in a safe manner is also essential (*EEOC v. Amego, Inc.*, Docket No. 96-1837, 1st Cir. Apr. 7, 1997). The ability to work cooperatively with a supervisor is essential (*Dazey v. Department of the Air Force*, 54 MSPR 658, 1992), as is regular attendance (*Mancini v. General Electric Co.*, 820 F. Supp. 141, D. Vt. 1993). Honesty is not only the best policy; it too is essential (*Hartman v. City of Petaluma*, 841 F. Supp. 946, N.D. Cal. 1994). The ability to conduct oneself in the work environment with an appropriate degree of socialization is also essential (*Bussey v. Togo D. West, Jr., Secretary, Department of the Army*, 1996.C04.1539). No employer is required to modify an essential job requirement.

Reasonable Accommodations

Reasonable accommodations are of three general types: (1) those required to ensure equal opportunity in the job application process, (2) those which enable the individual with a disability to perform the essential features of a job, and (3) those which enable individuals with disabilities to enjoy the same benefits and privileges as those available to individuals without disabilities.

Testing Accommodations

Testing accommodations in the workplace are available under the same conditions as testing accommodations in postsecondary education. Discriminatory testing is prohibited. Modifications that do not alter the essential nature of the test or pose an undue hardship are required.

Job Accommodations

Reasonable accommodations for ADHD can include any of the following. The EEOC has suggested that time off, modified work schedules, flex-time, and working at home might be appropriate, depending on the situation. Physical changes to workplace or equipment such as room dividers, partitions, soundproofing, or visual barriers might be appropriate for individuals who have disability-related limitations in concentration. Moving the individual to a quieter location, lowering the pitch of telephones, and permitting use of headphones to block distractions are also possibilities.

Modifications of workplace policies may be appropriate. The EEOC suggests that it would be a reasonable accommodation to allow an individual who has difficulty concentrating due to a disability to take detailed notes during client presentations even though company policy discourages employees from doing so.

Adjusting supervisory methods to ensure that assignments, instructions, and training are delivered by the medium that is most effective for the individual (e.g., writing, oral, or electronic mail) are reasonable accommodations. Increased feedback and structure are also reasonable accommodations. However, employer monitoring to ensure that required medications are taken is not a reasonable accommodation. Adjusting supervisory methods to provide more feedback has been held to be a reasonable accommodation (*Lynch v. Department of Education*, 52 MSPR 541, 1992).

Reassignment is sometimes an option. Under the ADA, reassignment to an appropriate vacant position must be considered as a reasonable accommodation when accommodation in the present job would constitute an undue hardship. Temporary assignment to a job with a light workload may be required where such assignments are provided to those returning to work after an illness.

Selecting the Accommodation

The employee and the employer are both required to cooperate reasonably in an interactive process of exploring the nature of a claimed disability and the appropriate accommodations (*Beck v. University of Wisconsin*, No. 95-2479, 7th Cir. Jan. 26, 1996). In the process of exploring appropriate accommodations, the employer must take into account the known mental limitations of the employee (*Bultemeyer v. Fort Wayne Community Schools*, Docket No. 96-1984, 7th Cir. Nov. 18, 1996). The duty to provide reasonable accommodations is not endless. An employer is not required to offer accommodations preferred by an employee where reasonable ones have been offered (*Hankins v. the Gap, Inc.*, 1996 FED App. 0151P). Finally, the interactive process is not required where no duty to accommodate exists (*Willis v. Conopco, Inc.*, Docket No. 96-8395, 11th Cir. 25 Mar. 1997).

By Reason of the Disability

It has long been held that an individual with a disability must also show that he or she has been denied employment, education, or access to a public accommodation by reason of the disability. In *Ross v. Beaumont Hospital* (687 F. Supp. 1115, E.D. Mich. 1988), a hospital terminated the privileges of a surgeon who suffered from narcolepsy despite the fact that her narcolepsy was largely controlled through medication. However, the surgeon also engaged in verbal abuse of nurses over a seven-year period. There was no evidence that the abuse was related to the narcolepsy. Accordingly, the termination was held to be lawful under the RA because it was based in major part on her unacceptable conduct.

In some cases, individuals with disabilities believe, perhaps with good reason, that their workplace is a hostile environment for individuals with disabilities and that, as a result, they have been forced to leave. This is often difficult to establish legally. In *Sinopoli v. Regula* (Docket No. 97-7229, 2nd Cir. Oct. 9, 1997), the court held that "To establish a constructive discharge, a plaintiff must show that the employer deliberately made [his] working conditions so intolerable that [he was] forced into an involuntary resignation. . . . Proof of a hostile work environment requires a showing that the workplace is permeated with discriminatory intimidation, ridicule and insult, that is sufficiently severe or pervasive to alter the conditions of the victim's employment." (*Harris v. Forklift Sys. Inc.*, 510 U.S. 17, 21, 1993).

Documentation, Disclosure, and Confidentiality

No person is required to disclose his or her disability, and no postsecondary institution, employer, governmental agency, or place of public accommodation is required to accommodate an unknown disability. The disclosure must be clear and should be accompanied by a clear request for specific accommodations. All requests for documentation must be reasonable. Documentation should demonstrate (1) that a disability exists, (2) how it affects the individual, and (3) what specific accommodations are required. Confidentiality of disability information is protected by law but is subject to various exceptions on a need-to-know basis.

Conclusion

This chapter provides an overview of *legal* rights for individuals with disabilities under federal anti-discrimination laws in education and employment settings. ADHD is a disability when it meets the criteria under the particular law involved. For an in-depth discussion of this topic, the following books are recommended: *Attention Deficit Hyperactivity Disorder and the Law* (second edition), *Documentation and the Law,* and *Succeeding in the Workplace,* all published by JKL Communications (202/223-5097).

Dispelling the Myths and Misconceptions about ADHD

MARY MCDONALD RICHARD

Advances in the field of ADHD are yielding benefits for individuals living with this disorder. Research investigations of associated neurological factors are providing information through which its symptoms are becoming better understood. Clinical studies are producing better tools and methodologies for use in diagnosis and treatment. New insights into the impact of ADHD on the daily functioning of people with the disorder are generating more effective approaches for improving school and workplace performance. However, in spite of this progress, myths about ADHD continue to circulate and receive an unacceptable level of public acceptance and media attention.

Myths about ADHD and other mental disorders perpetuate misinformation and foster inappropriate attitudes toward people with these conditions. The dissemination of research-based information is critical to dispelling myths and improving the lives of those living with this disorder. With respect to this situation, the following five thematic sections contain 21 common myths about ADHD and examples of the scientific findings that refute them.

Myths about the Existence of ADHD

ADHD is just normal childhood behavior.

It is not unusual for typical children to display individual symptoms of ADHD. Teachers in a study in which they were asked to evaluate behavior problems among their students reported that 42% of the girls and 57% of the boys were overactive (Lapouse & Monk, 1958). Since so many children display symptoms occasionally or one at at time, some people have incorrectly concluded that ADHD is normal. However, children who are considered overactive do not necessarily have ADHD Predominantly Hyperactive-Impulsive Type. Nor does the person described as a "daydreamer" necessarily have ADHD Predominantly Inattentive Type, unless daydreaming in combination with a number of other symptoms significantly impairs functioning in daily life. An individual must demonstrate a required number of symptoms and meet other diagnostic criteria in order to be diagnosed with ADHD. Such persons chronically experience significant levels of developmentally inappropriate activity, distractibility, impulsivity, difficulty with focusing, and problems in sustaining attention.

Contrary to the myth that ADHD is "normal childhood behavior" that is outgrown by puberty, research has revealed that in many cases the disorder continues into adolescence and adulthood. However, in such cases, its symptoms are often altered in a manner that parallels other behavioral changes associated with growth and development. For example, just as children demonstrate their emotions differently at different ages, so may the behavioral manifestations of ADHD be displayed differently. The symptoms of hyperactivity that appear as "bouncing off the walls" during elementary school may be converted to intense feelings of restlessness in an adolescent who will struggle internally in order to sit through movies, school assemblies, and classes. An adolescent whose bedroom, locker, and backpack display near-disastrous disorganization may become an adult who displays a level of vigilance approaching rigidity in implementing self-management strategies.

When symptoms are viewed strictly from a short-term perspective, they may be explained away as a child's "wild" behavior, an adolescent's "attitude," or an adult's "quirky" personality. The changing appearance of symptoms may mask the causal role of ADHD underlying a variety of problematic behaviors. This contributes to the diagnostic identification problems that often cause the disorder to go unrecognized well into adolescence and adulthood.

As a part of the diagnostic assessment of an adult, the emergence and appearance of symptoms from early childhood onward should be carefully investigated. Hallowell and Ratey (1994) reported that many adults who have been diagnosed with ADHD have felt that "something has been wrong for years." Clinical interviews and other evaluation tools may be used to assess these feelings and any relationship they may have to the presence and impact of ADHD symptoms. When ADHD is identified as the "something that has been wrong" in the life of an adult, it is very likely that both a history of symptoms as well as a history of their impact will be revealed.

Statements such as "ADHD is normal childhood behavior" are often used by groups, such as the Church of Scientology, which states that the disorder does not exist (Goldman, Genel, Bezman, & Slanetz, 1998). Similarities between typical children's behavior and changes over time in the appearance of ADHD symptoms inadvertently contribute to such statements. In addition, these groups cite the absence of definitive diagnostic laboratory tests for ADHD and other mental disorders as evidence that the disorder is not real.

Not only is ADHD not "normal childhood behavior," but it is also not a condition that can be detected using biopsies, X-rays, or blood and urine studies. Reliable diagnoses of this disorder are established on the basis of patient history and behavioral assessment. Professionals who are well-trained in the evaluation of ADHD can identify it accurately on the basis of well-researched diagnostic criteria. When the full set of criteria is properly applied, these criteria produce diagnostic results that are highly reliable (Goldman et al., 1998; Jensen, 1996; Shaffer, Fisher, & Dulcan, 1996).

ADHD is just immature behavior.

Studies have indicated that the maturational development of children with ADHD often lags behind that of their nondisabled agemates by as much as two to three years (Armin, Douglas, Mendelson, & Dufresne, 1993; Chelune, Ferguson, Koon, & Dickey, 1986; Dykens, Leckman, & Riddle, 1990). When parents and educators observe developmentally inappropriate behavior in children and adolescents with ADHD, it is likely that they are witnessing the effects of the neurodevelopmental lag associated with the disorder (Kinsbourne, 1973). Developmental delays may affect a number of areas of functioning, including judgment, organization, responsibility, patience, and persistence. Behavioral examples may range from preferences for activities associated with youth of younger ages to a lack of "common sense." Studies of adolescents with ADHD have indicated that neurodevelopmental lags in that stage of life may expose them to greater risks than they will experience at any other time (Barkley, Fischer, Edelbrock, & Smallish, 1990). In order to effectively assist young people with ADHD, those who work with them should be knowledgeable about the ways in which maturational lags can alter the typical time frames for developmental progress.

Another study looked at behavioral issues related to maturity. Psychologists investigated adaptive behavior in individuals with and without ADHD. They found that subjects with the disorder demonstrated levels of adaptive behavior that were unexpectedly low for their ages (Roisen, Blondis, Irwin, & Stein, 1994). These results are consistent with other findings related to deficits associated with maturational lags.

Inadequate development of adaptive behavior can significantly affect an individual's ability to apply knowledge to the activities of daily living. Examples range from a student who carefully completes a test, but forgets to write his or her name on it, to an adult who frequently misplaces car keys and other items that are used every day. Sam Goldstein (1990) aptly described such situations, saying: "It's not a problem of not knowing what to do—it's a problem of not doing what they know."

In physiological terms, the presence of neurological differences is implicated in maturational lags. This has been demonstrated by medical researchers studying the role of dopamine, the neurotransmitter that plays an important role in the brain's braking system. In the course of physical maturation, the brains of persons with ADHD do not seem to follow the normal developmental course of increasingly "putting the brakes" on behavior. The results may contribute to developmental lags. Research has indicated that the high concentration of dopamine in the brains of young children facilitates their ability to explore the environment (Castellanos, 1997). As most of these children grow into adulthood, their dopamine concentrations will gradually decrease. These reductions have been correlated with increases in inhibiting signals within the brain. However, in the brains of hyperactive boys with developmental lags, researchers have found inappropriately high concentrations of dopamine (Castellanos, 1997). This is consistent with the findings of other research that has compared the developmental processes in persons with and without ADHD (Hynd, Hern, Voeller, & Marshall, 1991).

ADHD is a cultural invention of the 1980s and 1990s.

Although the final two decades of the twentieth century were filled with cultural innovations, ADHD was not among them. Those who believe this myth may be inadvertently buying into a belief that was common at the turn of the twentieth century. At that time, behavior was considered to be solely the product of an individual's upbringing and environment (Goldstein, 1942). Since that time, however, research studies have found strong links between behavior and the functioning of various structures and circuits within the brain.

ADHD is not a cultural innovation; in fact, it is recognized as one of the best-researched disorders in medicine (Goldman et al., 1998). Since the turn of the twentieth century, an enormous body of literature about its core symptoms has accumulated in the fields of medicine and psychology. Samples from these records provide clear evidence that ADHD is not a fad and that its symptoms have not been recently invented. If a time line of the highlights of the early research progress were drawn, the following events would be noted:

1. 1902: George F. Still writes about the problems of children who demonstrated hyperactivity, inattentiveness, and behavior and learning problems. He attributes these children's excessive behaviors to organic and environmental factors.
2. 1922–1923: Hohman and Ebaugh note the same characteristics in children who survived an epidemic of encephalitis and attributed them to neurological changes caused by the disease.
3. 1947: Strauss and Lehtinen study the effects of brain injuries on the learning and behavior of children. They use the term "minimal brain damage syndrome" to describe a cluster of behavioral changes that include emotional instability, perceptual impairments, and poor impulse control.
4. 1957: Laufer and Denhoff use another term, "hyperkinetic impulse disorder," to describe a behavioral syndrome involving hyperactivity and impulsivity.
5. 1962: Clements and Peters use the term "minimal brain dysfunction."
6. 1966: A U.S. Department of Health, Education, and Welfare task force meets to review the terminology used in the identification and education of children who chronically display symptoms of minimal brain dysfunction (MBD). The task force describes MBD as a syndrome occurring in children who are of "near average, average, or above average general intelligence with certain learning or behavioral disabilities ranging from mild to severe, which are associated with deviations of function of the central nervous system." It describes the

symptoms as "various combinations of impairment in perception, conceptual-ization, language, memory and control of attention, impulse or motor func-tion" (Clements, 1966).

As research has contributed new information about ADHD, the terms used to describe it have changed. The current version of the *Diagnostic and Statistical Manual (DSM-IV)* lists three types subsumed under the term Attention Deficit/Hyper-activity Disorder (American Psychiatric Association, 1994). Two lists of criteria, one related to symptoms of inattention and the other to impulsivity, are associated with the three subtypes that are titled: ADHD Predominantly Inattentive Type, ADHD Predominantly Hyperactive-Impulsive Type, and ADHD Combined Type.

ADHD doesn't exist outside the United States.

Researchers have demonstrated that ADHD is not exclusively found in the United States. Rather, it has been found in every country in which studies have taken place (Barkley, 1998). Research that has been conducted in a number of coun-tries with children from a variety of backgrounds has found that ADHD exists across cultures, races, geographical boundaries, and socioeconomic classes. Differ-ences in the findings may be in part attributed to differences in the procedures used to identify the ADHD in each study. A few example of findings are the following:

1. Anderson, Williams, McGee, and Silva (1987): 6.75% of a sample of 792 11-year-old boys in New Zealand
2. Bird, Canino, and Rubio-Stipec (1988): 9.5% of Puerto Rican children ages 4 through 16
3. Szatmari, Offord, and Boyle (1989): 9.0% of boys ages 4–16 in Ontario
4. Bhatia, Nigam, Bohra, and Malik (1991): 15.7% boys, 4.1% girls—pediatric out-patients in India
5. Ferguson, Horwood, and Lynskey (1993): 2.8–3.0% of 15-year-olds in New Zealand
6. Gallucci, Bird, Berardi, and Gallai (1993): 3.9% of students in 9 fourth-grade classes in two regions of Italy
7. Baubaertel, Wolraich, and Dietrich (1995): 17.8% elementary school students in Germany
8. Leung, Luk, Ho, Taylor, Mak, and Bacon-Shone (1996): 8.9% of school-age boys in China

Myths about the Cause of ADHD

ADHD is caused by too much sugar (or aspartame, or preservatives, etc.) in the diet.

Among the causal myths about ADHD, some have targeted common dietary substances, including sugar, aspartame (an artificial sweetener), various food col-orings, and preservatives. However, the role of dietary factors has been investigated for three decades without producing evidence of a relationship. In 1982, at a consensus conference convened by the National Institutes of Health, researchers reviewed over 20 studies and found that no relationships existed between dietary variables and the symptoms of ADHD. Neither those studies nor others conducted since that time have yielded any evidence of a relationship between the consumption of specific substances and the symptoms of ADHD (Hoover & Milich, 1994; Shaywitz et al., 1994; Wolraich et al., 1994; Wolraich, Milich, Stumbo, & Schultz, 1985).

When a complete causal explanation of ADHD is established, it will not be so simple as the effects of ingesting sugar or artificial sweetener. Nor is it likely that it will involve a single cause. Just as a number of causal elements have been found for medical conditions such as heart and bone diseases, scientists believe multiple factors will ultimately be identified as causes of ADHD (LaHoste et al., 1996).

ADHD is caused by poor parenting.

Although some members of the public have stated that poor child-raising practices are responsible for causing ADHD, research has found no evidence to support this myth. However, research has revealed that in a significant number of cases, parents' genetic contributions to their children may "cause" ADHD. One study that investigated the role of genetic inheritance found that when one parent had ADHD, the risk to his or her offspring was 57% (Biederman et al., 1995). Although researchers have not identified a genetic link in all cases of ADHD, they have found that individuals with a family history of the disorder are more likely to have it themselves. This risk may be increased when combined with factors that parents may or may not be able to control, including prenatal health and environmental toxins (Milberger, Biederman, & Faraone, 1994; Sprich-Buckminster, Biederman, Milberger, Faraone, & Lehman, 1993).

Among the studies that have investigated the heritability of ADHD several have found that the parents and siblings of children diagnosed with ADHD are much more likely to have the disorder themselves (Cantwell, 1972; Biederman et al., 1992; Deutsch, Matthysse, Swanson, & Farkas, 1990; Faraone et al., 1993; Hechtman, 1994). Studies of twins have found that if one identical twin has ADHD, the chances have been estimated at 80–90% that the other twin will have it as well (Hechtman, 1994; Levy, Hay, McStephen, Wood, & Waldman, 1997). Findings of the same study indicated that if one non-identical twin has ADHD, there is a 30% chance that the sibling twin will have it as well. Other studies have demonstrated genetic transmission factors in children who have both ADHD and learning disabilities (Faraone et al., 1993; Gilger, Pennington, & DeFries, 1992; Gillis, Gilger, Pennington, & DeFries, 1992; Semrud-Clikeman et al., 1992).

Researchers are currently investigating the relationship of multiple genetic factors to ADHD. In 1995, a dopamine-related gene was linked to novelty-seeking behavior (Cook et al., 1995; Benjamin et al., 1996; Ebstein et al., 1996). Two years later, researchers confirmed that it is involved in some cases of ADHD (Gill, Daly, Heron, Hawi, & Fitzgerald, 1997; Swanson et al., 1997).

Although a causal link has not been demonstrated between parenting practices and ADHD, this is not necessarily the case for two other conditions that co-occur at a high rate of frequency with ADHD. Studies have indicated that two disorders associated with significantly difficult and negative behaviors, Oppositional Defiant Disorder (ODD) and Conduct Disorder (CD), may in some cases be connected with parents' behavior. The behaviors associated with ODD and CD appear to be precipitated or exacerbated by some parents' communication styles and child-rearing practices (Sprich-Buckminster et al., 1993).

ADHD does not have a physical cause.

Individuals who believe that ADHD has no physical cause and those who believe that it is a cultural invention should review the findings of the past 100 years' worth of research investigating its likely causal factors. The historical highlights from research literature provided earlier in this article give an overview of the progress that scientists have made in linking behavior to the functioning of various brain structures. Although the precise causes of ADHD have yet to be identified, clearly a great deal has been learned about the relationships between such physical structures as genes and the brain and the symptoms of ADHD (LaHoste et al., 1996).

The myth that ADHD has no physical cause may have continued to circulate since the outward manifestations of the disorder reveal very little about the internal workings that are responsible for its symptoms. However, the investigation of physical factors requires that scientists first determine what constitutes normalcy in the brain's structures and functions. In order to accomplish this, researchers are employing a wide range of advanced technology to examine normal brains and those of persons with diagnosed mental disorders. These applications include magnetic resonance imaging (MRI), single photon emission computed tomography (SPECT), positron emission tomography (PET), and sophisticated laboratory methodologies.

Some researchers investigating the relationship of brain to ADHD have focused on the structures that appear to support the executive functions. The involvement of the prefrontal cortex (the outer layer of gray matter covering the cerebral hemispheres) in executive functioning has been well established. These functions have been defined as the "abilities to prioritize, organize, and strategize" (Denckla, 1989) and as the "control processes involving inhibition and delay of responding that allow an individual to initiate, sustain, inhibit/stop, and shift" (Denckla, 1996). The executive function deficits in ADHD appear to involve a network linking various structures of the brain that are believed to be responsible for providing positive and negative feedback to various other parts (Alexander, DeLong, & Strick, 1986). Inadequate inhibition of traffic through these circuits is associated with not only ADHD, but also with Tourette's syndrome and obsessive–compulsive disorder (Alexander & Crutcher, 1990; Alexander, DeLong, & Strick, 1986). In addition to the prefrontal cortex, research has indicated that the following brain structures are related to the executive function and that disturbances in them may be associated with some of the symptoms of ADHD:

1. Basal ganglia: four collections of neurons located deep in the cerebral hemi-spheres
2. Cerebellum: a portion of the brain that interacts with the brain stem in execut-ing voluntary movement
3. Thalamus: a part of brain that receives input from all the senses (except smell), associates and synthesizes it, and relays it to other parts of the brain

Research was conducted to measure a number of regions of the brains of boys with ADHD, using anatomic MRI to see if their brain structures were different from those of normal subjects (Casey et al., 1997; Castellanos et al., 1994; Giedd et al., 1994). The following differences in the brains of subjects with ADHD were documented:

1. smaller cerebral volume
2. less asymmetry in the caudate
3. smaller right globus pallidus
4. smaller anterior frontal region
5. smaller cerebellum
6. a reversal of lateral ventricular asymmetry

Myths about the Diagnosis of ADHD

ADHD can be diagnosed within a 30-minute doctor's office appointment.

Although some insurance companies will cover no more than the costs of a rel-atively brief office visit, experts agree that the diagnosis of ADHD should not be conferred without a comprehensive evaluation. First and foremost, it is critical that such assessments be conducted by a qualified professional or combination of pro-fessionals who know how to evaluate the symptoms according to diagnostic crite-ria and can rule out alternative medical or psychological explanations for them.

A diagnosis should be established only after a careful clinical process has determined that symptoms meet the requirements of rigorous diagnostic criteria. ADHD cannot be diagnosed by any single laboratory or psychological test, but these procedures may be used to rule out other potential causes of symptoms. A number of other conditions can cause inattention, including hearing impairments, depression, seizure disorders, learning disabilities, Tourette's Syndrome, substance abuse, sleep and anxiety disorders, and the effects of abuse or neglect. Conditions that may produce hyperactivity include thyroid disorder, reactions to drugs, bipo-lar disorder, and Fragile X Syndrome (Greenhill, 1996).

The diagnostic assessment of ADHD generally involves a number of proce-dures and may include a comprehensive developmental and educational history, a structured interview with the patient (and patient's family in the case of a young child), a mental status examination, a medical evaluation of general health and neurological status, reports from observations, an evaluation of cognitive ability and achievement, neuropsychological tests, lab tests, and the review of collateral information collected from additional sources (Goldman et al., 1998). Several sets of professional diagnostic guidelines are currently in use. Among those circulated nationally by professional organizations are the Practice Parameters for the Assessment and Treatment of Attention Deficit/Hyperactivity Disorder (American Academy of Child & Adolescent Psychiatry, 1997) and those contained in the *Diagnostic & Statistical Manual of Mental Disorders (DSM-IV)* (American Psychiatric Association, 1994). Guidelines have also been prepared and cirulated nationally in connection with the requirements of the Educational Testing Service for diagnostic reports submitted to document the eligibility of students with ADHD for testing accommodations (Educational Testing Service, 1998).

Children are being overdiagnosed with ADHD.

In spite of a number of studies that have soundly refuted it, the myth that ADHD is being overdiagnosed has continued to circulate. A recent study published in the *Journal of the American Medical Association* involved a review of a National Library of Medicine database from 1975 to 1997 (Goldman et al., 1998). Investigators concluded that while 3% to 6% of the school-aged population may have ADHD, the percentage who are diagnosed and treated for the condition is at or below 3 percent.

A variety of factors have contributed to increases in total number of children diagnosed with ADHD. First, a number of parents of children who have displayed educational and behavioral difficulties have been proactive in obtaining evaluations to investigate these difficulties. Second, the federal and state departments of education have recognized the need of some children with ADHD for special education services. And third, a wider range of professionals in psychology, medicine, and education are receiving training related to recognizing and treating the disorder.

Although concerns about the number of children who have been diagnosed with ADHD in the past decade have been widely reported, very little has been mentioned about problems related to underdiagnosis. Geographical variances in the proportion of diagnosed schoolchildren have caused some experts to believe that problems may exist with both under- and over-diagnosis of ADHD (Jensen, 1996).

If a person wasn't diagnosed with ADHD in childhood, then he or she doesn't have it.

Many of the earlier responses to beliefs that ADHD is either normal childhood behavior or immaturity apply to this myth. According to diagnostic guidelines, the symptoms of ADHD should have appeared by age seven. However, for a variety of reasons they may not be recognized at the time. The symptoms of children who are "firsts" or "onlies" may not be recognized by parents who are inexperienced with children or unfamiliar with typical child development. Symptoms of inattentiveness are often subtle in appearance, making detection difficult. Difficulties in regulating internal focus and concentration, and their associated behaviors, may not be recognized until an individual has sustained enough damage from the symptoms that his or her resulting functional gaps are noticed. Although the symptoms of hyperactivity are often much more apparent, even children who usually display them in full force occasionally thwart identification. Some children who are virtual "whirlwinds" of activity may be temporarily subdued in the doctor's examination room. Such episodes of "good" behavior can often be ascribed to their wariness related to past experiences with immunization shots and other medical procedures that have taken place in this environment. And some children may be so active that their hyperactivity would seem obvious to almost anyone, but they may not be referred for assessment if they are considered "normal" by parents who manifested the same symptoms in childhood (Barkley, 1990).

ADHD can be diagnosed by taking a computer test or by using a checklist of symptoms.

A variety of questionnaires have been developed for use in diagnosing ADHD. Among these forms that are used for identifying and categorizing symptoms, some are interviewer-rated or prepared for use by parents and teachers. A few others are self-rated. However, none of these instruments can be used alone to diagnose ADHD (Barkley, 1988).

Several computer-based tests are available that measure patient responses to certain visual and auditory patterns. Although they may provide pertinent information, ADHD cannot be reliably diagnosed on the basis of any of these tests used alone. Diagnostic professionals often consider them to be valuable tools when used and interpreted in the context of other neuropsychological testing and a comprehensive clinical interview (Edwards, 1998; Fischer, Newby, & Gordon, 1995).

A positive response to stimulant medication confirms the diagnosis of ADHD.

It was once incorrectly believed that stimulant medications had a paradoxical effect on people with ADHD. This was based on the incorrect assumption that instead of stimulating them, these medications would have a calming effect on people with the disorder. This myth has persisted for 30 years beyond the time that scientists concluded that the clinical response of children with ADHD was qualitatively the same as the response of children without the disorder (Cole, 1969). Since then, other studies have found that subjects without ADHD have the same or similar responses to equivalent doses of stimulant medications as subjects with the disorder (Rapoport, Buchsbaum, & Weingartner, 1980; Swanson, McBurnett, Christian, & Wigal, 1995).

Myths about the Features of ADHD

Motor hyperactivity is the main problem of ADHD.

Although physical hyperactivity is the most noticeable characteristic associated with ADHD, in and of itself, hyperactivity is not the main problem associated with ADHD. In fact, hyperactivity often diminishes over the years, without resolution of other symptoms (Frick, Lahey, & Applegate, 1994; Hart, Lahey, & Loeber, 1995). For example, the large motor symptoms of hyperactivity that were obvious in childhood may be reduced to well-concealed, but uncomfortable feelings of physical restlessness in an adolescent or adult.

The work of Virginia Douglas and her colleagues redirected the focus of researchers from an emphasis on the symptoms of motor hyperactivity to those involved in attention and impulse control. In her 1972 presidential address to the Canadian Psychological Association, Douglas spoke about the results of her studies of hyperactive children, emphasizing that the major difficulties of these children stemmed from deficits related to sustained attention and impulse control (Douglas, 1972). Further studies of hyperactive children by Douglas and her colleagues provided more evidence that the primary deficits of the disorder involved an inability to sustain attention to task and manage impulses (Douglas & Parry, 1983; Douglas, 1985).

The diagnostic criteria published in the *Diagnostic and Statistical Manual (DSM-IV)* (1994) includes two lists of specific symptoms. The first describes behaviors associated with hyperactivity and impulsivity. The second list is composed of behaviors that demonstrate inattention.

Children outgrow ADHD when they enter puberty.

In the process of maturation, the appearance of an individual's symptoms of ADHD may change, but this does not always indicate that the disorder has been resolved. Decades of longitudinal research have shown that as many as 70–80% of children diagnosed with ADHD have ongoing problems during adolescence that include overactivity, poor school performance, and behavioral problems at home. Compared to matched control subjects, young adults with ADHD have significantly higher levels of impulsivity and restlessness, legal problems, and vocational and marital difficulties (Gittelman, Mannuzza, Shenker, & Bonagura, 1985; Klein & Mannuzza, 1991; Mannuzza, Klein, Bessler, Malloy, & LaPadula, 1993; Weiss & Hecktman, 1993; Weiss, Hechtman, Milroy, & Perlman, 1985). It is also well documented that adolescents (Klorman, Brumaghim, Fitzpatrick, & Borgstedt, 1992) and adults (Wender, Reimherr, & Wood, 1985) with ADHD continue to benefit from treatment with stimulant medication.

A number of adolescents with ADHD may continue to manifest the disorder in adulthood. In 1995, Wender wrote that between 2% and 7% of the adult population has the disorder. A study by Murphy and Barkley (1996) suggested that the incidence of ADHD in adults was 4.7%. Another study of male adults who were seen for hyperactivity at a child guidance clinic 25 years earlier found that these men were three to four times more likely than their non-hyperactive brothers to have had significant problems as adults with anxiety, depression, and relationships and jobs (Mannuzza et al., 1993). Scientists investigating symptom improvement in some adults believe it may be linked to the phenomenon of delayed maturing of the prefrontal circuits into the third decade of life, consistent with decreases in symptoms in some adults (Benton, 1991).

ADHD symptoms are consistent in appearance from person to person.

Russell Barkley, a leading researcher in the field of ADHD, once noted that the only thing consistent about ADHD is its inconsistency (CH.A.D.D. Educators Inservice Training Program, 1994). Indeed, the presentation of its symptoms is affected by many and varied characteristics of each person with the disorder. One element of this heterogeneity that has been investigated by researchers is the frequency of comorbid conditions (Biederman, Newcorn, & Sprich, 1991). Like people, individuals with ADHD vary in their interests, intelligence, personality type, learning style, education, and life experiences (Hechtman, 1991). Research data from a study that examined the personality characteristics of adults with ADHD suggested that there is no one personality type associated with the disorder and emphasized the importance of avoiding stereotypes about people with the disorder and dealing with them as individuals (Robin, Tezelepsis, & Bedway, 1997).

ADHD is found primarily in boys.

Most studies have found that ADHD occurs more frequently in males than in females, but girls and women are by no means exempted from the disorder. Studies of the population of individuals with ADHD have found other trends associated with gender (Gaub & Carlson, 1997). A 1997 study looked at differences in boys and girls with ADHD (Roisen, Blondis, Irwin, & Stein, 1994). It found a number of differences according to gender. Of the boys and girls in the study:

1. Forty-four percent of the boys had motor impairments in contrast to 25% of the girls.
2. Boys displayed more pronounced deficits in executive functioning in comparison to nondisabled boys than the girls displayed in comparison to nondisabled girls.
3. Of the girls, 17.1% had comorbid affective disorders compared to 2.3% of the boys.
4. Of the girls, 29.3% had the inattentive subtype compared to 2.3% of boys.
5. Girls were more likely than boys to have comorbid learning disabilities.

Myths about Treatment

Medication is the only treatment needed for the treatment of ADHD.

Behavior therapies are another accepted form of treatment for ADHD. They involve teaching parents, teachers, and sometimes the individuals with ADHD to apply rewards and consequences for on-task as opposed to off-task behavior (Swanson et al., 1992). When rigorously implemented, these treatments can help children control their behavior. However, much of the research evidence suggests that behavior therapies are not as effective as the stimulant medications, that they can be more difficult and expensive to implement, and that the related behavior improvements may not transfer across settings.

All treatments, whether medical or behavioral, should be adapted according to the unique needs of each person and integrated across the settings and circumstances of his or her life. The determination of any treatment or combination of treatments must be carefully made. The National Institute of Mental Health in partnership with the U.S. Department of Education has mounted a six-site study of about 600 children diagnosed with ADHD (Richters et al., 1995). The study is collecting data to compare state-of-the-art medical treatments, optimal regimens of behavioral treatment, combinations of the two treatments, and the standard clinical care available in the subjects' communities. The results of this study will be valuable in determining which treatment or combination of treatments work best on the basis of the profile of the individual child. They will also help determine the longer-term outcomes of each treatment or combination of treatments.

Medication is overprescribed for ADHD.

Some reports in the media have exaggerated the number of American children taking stimulant medication to treat the symptoms of ADHD. Government figures released in 1995 indicated an increase of 600% since 1990 in the number of children for whom methylphenidate (MPH) had been prescribed (Drug Enforcement Administration Office of Public Affairs, 1995). This figure was based on the increase in production quotas for methylphenidate from the Drug Enforcement Administration (DEA, 1995). However, in 1996 a study by Johns Hopkins University School of Medicine used a variety of databases to show that about 2.8% of children in the United States were taking MPH in 1995 (Safer, Zito, & Fine, 1996). This represented a 250% increase since 1990. The researchers who conducted the study stated that the methodology used in their study produced a more accurate picture of how many children actually took such medications than the methodology employed by the DEA. Another study conducted by the Council on Scientific Affairs of the American Medical Association (1998) concluded that at or below 3% of school-aged children in the United States were being treated for ADHD (Goldman et al., 1998).

Medications used in the treatment of the symptoms of ADHD stunt growth.

The number of studies that have investigated growth and stimulant treatment is indicative of the significant interest of clinicians in the topic. Among the studies, some initially suggested that children taking stimulant medication might experience less gain or even a reduction in expected height as compared to agemates. A recent study that revisited these concerns looked at height and weight records on 124 children and adolescents with ADHD who were treated with stimulants, and a non-ADHD control group of 109 children and adolescents. The study found that the adolescents showed no differences in height or weight in comparison to a control group, and concluded that height and weight deficits were not associated with stimulant treatment for ADHD (Spencer, Biederman, & Harding, 1996).

People treated with the stimulant medication most often prescribed for ADHD are at risk of becoming addicted to it.

This myth is a common example of the type of misinformation that has appeared in the press concerning methylphenidate (MPH), the medication most commonly prescribed to treat the symptoms of ADHD. Since MPH (brand name: Ritalin) is the most widely tested and studied medication available for prescription in the United States, it is difficult to rationally understand the amount of misinformation about it in circulation. A study conducted by the Council on Scientific Affairs of the American Medical Association (1998) that used a National Library of

Medicine database from 1975 to 1997 did not find stimulant abuse or diversion to be a significant problem among children treated for ADHD, but cautioned physicians to be mindful of the risk of abuse and to keep careful records of the medications they prescribe (Goldman et al., 1998).

Among the most alarming claims have been statements to the effect that MPH is "just like cocaine." Members of the public are vulnerable to being misled by such statements since few possess the knowledge of psychopharmocology required to understand the differences between these substances. Although stimulants as a class have a documented abuse potential, individually they vary in their ability to induce the euphoria that is associated with liability to abuse. Cocaine is known to be highly addictive, but MPH used in the treatment of ADHD has not yet been shown to be addictive when taken orally as prescribed for the treatment of symptoms. This was demonstrated in a study that was mounted to compare the effects of cocaine and MPH on the brains of humans and baboons. PET scans were employed to measure their respective binding sites and concentrations. The results indicated that MPH and cocaine acted in considerably different ways with respect to binding and the amount of clearance time required for each substance to leave the brain. An analysis of these findings indicated that these differences are associated with the presence of euphoria in cocaine use, and the absence of euphoria in the use of MPH (Volkow et al., 1995).

A few reports that have emphasized the abuse potential of stimulant treatments have intimated that ADHD is being promoted to increase the profits of pharamaceutical companies. In spite of the lack of factual support for these claims, they have fueled criticism of parents who administer prescribed stimulant treatments to their children. Whereas the amount of grief this causes to such children and their families cannot be measured, the harmful impact of inaccurate and ill-intended information is clearly evident in the testimonies of parents who have experienced it.

Medications for ADHD turn children into zombies.

This "Cuckoo's Nest" myth might be partially based on the erroneous assumption that anti-psychotic tranquilizers would be used to treat hyperactivity. It supports another myth that parents who agree to medical treatment for their children are drugging them into a stupor so they will be compliant and easily managed. The first-line medical treatments for ADHD are medications that stimulate the central nervous system, followed by several nonstimulant medications. Although side-effects from these medications are uncommon, were a child, adolescent, or adult to manifest "zombie-like" behavior, it is highly likely that the attending physician would adjust, discontinue, or change the treatment.

Stimulant medications have been used for over 55 years to treat the symptoms of ADHD (Swanson et al., 1995). They are used to treat between 60% and 90% of diagnosed cases of ADHD (Whalen & Henker, 1991). They are by far the most widely studied, clinically effective, and commonly prescribed treatments for ADHD (Goldman et al., 1998). These medications are widely regarded in the medical community as safe and highly effective psychopharmacological treatments for

ADHD (Davy & Rogers, 1989). Between 76% and 92% of the children for whom stimulants have been prescribed demonstrate significant improvement (Rapport, Denney, DuPaul, & Gardner, 1994).

Numerous studies have demonstrated the short-term effectiveness of stimulants in reducing a range of core ADHD symptoms (Abikoff & Gittelman, 1985; Jacobvitz, Stoufe, Stewart, & Leffert, 1990; Pelham, 1982), as well as their effectiveness in improving parent-child interactions (Barkley & Cunningham, 1979), problem-solving and interactions with peers (Whalen, Henker, Collins, McAuliffe, & Vaux, 1979; Granger, Whalen, & Henker, 1993), and performance on laboratory tasks (Conners, Eisenberg, & Sharpe, 1964; Gan & Cantwell, 1982; Swanson & Kinsbourne, 1976).

The study and use of stimulants in the treatment of hyperactive behavior are not a new or recent development. In 1937 an article described the effects of a central nervous system stimulant drug, Benzedrine, on a group of children who demonstrated a high level of problems with hyperactivity, inattentiveness, and emotionality in school (Bradley, 1937). It found that about half of the children in the study showed improvement when treated with Benzedrine. Moreover, an enormous body of scientific literature exists on the use of stimulant medication to treat ADHD. In 1993 a "review of reviews" of journal articles was published on the topic of stimulant treatment for ADHD. Its authors looked at original work published between 1937 and 1993 and found, among other things, that the reviews showed a "surprising consensus" regarding the efficacy of stimulant treatment (Swanson et al., 1993).

The action of stimulant medication has also been investigated by researchers who have looked at its effect on dopamine activity in the brain. They have done this by measuring the concentrations of its metabolite, homovanillic acid, in the cerebrospinal fluid of subjects with and without ADHD (Reimherr, Wender, Ebert, & Wood, 1984; Shaywitz, Cohen, & Bowers, 1977; Shaywitz, Cohen, Leckman, Young, & Bowers, 1980; Shetty & Chase, 1976; Wender, 1973). The results of a relatively recent study clearly indicated that changes in its amount correlated with reductions in hyperactivity resulting from treatment with stimulant medication. Researchers found that the reductions occurred following the administration of a stimulant also correlated with decreases in hyperactivity, and were, at least in part, related to decreasing dopamine turnover (Castellanos, Elia, et al., 1996).

Looking to the Future

How did these myths about ADHD originate? Many of them may have started as misconceptions based on assumptions that were common at the time they were conceived. For example, the notion that sugary food caused hyperactivity was conceived during an era in which athletes, just as mistakenly, believed they could boost their energy levels by consuming candy bars just before competing in races. However, although these myths have been disproven by scientific information, many of them have been perpetuated to serve agendas that are less concerned with the truth than with their own interests. These have included the promotion of treatments of unproven efficacy, "parent bashing," and the rationalization of inept, substandard, or discriminatory educational practices.

Few outcomes of scientific progress in the field of ADHD would be more important to those living with it than the achievement of an environment in which they are treated with understanding and fairness. Attitudes that stem from misinformation hamper the progress of individuals with the disorder and many often cause their potential contributions to be lost to our society. Although there is an abundance of scientific findings to correct the myths in circulation, at times they seem to receive more press than does well-founded evidence. Efforts to promote the dissemination of research-based information about ADHD are critical to dispelling the myths about this disorder. And as the public media increasingly distribute well-validated information, the more likely it is that health care systems, education programs, and society at large will deal fairly with those living with it.

In concluding this article about myths and misconceptions, it seems appropriate to repeat a bit of wisdom quoted by Peter S. Jensen, Chief of the Child and Adolescent Research Branch of the National Institute of Mental Health (Jensen, 1998). He recalled first hearing this aphorism from the late Dennis Cantwell, an esteemed pioneering researcher in the field of ADHD, who said: "In God we trust, but from all others, demand data!"

References

Abikoff, H., & Gittelman, R. (1985). The normalizing effects of methylphenidate on the classroom behavior of hyperactive children. *Journal of Abnormal Child Psychology, 13*, 33–44.

Alexander, G. E., & Crutcher, M. D. (1990). Functional architecture of basal ganglia circuits: Neural substrates of parallel processing. *Trends in Neuroscience, 13*, 266–271.

Alexander, G. E., DeLong, M. R., & Strick, P. L. (1986). Parallel organization of functionally segregated circuits linking basal ganglia to the frontal cortex. *Annual Review of Neuroscience, 9*, 357–381.

American Academy of Child & Adolescent Psychiatry. (1997). Practice parameters for the assessment and treatment of children, adolescents, and adults with Attention-Deficit/Hyperactivity Disorder. *Journal of the American Academy of Child and Adolescent Psychiatry, 36* (10, supplement), 85S–121S.

American Psychiatric Association. (1994). *Diagnostic and statistical manual of mental disorders* (4th ed.). Washington, DC: Author.

Anderson, J. C., Williams, S., McGee, R., & Silva, P. A. (1987). DSM-III disorders in preadolescent children. *Archives of General Psychiatry, 44*, 69–76.

Armin, K., Douglas, V. I., Mendelson, M. J., & Dufresne, J. (1993). Separable/integral classification by hyperactive and normal children. *Developmental Psychopathology, 5*, 415–431.

Barkley, R. (1988). Child behavior rating scales and checklists. In M. Rutter, H. Tuma, and I. Lann (Eds.), *Assessment and Diagnosis in Child Psychopathology* (pp. 113–155). New York: Guilford.

Barkley, R. A. (1990). *Attention Deficit Hyperactivity Disorder: A handbook for diagnosis and treatment.* New York: Guilford.

Barkley, R. A. (1998). The prevalence of ADHD: Is it just a US disorder? *The ADHD Report, 6,* (2), 1–6.

Barkley, R. A., & Cunningham, C. E. (1979). The effects of methylphenidate on the mother–child interactions of hyperactive children. *Archives of General Psychiatry, 36,* 85–92.

Barkley, R. A., Fischer, M., Edelbrock, C. S., & Smallish, L. (1990). The adolescent outcome of hyperactive children diagnosed by research criteria: I. An 8-year prospective follow-up study. *Journal of the American Academy of Child and Adolescent Psychiatry, 29,* 546–557.

Baumbaertel, A., Wolraich, M. L., & Dietrich, M. (1995). Comparison of diagnostic criteria for attention deficit disorders in a German elementary school sample. *Journal of the Academy of Child and Adolescent Psychiatry, 34,* 629–638.

Benjamin, J., Li, L., Patterson, C., Greenberg, B. D., Murphy, D. L., & Hamer, D. H. (1996). Population and familial association between the D4 dopamine receptor gene and measures of novelty seeking. *Nature Genetics, 12,* 81–84.

Benton, D. F. (1991). The role of frontal dysfunction in attention deficit hyperactivity disorder. *Journal of Child Neurology, 6* (supplement), 9–12.

Bhatia, M. S., Nigam, V. R., Bohra, N., & Malik, S. C. (1991). Attention deficit disorder with hyperactivity among paediatric outpatients. *Journal of Child Psychology and Psychiatry, 145,* 185–190.

Biederman, J., Faraone, S., Keenan, K., Benjamin, J., Krifcher, B., Moore, C., & Sprich-Buckminster, S. (1992). Further evidence for family–genetic risk factors in attention deficit hyperactivity disorder: Patterns of comorbidity in probands and relatives in psychiatrically and pediatrically referred samples. *Archives of General Psychiatry, 49,* 728–738.

Biederman, J., Faraone, S. V., Mick, E., Spencer, T., Wilens, T., Kiely, K., Guite, J., Ablon, J. S., Reed, E., & Warburton, R. (1995). High risk for attention deficit hyperactivity disorder among children of parents with childhood onset of the disorder: A pilot study. *American Journal of Pyschiatry, 152,* 431–435.

Biederman, J., Newcorn, J., & Sprich, S. (1991). Comorbidity of attention deficit hyperactivity disorder with conduct, depressive, anxiety, and other disorders. *American Journal of Psychiatry, 48,* 564–567.

Bird, H., Canino, G., & Rubio-Stipec, M. (1988). Estimates of the prevalence of childhood maladjustment in a community survey in Puerto Rico. *Archives of General Psychiatry, 45,* 1120–1126.

Bradley, C. (1937). The behavior of children receiving Benzedrine. *American Journal of Psychiatry, 94,* 577–585.

Cantwell, D. (1972). Psychiatric illness in the families of hyperactive children. *Archives of General Psychiatry, 27,* 414–427.

Castellanos, F. X. (1997). Toward a pathophysiology of Attention-Deficit/Hyperactivity Disorder. *Clinical Pediatrics, 36*(7), 381–393.

Castellanos, F. X., Elia, J., Kruesi, M. J., Gulotta, C. S. Mefford, I. N., Potter, W. Z., Ritchie, G. F., & Rapoport, J. L. (1994). Cerebrospinal fluid monoamine metabolites in boys with Attention Deficit Hyperactivity Disorder. *Psychiatry Research, 52,* 305–316.

Castellanos, F. X., Elia, J., Kruesi, M. J., Marsh, W. L., Gulotta, C. S., Potter, W. Z., Ritchie, G. F., Hamburger, S. D., & Rapoport, J. L. (1996). Cerebrospinal fluid homovanillic acid predicts behavioral response to stimulants in 45 boys with attention deficit hyperactivity disorder. *Neuropsychopharmacology, 14*(2), 125–137.

CH.A.D.D. (1994). Educators Inservice Training Program. Plantation, FL: Author.

Chelune, G. J., Ferguson, W., Koon, R., & Dickey, T. O. (1986). Frontal lobe disinhibition in attention deficit disorder. *Child Psychiatry and Human Development, 16,* 221–234.

Clements, S. D. (1966). Minimal brain dysfunction in children. NINDB Monograph No. 3. U.S. Department of Health, Education, and Welfare, Public Health Service.

Clements, S. D., & Peters, J. E. (1962). Minimal brain dysfunctions in the school-age child. *Archives of General Psychiatry, 6,* 185–197.

Cole, J. (1969). The amphetamines in child psychiatry: A review. *Seminars in Psychiatry, 1,* 174–178.

Conners, C. K., Eisenberg, L., & Sharpe, L. (1964). The effects of methylphenidate on paired associate learning and Porteus maze performance in emotionally disturbed children. *Journal of Consulting Psychology, 28,* 14–22.

Cook, E. H., Stein, M. A., Drasowski, M. D., Cox, N. J., Olkon, D. M., Kieffer, J. E., & Leventhal, B. L. (1995). Association of Attention Deficit Disorder and the dopamine transporter gene. *American Journal of Human Genetics, 56,* 593–598.

Davy, T., & Rodgers, C. L. (1989). Stimulant medication and short attention span: A clinical approach. *Developmental and Behavioral Pediatrics, 10*(6), 313–318.

Denckla, M. B. (1989). Biological correlates of learning and attention: What is relevant to learning disability and Attention-Deficit Hyperactivity Disorder? *Developmental and Behavioral Pediatrics, 17*(2), 114–119.

Denckla, M. B. (1996). A theory and model of executive function. A neuropsychological perspective. In G. R. Lyon & N. A. Krasnegor (Eds.), *Attention, memory, and executive function* (pp. 263–278. Baltimore: Brookes.

Deutsch, C. K., Matthysse, S., Swanson, J. M., & Farkas, L. G. (1990). Genetic latent structure analysis of dysmorphology in Attention Deficit Disorder. *Journal of the American Academy of Child & Adolescent Psychiatry, 29*(2), 189–194.

Douglas, V. I. (1972). Stop, look and listen: The problem of sustained attention and impulse control in hyperactive and normal children. *Canadian Journal of Behavioral Science, 4,* 258–282.

Douglas, V. I. (1985). The response of ADD children to reinforcement: Theoretical and clinical implications. In L. M. Bloomingdale (Ed.), *Attention Deficit Disorder: Identification, course and rationale.* New York: Spectrum.

Douglas, V. I., & Parry, P. A. (1983). Effects of reward on delayed reaction time task performance of hyperactive children. *Journal of Abnormal Child Psychology, 11,* 313–326.

Dykens, K., Leckman, J. R., & Riddle, M. (1990). Intellectual, academic, and adaptive funtioning of Tourette's Syndrome children with and without Attention Deficit Disorder. *Journal of Abnormal Child Psychology, 18,* 607–615.

Ebaugh, F. G. (1923). Neuropsychiatric sequelae of acute epidemic encephalitus in children. *American Journal of Diseases in Children, 25,* 89–97.

Ebstein, R. P., Novick, O., Umansky, R., Priel, B., Osher, Y., Blaine, D., Bennett, E. R., Nemanov, L., Katz, M., & Belmaker, R. H. (1996). Dopamine D4 receptor (D4DR) exon III polymorphism associated with the human personality trait of novelty seeking. *Nature Genetics, 12,* 78–80.

Educational Testing Service. 1998. *Policy statement for documentation of Attention-Deficit/Hyperactivity Disorder in adolescents and adults.* Princeton, NJ: Author.

Edwards, G. (1998). Determining the role of a new continuous performance test in the diagnostic evaluation for ADHD. *ADHD Report, 6*(3), 11–13.

Faraone, S. V., Biederman, J., Lehman, B. K., Keenan, K., Norman, D., Seidman, L. J., Kolodny, R., Kraus, I., Perrin, J., & Chen, W. J. (1993). Evidence for the independent familial transmission of Attention Deficit Hyperactivity Disorder and learning disabilities: Results from a family genetic study. *American Journal of Psychiatry, 150*(6), 891–895.

Ferguson, D. M., Horwood, L. J., & Lynskey, M. T. (1993). Prevalence and comorbidity of DSM-III-R diagnoses in a birth cohort of 15 year olds. *Journal of the American Academy of Child and Adolescent Psychiatry, 32,* 1127–1134.

Fischer, M., Newby, R. F., & Gordon, M. (1995). Who are the false negatives on continuous performance tests? *Journal of Clinical Child Psychology, 24,* 427–433.

Frick, P. J., Lahey, B. B., & Applegate, B. (1994). DSM-IV field trials for the disruptive behavior disorders: Symptom utility estimates. *Journal of the American Academy of Child and Adolescent Psychiatry, 33,* 529–539.

Gallucci, F., Bird, H. R., Berardi, C., & Gallai, V. (1993). Symptoms of Attention-Deficit Hyperactivity Disorder in an Italian school sample: Findings of a pilot study. *Journal of the American Academy of Child and Adolescent Psychiatry, 31*(5), 1051–1058.

Gan, J., & Cantwell, D. P. (1982). Dosage effects of methylphenidate on paired-associate learning: Positive/negative placebo responders. *Journal of the American Academy of Child Psychiatry, 21,* 237–242.

Gaub, M., & Carlson, G. (1997). Gender differences in ADHD: A meta-analysis and critical review. *Journal of the American Academy of Child and Adolescent Psychiatry, 36,* 1036–1045.

Giedd, J. N., Castellanos, F. X., Casey, B. J., Kozuch, P., King, A. C., Hamburger, S. D., & Rapoport, J. L. (1994) Quantitative morphology of the corpus callosum in Attention Deficit Hyperactivity Disorder. *American Journal of Psychiatry, 151,* 665–669.

Gilger, J. W., Pennington, B. F., & DeFries, J. C. (1992). A twin study of the etiology of comorbidity: Attention-Deficit Hyperactivity Disorder and dyslexia. *Journal of the American Academy of Child and Adolescent Psychiatry, 31,* 343–348.

Gill, M., Daly, G., Heron, S., Hawi, Z., & Fitzgerald, M. (1997). Confirmation of association between Attention Deficit Hyperactivity Disorder and a dopamine transporter polymorphism. *Molecular Psychiatry, 2,* 311–313.

Gillis, J. J., Gilger, J. W., Pennington, B. F., & DeFries, J. C. (1992). Attention Deficit Disorder in reading-disabled twins: Evidence for a genetic etiology. *Journal of Abnormal Child Psychology, 20,* 303–315.

Gittelman, R., Mannuzza, S., Shenker, R., & Bonagura, N. (1985). Hyperactive boys almost grown up: I. Psychiatric status. *Archives of General Psychiatry, 42,* 937–947.

Goldman, L. S., Genel, M., Bezman, R. J., & Slanetz, P. J. (1998). Report on MPH for the Council on Scientific Affairs, American Medical Association. *Journal of the American Medical Association, 279,* 1100–1107.

Goldstein, K. (1942). *After effects of brain injuries in war.* New York: Grune & Stratton.

Goldstein, S., & Goldstein, M. (1990). *Managing attention disorders in children: A guide for practitioners.* New York: Wiley.

Granger, D. A., Whalen, C. K., & Henker, B. (1993). Perceptions of methlyphenidate effects on hyperactive children's peer interactions. *Journal of Abnormal Child Psychology, 21,* 535–550.

Greenhill, L. L. (1996, December). *The use of stimulants in the treatment of AD/HD.* Paper presented at the Drug Enforcement Administration Conference, San Antonio, TX.

Hallowell, E. M., & Ratey, J. J. (1994). *Driven to distraction.* New York: Pantheon.

Hart, E. D., Lahey, B. B., & Loeber, R. (1995). Developmental change in AD/HD in boys: A four year longitudinal study. *Journal of Child and Adolescent Psychology, 23,* 729–749.

Hechtman, L. (1991). Resilience and vulnerability and long term outcome of Attention Deficit Hyperactivity Disorder. *Canadian Journal of Psychiatry, 36,* 415–421.

Hechtman, L. (1994). Genetic and neurobiological aspects of Attention Deficit Hyperactivity Disorder: A review. *Journal of Psychiatric Neuroscience, 19,* 193–201.

Hohman, L. B. (1922). Post encephalitic behavior disorder in children. *Bulletin of Johns Hopkins Hospital, 380,* 372–375.

Hoover, D. W., & Milich, R. (1994). Effects of sugar ingestion expectancies on mother–child interactions. *Journal of Abnormal Child Psychology, 22,* 501–515.

Hynd, G. W., Hern, K. L., Voeller, K. K., & Marshall, R. M. (1991). Neurobiological basis of Attention-Deficit Hyperactivity Disorder (ADHD). *School Psychology Review, 20*(2), 174–186.

Jacobvitz, D., Stoufe, L. A., Stewart, M., & Leffert, N. (1990). Treatment of attentional and hyperactivity problems in children with symphomimetric drugs: A comprehensive review. *Journal of the American Academy of Child and Adolescent Psychiatry, 29,* 677–688.

Jensen, P. S. (1996). Testimony before the Human Resources and Intergovernmental Relations Subcommittee of the U.S. House Committee on Government Reform and Oversight. July 16, 1996.

Jensen, P. S. (1998). NIH sets consensus development conference on the diagnosis and treatment of AD/HD. Attention (Spring issue), 10–11.

Kinsbourne, M. (1973). Minimal brain dysfunction as a neurodevelopmental lag. *Annals of the New York Academy of Sciences, 205,* 263–273.

Klein, R. G., & Mannuzza, S. (1991). Long term follow-up of hyperactive children: A review. *Journal of the American Academy of Child and Adolescent Psychiatry, 30,* 383–387.

Klorman, R., Brumaghim, J. T., Fitzpatrick, P. A., & Borgstedt, A. D., (1992). Methylphenidate reduces abnormalities of stimulus classification in adolescents with Attention Deficit Disorder. *Journal of Abnormal Psychology, 101*(1), 130–138.

LaHoste, G. J., Swanson, J. L., Wigal, S. B., Glabe, C., Wigal, T., King, N., & Kennedy, J. L. (1996). Dopamine D4 receptor gene polymorphism is associated with attention deficit hyperactivity disorder. *Journal of Molecular Psychiatry, 1,* 121–124.

Lapouse, R., & Monk, M. (1958). An epidemiological study of behavior characteristics in children. *American Journal of Public Health, 48,* 1134-1144.

Laufer, M. W., & Denhoff, E. (1957). Hyperkinetic behavior syndrome in children. *Journal of Pediatrics, 50,* 463–474.

Leung, P. W. L., Luk, S. L., Ho, T. P., Taylor, E., Mak, F. L., & Bacon-Shone, J. (1996). The diagnosis and prevalence of hyperactivity in Chinese schoolboys. *British Journal of Psychiatry, 168,* 486–496.

Levy, F., Hay, D. A., McStephen, M., Wood, C., & Waldman, I. (1997). Attention Deficit Hyperacvity Disorder: A category or a continuum? Genetic analysis of a large-scale twin study. *Journal of the American Academy of Child and Adolescent Psychiatry, 36,* 737–744.

Mannuzza, S., Klein, R. G., Bessler, A., Malloy, P., & LaPadula, M. (1993). Adult outcome of hyperactive boys. *Archives of General Psychiatry, 50,* 565–576.

Milberger, S., Biederman, J., & Faraone, S. V. (1994). Pregnancy, delivery and infancy complications and Attention Deficit Hyperactivity Disorder: Issues of gene–environment interaction. *Scientific Proceedings of the Annual Meeting, American Academy of Child and Adolescent Psychiatry, 10*(66): Abstract.

Murphy, K., & Barkley, R. A. (1996). Prevalence of DSM-IV symptoms of ADHD in adult licensed drivers: Implications for clinical diagnosis. *Journal of Attention Disorders, 1,* 147–161.

Office of Public Affairs, Drug Enforcement Administration, Department of Justice. (1995). *Methylphenidate yearly production quota (1975–1995).* Washington, DC: U.S. Government Printing Office.

Pelham, W. E. (1982). Childhood hyperactivity: Diagnosis, etiology, nature and treatment. *Behavioral Medicine and Clinical Psychology: Overlapping Principles,* 261–327.

Rapoport, J. L., Buchsbaum, M. S., & Weingartner, H. (1980). Dextroamphetamine: Cognitive and behavioral effects in normal and hyperactive boys and men. *Archives of General Psychiatry, 37,* 933–943.

Rapport, M. D., Denney, C., DuPaul, G. I., & Gardner, M. J. (1994). Attention Deficit Disorder and methylphenidate normalization rates, clinical effectiveness, and response prediction in 76 children. *Journal of the American Academy of Child and Adolescent Psychiatry, 33,* 882-893.

Reimherr, F. W., Wender, P. H., Ebert, M. H., & Wood, D. R. (1984). Cerebrospinal fluid homovanillic acid and 5 hydroxyindoleacetic acid in adults with Attention Deficit Disorder, residual type. *Psychiatry Research, 11,* 71–78

Richters, J. E., Arnold, L. E., Jensen, P. S., Abikoff, H., Conners, C. K., Greenhill, L. L., Hechtman, L., Hinshaw, S. P., Pelham, W. E., & Swanson, J. M. (1995). NIMH collaborative multisite, multimodal treatment study of children with ADHD: I. Background and rationale. *Journal of the American Academy of Child and Adolescent Psychiatry, 34*(8), 987–1000.

Robin, A., Tzelepis, A., & Bedway, M. (1997, October). Understanding the personality of adults with AD/HD: A pilot study. Paper presented at the Ninth International Conference on Attention Deficit Disorders, San Antonio, TX.

Roisen, N. J., Blondis, T. A., Irwin, M., & Stein, M. (1994). Adaptive functioning in children with Attention-Deficit hyperactivity disorder. *Archives of Pediatric and Adolescent Medicine, 148,* 1137–1142.

Safer, D. J., Zito, J. M., & Fine, E. M. (1996). Increased methylphenidate usage for Attention Deficit Hyperactivity Disorder in the 1990's. *Pediatrics, 98,* 1084–1088.

Semrud-Clikeman, M. S., Biederman, J., Sprich, S., Krifcher, B., Norman, D., & Faraone, S. (1992). Comorbidity between ADDH and learning disability: A review and report in a clinically referred sample. *Journal of Consulting Clinical Psychology, 58,* 439–448.

Shaffer, D., Fisher, P., & Dulcan, M. K. (1996). The NIMH diagnostic interview schedule for children, version 2.3: Description, acceptability, prevalence rates, and performance in the MECA study. *Journal of the American Academy of Child & Adolescent Psychiatry, 35,* 865–877.

Shaywitz, B. A., Cohen, D. J., & Bowers, M. B. (1977). CSF monomamine metabolites in children with minimal brain dysfunction: Evidence for alteration of d/brain dopamine. *Journal of Pediatrics, 90,* 67–71.

Shaywitz, B. A., Cohen, D. J., Leckman, J. F., Young, J. G., & Bowers, M. B., Jr. (1980). Ontogeny of dopamine and serotonin metabolites in the cerebrospinal fluid of children with neurologic disorders. *Developmental Medicine and Child Neurology, 22,* 748-754.

Shaywitz, B. A., Sullivan, C. M., Anderson, G. M., Gillespie, S. M., Sullivan, B., & Shaywitz, S. E. (1994). Aspartame, behavior, and cognitive function of children with Attention Deficit Disorder. *Pediatrics, 93*(1), 70–75.

Shetty, T., & Chase, T. N. (1976). Central monoamines and hyperkinesis of childhood. *Neurology, 26,* 1000–1002.

Spencer, T., Biederman, J., & Harding, M. (1996). Growth deficits in ADHD revisited: Evidence for disorders-associated growth delays. *Journal of the American Academy of Child & Adolescent Psychiatry, 35,* 1460–1469.

Sprich-Buckminster, S., Biederman, J., Milberger, S., Faraone, S. B., & Lehman, B. K. (1993). Are perinatal complications relevant to the manifestation of ADHD? Issues of comorbidity and familiarity. *Journal of the American Academy of Child & Adolescent Psychiatry, 32,* 1032–1037.

Still, G. F. (1902). The Coulstonian Lectures on some abnormal physical conditions in children. *Lancet, 1,* 1008–1012, 1077–1082, 1163–1168.

Strauss, A. A., & Lehtinen, L. E. (1947). *Psychopathology and education of the brain-injured child.* New York: Grune & Stratton.

Swanson, J. M., Cantwell, D., Lerner, M., McBurnett, K., Pfiffner, L., & Kotkin, R. (1992). Treatment of ADHD: Beyond medication. *Beyond Behavior, 4,* 13–22.

Swanson, J. M., & Kinsbourne, M. (1976). Stimulant-related state-dependent learning in hyperactive children. *Science, 192,* 1754–1755.

Swanson, J. M., McBurnett, K., Christian, D. L., & Wigal, T. (1995). Stimulant medications and the treatment of children with AD/HD. In Ollendick & Prinz (Eds.), *Advances in Clinical Child Psychology* (Vol. 17), New York: Plenum.

Swanson, J. M., McBurnett, K., Wigal, T., Pfiffner, L. J., Lerner, M. A., Williams, L., Christian, D. L., Tamm, L., Willcutt, E., Crowley, K., Clevenger, W., Nader, K., Woo, C., Crinella, F. M., & Fisher, T. D. (1993). Effect of stimulant medication on children with Attention Deficit Disorder: A "review of reviews." *Exceptional Children, 60,* 154–162.

Swanson, J. M., Sunohara, G. A., Kennedy, J. L., Regino, R., Fineberg, E., Wigal, E., LaHoste, G. J., & Wigal, S. (1997). *Association of the dopamine receptor D4 (DRD4) gene with a refined phenotype of Attention Deficit Hyperactivity Disorder (ADHD): A family-based approach.* Manuscript submitted for publication.

Szatmari, P., Offord, D. R., & Boyle, M. H. (1989). Ontario Health Study: Prevalence of Attention Deficit Disorder with hyperactivity. *Journal of Child Psychology & Psychiatry & Allied Disciplines, 30*(2), 219–230.

Volkow, N. D., Ding, Y., Fowlder, J. S., Wang, G., Logan, J., Fatley, J., Dewey, S., Ashby, C., Liebermann, J. S., Hitzemann, R., & Wolf, A. P. (1995). Is methylphenidate like cocaine? Studies on their pharmacokinetics and distribution in the human brain. *Archives of General Psychiatry, 52,* 456–463.

Weiss, G., & Hechtman, L. T. (1993). *Hyperactive children grown up: ADHD in children, adolescents, and adults* (2nd ed.). New York: Guilford.

Weiss, G., Hechtman, L., Milroy, T., & Perlman, T. (1985). Psychiatric status of hyperactive children as adults: A controlled 15-year follow-up of 63 hyperactive children. *Journal of the American Academy of Child Psychiatry, 24,* 211–220.

Wender, P. H. (1973). Some speculations concerning a possible biochemical basis of minimal brain dysfunction. *Annals of the New York Academy of Science, 205,* 21–28.

Wender, P. (1995). Prevalence of ADHD in adults. In *Attention-Deficit Hyperactivity Disorder in adults* (pp. 41–74). New York: Oxford University Press.

Wender, P. A., Reimherr, F. W., & Wood, D. R. (1985). Controlled study of methylphenidate in the treatment of Attention Deficit Disorder, residual type in adults. *American Journal of Psychiatry, 142,* 547–552.

Whalen, C. K., & Henker, B. (1991). Therapies for hyperactive children: Comparisons, combinations, and compromises. *Journal of Consulting and Clinical Psychology, 59,* 126–137.

Whalen, C. K., Henker, B., Collins, B. E., McAuliffe, S., & Vaux, A. (1979). Peer interaction in a structured communication task: Comparisons of normal and hyperactive boys and of methylphenidate (Ritalin) and placebo effects. *Child Development, 50,* 388–401.

Wolraich, M. L., Lindgren, S. D., Stumbo, P. J., Stegink, L. D., Appelbaum, M. I., & Kiritsy, M. C. (1994). Effects of diets high in sucrose or aspartame on the behavior and cognitive performance of children. *New England Journal of Medicine, 330,* 301–307.

Wolraich, M. L., Milich, R., Stumbo, P., & Schultz, F. (1985). The effects of sucrose ingestion on the behavior of hyperactive boys. *Pediatrics, 106,* 675–682.

Appendix A

Famous People with ADHD and/or LD

BARBARA PRIDDY GUYER   *KENNETH E. GUYER*

Throughout human history there have been those who have exhibited symptoms of what we currently refer to as Attention Deficit Hyperactivity Disorder (ADHD) and learning disabilities (LD). Of course, test results are not available to us so that we may clarify whether one or both of these conditions actually existed in these people. For our purposes here, however, it seems worthwhile to look at some of the people in history who became very successful in spite of possibly having ADHD and/or LD. We will examine some of their strengths as well as characteristics that may have required many compensatory skills.

- **George Patton:** Patton never learned to read well enough to read textbooks. His mother read to him until he left home to attend West Point. When he was a cadet, he paid classmates to read to him. Some have believed that the social–emotional problems that he exhibited during World War II were the result of the trauma he experienced pursuant to his failure to read. The creative genius that he possessed in planning battle strategy has been equaled by few other people in history.
- **Greg Louganis:** This Olympic gold-medal-winning diver said, "When you are told that you are lazy when you are 6, 7 or 8 years old and you're told enough times, you begin to believe it. The only place I really felt comfortable was with athletics and especially in the water."
- **F. W. Woolworth:** Woolworth had a job in a yard goods store when he was 21 years old, but his employers wouldn't let him wait on customers because he "didn't have enough sense." Woolworth sometimes spoke before he thought about what he was going to say, and one wonders if his possible impulsivity

could have been a symptom of ADHD. This didn't keep him from becoming one of the world's wealthiest men, we must hasten to note.

- **Walt Disney:** A newspaper editor fired him because he had "no good ideas." Also, he went bankrupt for seven years in succession. He was dishonorably discharged from the military because he had so much difficulty in following directions. Disney is another example of a person possessing creative ideas far beyond what is found in the general population. His introduction of Mickey Mouse to the world has certainly changed entertainment significantly.

- **J. C. Penney:** At the age of 57 he was in a psychiatric ward, diagnosed as "crazy" and left alone. He owed $6,000,000, but when he died at the age of 92, his fortune had changed drastically and he was a multimillionaire. Penney was easily distracted and had a short attention span at times. However, he was able to hyperfocus when something interested him intensely.

- **Leo Tolstoy:** He was a brilliant novelist and philosopher who managed to flunk out of college. He was rather disorganized and had difficulty in focusing on one topic for any length of time. He was a celebrated Russian writer of fiction, as well as a great moral thinker and social reformer. His two most notable books, *War and Peace* and *Anna Karenina,* have been enjoyed by people throughout the world. He seemed to possess a gift of empathy and was able to beautifully describe how people felt when they experienced love, fear, hatred, hunger, etc.

- **Werner von Braun:** He was a gifted rocket engineer who failed math when he was in school. His mother never seemed to lose patience with him and tried to help Werner as much as she could. Von Braun is another example of a creative genius who had difficulty with some of the more mundane requirements of life, such as multiplication and division.

- **Amadeus Mozart:** Mozart is a classic example of someone with ADHD. He was impatient, impulsive, emotionally immature, distractible, very energetic, creative (which he put to good use in writing music), and a maverick. Hallowell (1994) wrote that Mozart's work "shows how beautifully structure can capture the dart-here, dart-there genius of the ADHD mind. In fact, there is a powerfully positive aspect . . . you might describe many with ADHD as having a 'special something,' a hard-to-pin-down, yet undeniable potential. If that potential can be tapped, the results can be spectacular."

- **Louisa May Alcott:** Alcott was a popular American novelist who was told by an editor that she could never write well enough to have anything that would appeal to large groups of people. She later wrote the classic *Little Women* among other popular books and is regarded by many as a great author.

- **Harvey Cushing:** Dr. Cushing was a famous surgeon and Pulitzer Prize winner for his biography of William Osler. Dr. Cushing was also a dyslexic who had serious problems with spelling. He had someone write his thesis for the M.D. degree for him (Cushing did the work), but at the last minute he decided to make a few changes by writing in the margins. His additions were full of reversals and "creatively" spelled words.

- **Paul Ehrlich:** He was a famous German bacteriologist who almost failed to graduate from preparatory school, much less college. He experienced a great deal of difficulty with written examinations and was diagnosed as having what we now refer to as dyslexia when he was a child.
- **Louis Pasteur:** He was a gifted French chemist who made important discoveries in microbiology and immunology. He was rated as a mediocre student when he was in school, but his teachers felt that he was capable of performing on a much higher level. He was disorganized and seemed "to march to a different drummer."

In More Recent Years

- **P. Buckley Moss:** She is a famous artist whose watercolors feature life and scenes of the Shenandoah Valley of Virginia and often the Amish people. When she was in school, she was described as being hyperactive, inattentive, a slow learner, and, finally, stupid. She tried very hard, but throughout school the only compliments she ever received were for her drawings. Today she is known all over the world, and she helps organizations interested in LD and ADHD raise money by donating her paintings.
- **Jay Leno:** He is a popular comedian who has a gift with oral expression but not written language. Diagnosed as a dyslexic, he has problems with reversals and transpositions and is a very poor speller. His creative ideas help to make him a success on *The Tonight Show.* In watching him on TV, one wonders if he was hyperactive as a child. He does appear to have a high energy level, but we do not know if he also has ADHD.
- **Edward Hallowell:** Many adults who have ADHD have been helped by reading Dr. Hallowell's books on that topic (*Driven to Distraction* and *Answers to Distraction*). Although he has been diagnosed as having ADHD, he has been able to acquire and maintain his position as a professor in the Psychiatry Department of the Harvard University School of Medicine. He has served as a source of inspiration to many who have ADHD and have dreams for the future. Hallowell has said that his relationship with words is founded on unpredictability. One moment he (and others with ADHD) are like Abraham Lincoln composing a Gettysburg Address, and the next moment the relationship with words is as clumsy as a boy on his first date.
- **Donald Coffey:** Dr. Coffey is a distinguished professor of urology, oncology, pharmacology, and molecular sciences at the Johns Hopkins University School of Medicine. He had an unusual school career but was so obviously gifted that he was able to persuade influential people to allow him to do what he felt he needed to do. He has published almost 250 articles in scientific journals. In 1990 he was selected by the Lab School of Washington, D.C. (a prestigious school for students with LD/ADHD), as the recipient of the Outstanding Achiever Award. This award goes to a person who has a learn-

ing disability, and often ADHD, who has made an outstanding contribution to our society.

- **Henry Winkler:** He is probably best known for his role as the "Fonz." Henry Winkler has stated that the Fonz is very much like himself. He said that he was hyperactive when he was younger, he was easily distracted, he was definitely impulsive (act first, think later!), and he had a short attention span. He has used the creativity that often accompanies LD/ADHD to good advantage by becoming a highly respected actor, director, and producer.
- **Jackie Stewart:** He is certainly one of the most successful Grand Prix drivers in racing history. Today he cannot recite the alphabet and is functionally illiterate. He is a consultant for Goodyear and test-drives their new tires, advising the designers what changes need to be made. He continues to desire to learn to read and regrets that the world of written language seems to be "off limits" for him. Fortunately, Jackie Stewart has found a profession where his difficulty with written language is not a hindrance to his success.
- **Kate Kelly and Peggy Ramundo:** These two women wrote a very popular and helpful book, *You Mean I'm Not Lazy, Stupid or Crazy?* They were both diagnosed as having ADHD when they were adults and have used their experiences to help others learn to survive. They both help adults learn to cope with life successfully and encourage them to concentrate on the assets of ADHD rather than to bemoan the problems that ADHD causes them to have. We are fortunate to have Peggy Ramundo as one of the authors in this book.

Recommended Readings

Fleming, E. (1982). *Believe the Heart: Our dyslexic days.* San Francisco: Strawberry Hill.

Guyer, B. (1988). Dyslexic doctors: A resource in need of discovery. *Southern Medical Journal, 81,*1151–1154.

Guyer, B. P. (1997). *The pretenders: Gifted people who have difficulty learning.* Homewood, IL: High Tide.

Hallowell, E. M., & Ratey, J. J. (1994). *Driven to distraction: Recognizing and coping with Attention*

Deficit Disorder from childhood through adulthood. New York: Random.

Kelly, K., & Ramundo, P. (1993). *You mean I'm not lazy, stupid or crazy? A self-help book for adults with Attention Deficit Disorder.* New York: Scribner.

Thompson, L. (1969). Language disabilities among men of eminence. *Bulletin of the Orton Society, 19,*113–120.

Appendix *B*

Resources for ADHD

COMPILED BY BARBARA P. GUYER

Videotapes and Audiotapes

All Children Learn Differently. Narrated by Steve Allen. Interviews with 12 specialists in medicine, perception, language, and education. Available from LDA, 4156 Library Rd., Pittsburgh, PA 15234. (412) 341-1515.

A Child's First Words. How speech and language development in young children can affect their ability to learn. Available from LDA, 4156 Library Rd., Pittsburgh, PA 15234. (412) 341-1515.

The Employment Interview and Disclosure. Tips for job seekers with LD/ADHD. Available from LDA, 4156 Library Rd., Pittsburgh, PA 15234. (412) 341-1515.

How Difficult Can This Be? (Understanding Learning Disabilities through the F.A.T. City Workshop) A classic in the LD/ADHD field with Rick Lavoie. 57 Min. Available from P.B.S. Video, (800) 424-7963.

How to Recognize ADD/ADHD as Distinct from LD. Vineyard Video Productions, P.O. Box 370, W. Teasbury, MA 02575. (800) 664-6119.

I'm Not Stupid. A 53-min. video that gives an overview of LD in children and adults. Available from LDA, 4156 Library Road, Pittsburgh, PA 15234. (412) 341-1515.

A Leader's Guide for Youth with Learning Disabilities. How leaders of groups can integrate those with LD/ADHD into regular programs, including scouts. $24 from LDA, 4156 Library Rd., Pittsburgh, PA 15234. (412) 341-1515.

Managing Oppositional Youth: Effective, Practical Strategies for Managing the Behavior of Hard to Manage Kids and Teens! A. Robin and S. Weiss. 53-min. video. $38. ADD Warehouse. (800) 233-9273.

National Council of Juvenile and Family Judges (audiotapes). Speeches presented by several renowned judges on LD/ADHD and delinquency. (702) 784-6012.

We Can Learn: Understanding and Helping Children with LD. $44 from NCLD, 381 Park Ave., Suite 1420, New York, NY 10016. (212) 545-7510.

What Every Teacher Should Know about ADD. Strategies on how to manage behavior with students who have ADD. Stresses teamwork approach. Research Press, P.O. Box 9177, Champaign, IL 61826. Internet: http://www.researchpress.com

Government Agencies

National Adult Literacy and Learning Disabilities Center (National ALLD Center)
Academy for Educational Development
1875 Connecticut Avenue, N.W.
Washington, DC 20009-1202
Phone: (202) 8184-8175 or (800) 953-2553. Fax: (202) 884-8422.
E-mail: info@nalldc.aed.org

National Institute of Child Health and Human Development
6100 Bldg.
9000 Rockville Pike
Bethesda, MD 20892

National Institute of Mental Health (NIMH)
5600 Fisher Lane
Rockville, MD 20857

Office of the Americans with Disabilities Act Civil Rights Division
U.S. Department of Justice
P.O. Box 66738
Washington, DC 20035-6118
ADA information line: (800) 514-0301

Office of Special Education and Rehabilitation Services
Room 3090, Switzer Building
330 C Street, S.W.
Washington, DC 20202

President's Committee on the Employment of People with Disabilities
1331 F Street, NW
Washington, DC 20036
Phone: (202) 376-6200. Fax: (202) 376-6859

National Organizations for ADHD and/or Learning Disabilities

ADDult Support Network
26210 Ivy Place
West Peabody, MA 01960-7277
Phone: (508) 535-3366.
Information only: (888) 239-4737.
Fax: (508) 535-3276.

Referrals to parent support groups. Will refer appropriate requests to professional advisors. Publishes a bi-monthly newsletter on ADHD issues.

Association on Higher Education for Adults with Disabilities (AHEAD)
University of Massachusetts
Boston, MA 02125
Phone: (617) 287-3880. Fax: (617) 287-3881.
Internet: www.ahead.gov.
Email: ahead@umb.org

Organization of professionals that attempts to help people with disabilities attend college. Group offers training programs, workshops, publications, and an annual conference.

The Attention Deficit Information Network, Inc. (AD-IN)
475 Hillside Avenue
Needham, MA 02194
Phone: (617) 455-9895

Offers support and information to families of children and adults with ADHD, as well as to the professionals who work with them. Information packets (60 chapters).

Children & Adults with ADD (CHADD)
499 NW 70th Avenue #308
Plantation, FL 33317
Phone: (305) 587-3700 or (800) 233-4050. Web site: http://www.chadd.org

A parent-based organization that dispenses information on ADHD and coordinates more than 460 parent support groups. Their semi-annual magazine, *Chadder*, and newsletter, *Chadderbox*, make worthwhile contributions to the field.

Council for Exceptional Children
1920 Association Drive
Reston, VA 20191
Phone: (888) 232-7733. Web site: http://www.cec.sped.org

A professional organization dedicated to improving educational outcomes for individuals with exceptionalities–students with disabilities and/or the gifted.

ERIC Clearinghouse on Disabilities and Gifted Education

Federally funded information clearinghouse that disseminates information on the education of students with disabilities and/or those who are gifted. Phone: (800) 328-0272. Web site: http://www.ericec.org. E–mail: ericec@cec.sped.org

General Education Development Testing Service (GEDTS)
Sponsored by American Council on Education
One Dupont Circle
Washington, DC 20036
GED hotline: (800) 642-2670 or (202) 939-9490. Fax: (202) 775-8578.

Has a 24-hour operator service that provides information on GED classes and testing services. GEDTS publishes a bi-monthly newsletter for examiners and adult education instructors.

Heath Resource Center
One Dupont Circle, Suite 800
Washington, DC 20036
Phone: (800) 544-3284 or (202) 939-9320. Fax: (202) 833-4760.
E-mail: heath@ace.nche.edu

Provides resource papers, directories, information on national organizations, and a resource directory for postsecondary people with disabilities. A valuable program of the American Council on Education.

International Dyslexia Association
8600 LaSalle Road, Suite 382, Chester Bldg.
Baltimore, MD 21286-2044
Phone: (800) 222-3123 or (410) 296-0232. Fax: (410) 321-5069.
Internet: http://www.ida.org

Information is provided on publications about dyslexia, referrals for testing and tutors, branches of IDA, and workshops and conferences. Informative quarterly newsletter and journal *(Annals of Dyslexia).*

Job Accommodations Network
(800) 526-7324

Provides information on equipment methods and modifications for those with LD or ADHD so that they can improve their work environment.

LD Online

Excellent informative resource on the Internet for parents and professionals. To subscribe to this free service, visit their home page and click on "Sign up for the LD Online Newsletter."
Internet: http://www.ldonline.org

Learning Disabilities Association of America
4156 Library Road
Pittsburgh, PA 15234
(412) 341-1515. Internet:http://www.ldanatl.org

Referrals, information on state organizations, support groups, very helpful newsletter and journal.

Learning Resources Network
Phone: (800) 678-5376. Fax: (913) 539-7766. E-mail: ihq@lern.com

Provides consulting information, takes orders for publications, and furnishes information regarding associations and organizations that deal with LD.

National Association for Adults with Special Learning Needs
808 17th Street, N.W., Suite 200
Washington, DC 20006
Phone: (202) 223-9669. Fax: (202) 223-9569.

National association that has an annual conference and journal.

National Attention Deficit Disorder Association (ADDA)
1788 Second Street, Suite 200
Highland Park, IL 60035
Phone: (847) 432-ADDA. Fax: (847) 432-5874. Internet: http://www.add.org

National Center for Learning Disabilities
381 Park Avenue South, Suite 1420
New York, NY 10016
Phone: (888) 575-7373. Fax: (212) 545-9665. Internet: http://www.ncld.org

Committed to improving lives of those with LD and related problems. Serves children and adults, their families, teachers, and other professionals. NCLD's annual publication is *Their World*.

National Center for Research in Vocational Education
(800) 762-4093

Provides information on products and vocational education. Catalog and newsletter are also available.

National Literacy Hotline
(800) 228-8813

Provides information on literacy education classes, GED testing services, and volunteer organizations.

Rebus Institute
1499 Bayshore Blvd., Suite 146
Burlingame, CA 94010
Phone: (415) 697-7424. Fax: (415) 697-3734.

Devoted to study and dissemination of information on adult issues related to ADD and LD. Publishes a quarterly newsletter and has an annual conference on adult issues.

Recordings for the Blind and Dyslexic
20 Roszel Road
Princeton, NJ 08540
Phone: (800) 221-4792. Fax: (609) 987-8116. E-mail: info@rfbd.org

Has over 80,000 textbooks on 4-track cassettes and increasing services on computer disks. Operators from 8:30 A.M. to 7 P.M. Services for fourth grade through post-graduate levels. Minimal fees.

Books

Burns, D. (1993). *Ten days to self-esteem.* New York: Quill/William Morrow.

Covey, S. (1990). *The seven habits of highly effective people.* New York: Simon & Schuster.

Fowler, R. (1992). *Honey, are you listening?* Nelson Pulishers. To order: 1-800-New Hope.

Gregg, N. (1996). *Adults with learning disabilities.* New York: Guilford.

Guyer, B. (1997).*The pretenders: Gifted people who have difficulty learning.* Homewood, IL: High Tide.

Hagin, R., & Silver, A. (1991). *Disorders of learning in childhood.* New York: Wiley.

Hallowell, E., & Ratey, J. (1994). *Driven to distraction.* New York: Pantheon.

Hartman, T. (1997). *ADD success stories.* Plantation, FL: ADD Warehouse.

Kelly, K., & Ramundo, P. (1995).*You mean I'm not lazy, crazy or stupid?* New York: Scribner.

Latham, P., & Latham, P. (1992). *Attention Deficit Disorder and the law.* Washington, DC: JKL.

Latham, P., & Latham, P. (1996). *Documentation and the law.* Washington, DC: JKL.

Nadeau, K. (1994). *Survival guide for college students with ADD or LD.* New York: Magination.

Nadeau, K. (Ed.). (1995). *A comprehensive guide to Attention Deficit Disorder in adults: Research, diagnosis and treatment.* New York: Brunner/Mazel.

Parker, H. (1996). *The ADD hyperactivity workbook for parents, teachers, and kids.* Plantation, FL: ADD Warehouse.

Ramundo, P., & Kelly, K. (1993). *You mean I'm not lazy, stupid or crazy?! A self-help book for adults with Attention Deficit Disorder.* Cincinnati: Tyrell & Jerem.

Schmidt, A. (1992). *Brilliant idiot: An autobiography of a dyslexic.* Intercourse, PA: Good.

Silver, L. (1994). *Attention Deficit Disorder: A clinical guide to diagnosis and treatment.* Washington, DC: American Psychiatric Press.

Silver, L. (1998). *The misunderstood child: Understanding and coping with your child's learning disabilities.* New York: Times Books.

Silver, L. (1998). *Dr. Larry Silver's advice to parents.* New York: Random House.

Stevens, S. (1997). *Classroom success for the LD and the ADHD child.* Winston-Salem, NC: Blair.

Booklets and Newsletters

ADDult News
2620 Ivy Place
Toledo, OH 43613

The ADHD Report
The Guilford Press
72 Spring Street
New York, NY 10012
(Russell A. Barkley, Editor)

Centegram
Ohio State University
1900 Kenny Road
Columbus, OH 43210-1090

Information on education and training issues. Published annually. No charge.

Closing the Gap
P.O. Box 68
Henderson, MN 56044
(507) 248-3294
E-mail: info@closingthegap.com

A bi-monthly newsletter on the use of computer technology in special education and rehabilitation.

A Guide to Understanding Attention Deficit Hyperactivity Disorder in Adults
(Ciba-Geigy Corp. Publication, 1994)
Available through CHADD
499 Northwest 70th Avenue, Suite 109
Plantation, FL 33317
(800) 233-4050

Materials and Games to Be Used in Teaching

Alphadeck. Twenty-one letter card games.
    Educators Publishing Service, 31 Smith Place, Cambridge, MA 02138-1089. (800) 225-5750. Internet: www.epsbooks. com
Angry Monster Machine. Teaches children to channel anger into a more appropriate form of expression and to talk about anger rather than acting it out.
    ADD Warehouse, (800) 233-9273.

Arkenstone WYNN. A software program that helps one read, study, and comprehend text more easily and quickly. Used with standard PC. Can insert notes, highlight sections, and look up words in dictionary.
Internet: www.arkenstone.org
E-mail: info@arkenstone.org
(800) 444-4443.

Classroom Behavior Game. Reinforces 12 positive classroom behaviors such as raising hand and taking turns.
ADD Warehouse, (800) 233-9273.

Flipping Phonics. A fun way for students to practice decoding skills, gain confidence to attack new words, and increase sight vocabulary. Thousands of letter combinations can be formed by flipping over each containing a consonant or vowel.
New Readers Press
U.S. Publishing Division of Laubach Literacy
Dept. S99
P.O. Box 888
Syracuse, NY 13210-0888
(800) 448-8878.

Language Tune-Up Kit at Home.
Jwor Enterprises, Inc., 4729 Maize Road, Columbus, OH 43229
(888) 431-6310
Internet: http://www.jwor.com

A multi-sensory computer approach to self-direction learning that takes student from beginning to eighth grade-level reading. IBM-compatible CD-ROM.

LEAD (Literacy, Education & Academic Development). Systematic sequential phonetic reading/spelling program on computer disk.
LEAD Educational Resources, 144 Main Street, N., Bridgewater, CT 06752. (800) 355-1516.

Rule-ette. Spelling game that teaches and reinforces basic spelling rules. Educators Publishing Service, 31 Smith Place, Cambridge, MA 02138-10089. (800) 114-4740.

The Social Skills Game. Students learn to use self-talk to reflect on social experiences.
ADD Warehouse, (800) 233-9273.

Sound Out! A multisensory card game to improve knowledge of phonemes.
J. Williams, 6617 Weymouth Ct., Baltimore, MD 21212-2487. (410) 377-2487. $15/deck.

Study Smart. For grades 5–12. Reinforces comprehension and use of 10 study skills.
ADD Warehouse, (800) 233-9273.

Word Demons. Game that helps students learn to master 86 non-phonetic words.
Educators Publishing Service, 31 Smith Place, Cambridge, MA 02138-1089.
(800) 114-4740. Internet: http://www.epsbooks.com

Words for Windows. Intensive training in reading longer words for teens and adults.
Runs in Windows 3.1 or higher with sound card.
The Word Workshop, 1317 Shawnee Drive, Yellow Springs, OH 45387. (937) 767-1142.
Internet: http://www.yellowsprings.com/wordworkshop

Technology

ABLEDATA and NARIC
8455 Colesville Road, Suite 935
Silver Spring, MD 20910-3319
Phone: (800) 227-0216. Fax: (301) 587-1967.

ABLEDATA database contains descriptions of more than 17,000 commercially available products for rehabilitation and independent living.

Alliance for Technology Access (ATA)
2175 E. Francisco Blvd., Suite L
San Rafael, CA 94901
Phone: (415) 455-4575. Fax: (415) 455-0654.
E-mail: atainfo@ataccess.org

Provides access to technology for people with disabilities through its coalition of 40 community-based resource centers. Each center provides information, awareness, and training for professionals and provides technical assistance for individuals with disabilities and for family members.

Job Accommodation Network (JAN)
West Virginia University
918 Chestnut Ridge Road
P.O. Box 6080
Morgantown, WV 26506
(800) 526-7234
E-mail: jan@jan.icdi.wvu.edu

Provides information on equipment, methods, and modifications so that job performance may be improved.

National Library Services for the Blind and Physically Handicapped
1291 Taylor Street, NW
Washington, DC 20542
(202) 707-5100
E-mail: nls@loc.gov

RESNA Technical Assistance Project
1700 N. Moore Street, Suite 1540
Arlington, VA 22209
(703) 524-6686
E-mail: ifloyd@resna.org

Provides technical assistance to states on the development and use of state technological programs for the disabled.

Appendix C

Rating Scales for Attention-Deficit/Hyperactivity Disorder

COMPILED BY DEBORAH PAINTER

1. Attention-Deficit/Hyperactivity Disorder Test (ADHDT) by James E. Gilliman. The ADHDT is an effective instrument for identifying and evaluating ADHD in persons ages 3.0 to 23.0. Designed for use in schools and clinics, the test contains 36 items, is easily completed by teachers, parents, and others who are knowledgeable about the referred individual, and is based on *DSM-IV* criteria.

> Catalog: Stoelting Co.
>   620 Wheat Lane
>   Wood Dale, IL 60191
>   Phone: (630) 860-9700
>   Fax: (630) 860-9775

2. Child Symptom Inventory-4 (CSI-4) by Kenneth D. Gadow and Joyce Sprafkin. The Child Symptom Inventories are parent and teacher rating scales that provide an efficient (completed in 10 minutes) and cost-effective method to screen for ADHD and other emotional and behavioral problems in children 5 to 12 years old. Items are based on *DSM-IV* criteria.

> Catalog: Stoelting Co.
>   620 Wheat Lane
>   Wood Dale, IL 60191
>   Phone: (630) 860-9700
>   Fax: (630) 860-9775

3. Spadafore ADHD Rating Scale (S-ADHD-RS) by Gerald J. Spadafore and Sharon J. Spadafore. The S-ADHD-RS provides a quick, easy, and accurate way to tell not only whether a child shows ADHD behaviors, but also the severity of the problem. The scale is completed by the classroom teacher, and the results are used by the school psychologists along with other useful information when devising effective IEPs for 5.0–19.0-year-olds.

> Catalog: Stoelting Co.
>   620 Wheat Lane
>   Wood Dale, IL 60191
>   Phone: (630) 860-9700
>   Fax: (630) 860-9775

4. ADHD Symptom Checklist-4 (ADHD-SC4) by Kenneth D. Gadow and Joyce Sprafkin. The ADHD-SC4 is a 50-item rating scale completed by parents and teachers to screen for ADHD and Oppositional Defiant Disorder for individuals 5–19 years old. Items are based on *DSM-IV* criteria.

> Catalog: Stoelting Co.
>   620 Wheat Lane
>   Wood Dale, IL 60191
>   Phone: (630) 860-9700
>   Fax: (630) 860-9775

5. ADHD School Observation Code (ADHD SOC) by Kenneth D. Gadow, Joyce Sprafkin, and Edith E. Nolan. Assesses the behavioral symptoms of ADHD, oppositional disorder, and conduct disorder in structured settings (e.g., academic seat work activities), semistructured settings (e.g., lunchroom), and unstructured settings (e.g., playground).

> Catalog: Stoelting Co.
>   620 Wheat Lane
>   Wood Dale, IL 60191
>   Phone: (630) 860-9700
>   Fax: (630) 860-9775

6. The ADD-H: Comprehensive Teacher/Parent Rating Scale (ACTeRS) by Rina K. Ullmann, Esther K. Sleator, and Robert L. Sprague. The teacher evaluation for kindergarten through grade 8 is intended for diagnosing and monitoring the behavior of the child who manifests a deficit in attention in the classroom or is unusually active or restless. The parent form, kindergarten through grade 12, in addition to the subscales on the teacher form, also focuses on early childhood.

> Catalog: A.D.D. Warehouse
>   300 Northwest 70th Avenue, Suite 102
>   Plantation, FL 33317
>   Phone: (800) 233-9273
>   Fax: (954) 792-8545

7. Conners' Rating Scales—Revised (CRS-R) by C. Keith Conners. The revised Conners' Scales are a result of 30 years of research on childhood and adolescent psychopathology and problem behavior that evaluate problem behaviors as reported by the teacher, parents, and adolescents. Norms are available for children and adolescents aged 3 to 17 on the parent and teacher forms and 12 to 17 on the adolescent self-report forms.

Catalog: A.D.D. Warehouse
  300 Northwest 70th Avenue, Suite 102
  Plantation, FL 33317
  Phone: (800) 233-9273
  Fax: (954) 792-8545

8. Copeland Symptom Checklist for Attention Deficit Disorders by Edna D. Copeland. The Copeland is available in two versions, the Child and Adolescent Version and the Adult Version. They were designed to help educators and health care professionals assess whether a child, adolescent, or adult has symptoms characteristic of ADD, to what degree, and which areas of functioning are most seriously affected.

Catalog: A.D.D. Warehouse
  300 Northwest 70th Avenue, Suite 102
  Plantation, FL 33317
  Phone: (800) 233-9273
  Fax: (954) 792-8545

9. Attention-Deficit Scales for Adults (ADSA) by Santo James Triolo and Kevin Richard Murphy. Consisting of 54 items, the instrument addresses symptoms associated with ADHD in adults by asking the client to select one of five choices with respect to each item.

Catalog: A.D.D. Warehouse
  300 Northwest 70th Avenue, Suite 102
  Plantation, FL 33317
  Phone: (800) 233-9273
  Fax: (954) 792-8545

10. Attention Deficit Hyperactivity Disorder: A Clinical Workbook by Russell A. Barkley. This is a master set of interview forms and rating scales for both children and adults with ADHD that Dr. Barkley has featured in his text, *Attention Deficit Hyperactivity Disorder: A Handbook for Diagnosis and Treatment.*

Catalog: A.D.D. Warehouse
  300 Northwest 70th Avenue, Suite 102
  Plantation, FL 33317
  Phone: (800) 233-9273
  Fax: (954) 792-8545

11. Brown Attention-Deficit Disorder Scales by Thomas E. Brown. The Brown Scales are clinician-administered instruments that allow quick screening for indications of Attention Deficit Disorder. They examine not only the ability to sustain attention, but also the ability to activate and organize work tasks, sustain energy to complete tasks, regulate moods, use short-term working memory, and recall learned material. Two forms are offered: one for adolescents ages 12–18 years and the other form for adults.

> Catalog: PAR, Psychological Assessment Resources, Inc.
> P.O. Box 998
> Odessa, FL 33556
> Phone: (800) 331-TEST (8378)
> Fax: (800) 727-9329

12. Attention Disorder in Children, School-Based Assessment: Diagnosis, and Treatment by Richard Morriss. This handbook gives school practitioners the information they need to diagnosis and treat ADD. It explains differential diagnosis, presents useful screeners and rating scales, shows how to report results to parents, and provides treatment strategies.

> Catalog: Western Psychological Services
> 12031 Wilshire Boulevard
> Los Angeles, CA 90025-1251
> Phone: (800) 648-8857
> Fax: (310) 478-7838

13. The Attention Deficit Disorders Evaluation Scale (ADDES), second edition, by Stephen B. McCarney. The scale includes subscales of inattention, impulsivity, and hyperactivity. The results are commensurate with criteria used by educational, psychiatric, and pediatric personnel for students aged 4.5 to 18 years. The scale comes in both a school version for educators and home version for parents. A computerized quick-score program is available.

> Catalog: Hawthorne Educational Services, Inc.
> 800 Gray Oak Drive
> Columbia, MO 65201
> Phone: (800) 542-1673
> Fax: (800) 442-9509

14. The Attention Deficit Disorders Evaluation Scale Secondary-Age Student (ADDES-S) by Stephen B. McCarney. The scale was developed to assist secondary educators with norms for students 11.5 through 18 years of age by using input provided by teachers and parents. A computerized quick-score program is available.

> Catalog: Hawthorne Educational Services, Inc.
> 800 Gray Oak Drive
> Columbia, MO 65201

Phone: (800) 542-1673
Fax: (800) 442-9509

15. Adult Attention Deficit Disorders Evaluation Scale (A-ADDES) by Stephen B. McCarney. The A-ADDES provides psychologists, psychiatrists, and other medical personnel the opportunity to evaluate and diagnose Attention-Deficit/Hyperactivity Disorder in adults from input provided by a self-report form, a work version completed by a supervisor in the workplace, and a home version completed by a significant other in the home environment.

Catalog: Hawthorne Educational Services, Inc.
800 Gray Oak Drive
Columbia, MO 65201
Phone: (800) 542-1673
Fax: (800) 442-9509

16. The Early Childhood Attention Deficit Disorders Evaluation Scale (ECADDES) by Stephen B. McCarney. The ECADDES is normed for children 24 through 84 months with information provided by teachers and parents/guardians who are the primary observers of behavior. The scale comes in both a school version and a home version. Two manuals are also available with this resource, *Parent's Guide to Early Childhood Attention Deficit Disorders* and *Early Childhood Attention Deficit Disorders Intervention Manual*. A computerized quick-score program is available.

Catalog: Hawthorne Educational Services, Inc.
800 Gray Oak Drive
Columbia, MO 65201
Phone: (800) 542-1673
Fax: (800) 442-9509

17. The Pediatric Assessment Systems developed under the direction of Melvin D. Levine. The *Anser System, Aggregate Neurobehavioral Student Health and Educational Review* is a series of questionnaires for parents, clinicians, and schools to assess the development, behavior, and health of children from age three through adolescence. It is intended for health care settings, guidance and counseling centers, or schools to evaluate children thought to have specific learning disabilities and/or behavior disorders.

Catalog: Educators Publishing Service, Inc.
31 Smith Place
Cambridge, MA 02138-1089
Phone: (800) 225-5750
Fax: (617) 547-0412

18. Children's Attention & Adjustment Survey (CAAS) by Nadine Lambert and Jonathan Sandoval. The CAAS can help professionals assess specific behavior problems related to hyperactivity and attention problems, both at home and at school through two forms, the home form and the school form.

Catalog: Hawthorne Educational Services, Inc.
    800 Gray Oak Drive
    Columbia, MO 65201
    Phone: (800) 542-1673
    Fax: (800) 442-9509

19. ADD/ADHD Checklist by Sandra Rief. Written in a simple, concise, easy-to-read checklist format, the book is packed with practical advice and is organized into five sections: checklists for basic information, checklists for parents, checklists for teachers, academic strategies for home and school, and other checklists for parents and teachers.

Catalog: American Guidance Service
    4201 Woodland Road
    P.O. Box 99
    Circle Pines, MN 55014-1796
    Phone: (800) 328-2560
    Fax: (800) 471-8457

20. BASC Monitor for ADHD by Randy W. Kamphaus and Cecil R. Reynolds. BASC Monitor for ADHD is a tool to help evaluate the effectiveness of ADHD treatments. It offers three important capabilities: evaluates behavior, tracks treatment, and maintains data. Brief rating scales for teachers and parents are used. Software collects and organizes behavior and treatment data, generates reports and graphs, and maintains the data for months or years.

Catalog: American Guidance Service
    4201 Woodland Road
    P.O. Box 99
    Circle Pines, MN 55014-1796
    Phone: (800) 328-2560
    Fax: (800) 471-8457

21. BASC: Behavior Assessment System for Children by Cecil R. Reynolds and Randy W. Kamphaus. This is a set of rating scales and self-report forms for describing the behaviors and emotions of children and adolescents. It provides teacher, parent, and self-reports, includes structured developmental history and directly observed classroom behavior. It measures aspects of behavior and personality, including adaptive and problematic dimensions, as well as behaviors linked to ADD and ADHD. Computer and hand-scoring options as well as a Spanish version of the parent scales are available.

Catalog: American Guidance Service
    4201 Woodland Road
    P.O. Box 99
    Circle Pines, MN 55014-1796
    Phone: (800) 328-2560
    Fax: (800) 471-8457

Computer-Based Assessment Instruments for ADHD

1. Test of Variables of Attention (T.O.V.A. and T.O.V.A.-A.) by Lawrence Greenberg, Robert A. Leark, Tammy R. Dupuy, Clifford L. Corman, Carol L. Kindschi, and Michael Cenedela. The T.O.V.A. is the visual version, and the T.O.V.A.-A. is the auditory version. These are non-language-based, computerized tests that require no left–right discrimination or sequencing and have no appreciable practice effects. They were developed to measure attentional and impulse control processes in four areas: inattention or omissions, impulse control or commissions, response time, and response time variability.

> Catalog: PAR, Psychological Assessment Resources, Inc.
> P.O. Box 998
> Odessa, FL 33556
> Phone: (800) 331-TEST (8378)
> Fax: (800) 727-9329

2. Integrated Visual and Auditory Continuous Performance Test (IVA) by Joseph A. Sandford and Ann Turner. This is a continuous performance test that combines visual and auditory stimuli to assess impulsivity, inattention, and hyperactivity in individuals from age 5 through adulthood in 13 minutes.

> Catalog: A.D.D. Warehouse
> 300 Northwest 70th Avenue, Suite 102
> Plantation, FL 33317
> Phone: (800) 233-9273
> Fax: (954) 792-8545

3. The Continuous Performance Test (CPT) Computer Program 3.11 by C. Keith Conners. The CPT provides timed-response assessments for individuals ages 4–19+ years suspected of having attention problems. It is a vigilance, or attention, test that is presented in a game-like format.

> Catalog: A.D.D. Warehouse
> 300 Northwest 70th Avenue, Suite 102
> Plantation, FL 33317
> Phone: (800) 233-9273
> Fax: (954) 792-8545

4. Conners' Rating Scales (CRS): Computer Program. Multi-Health Systems, Inc. This menu-driven program administers and scores the Conners' Parent and Teacher Rating Scales. Parents or teachers can enter their responses directly into the computer, or responses can be entered from a completed rating form.

> Catalog: PAR, Psychological Assessment Resources, Inc.
> P.O. Box 998
> Odessa, FL 33556
> Phone: (800) 331-TEST (8378)
> Fax: (800) 727-9329

5. Gordon Diagnostic System (GDS) by Michael Gordon. The GDS is an assessment device that aids in the diagnosis of attention deficits in both children and adults. It provides standardized, objective data about an individual's ability to sustain attention and exert self-control and is also used to monitor the effects of pharmacotherapy.

Catalog: A.D.D. Warehouse
      300 Northwest 70th Avenue, Suite 102
      Plantation, FL 33317
      Phone: (800) 233-9273
      Fax: (954) 792-8545

Appreciation is expressed to Deborah Painter, Coordinator of Diagnostic Testing, H.E.L.P. Program, Marshall University, for her assistance in compiling the information regarding tests for ADHD.

Index